FEUDALISM TO CAPITALISM: P[...]
IN ENGLISH AGRARIAN DEVEL[...]

STUDIES IN HISTORICAL SOCIOLOGY

This series was begun by Philip Abrams, whose intent it was to reconstitute history and sociology and historical sociology. Both disciplines have a common project: a sustained, diverse attempt to deal with the problematic of structuring; and the books in the series will attempt to do this by examining a wide range of issues.

Published titles

Forthcoming titles

FEUDALISM TO CAPITALISM

Peasant and Landlord in English Agrarian
Development

John E. Martin

MACMILLAN
PRESS

First edition 1983
Reprinted (with corrections) 1986

Published by
MACMILLAN PRESS LTD
Houndmills, Basingstoke, Hampshire RG21 2XS
and London
Companies and representatives
throughout the world

Printed in Hong Kong

ISBN 0–333–32504–4 (hardcover)
ISBN 0–333–40476–9 (paperback)

To my parents

Contents

List of Maps

List of Tables

List of Figures

List of Figures

Preface

This book arises out of my doctoral thesis, entitled 'Peasant and Landlord in the Development of Feudalism and the Transition to Capitalism in England'. This was submitted in 1979 at the University of Lancaster in England. Several years earlier, I had arrived there from New Zealand as a rather apprehensive recent graduate in sociology with little knowledge of English agrarian history, but with some grandiose theoretical schemas which I thought could be put to the test. However, my sights rapidly became readjusted towards more realistic goals through the good counsel of my two supervisors, John Urry of the Department of Sociology and Lee Beier of the Department of History. I am greatly indebted to them both. Through their joint assistance, my theoretical framework gained in rigour and in substance, while the role of history was no longer merely illustrative but constituted an integral part of my argument. In many respects, I had an ideal supervisory team. Their combination of analytic ability and empirical knowledge and focus, together with their general underlying sympathy for my own goals, made my task much easier than it would otherwise have been. In particular, I am most grateful to Lee Beier for pointing me towards the little-recognised Midlands Revolt of 1607 – it proved to be a key part of my overall argument. When I seemed to be immersed in a welter of impenetrable detail, John Urry was always available to point the way out. Both required much patience to work through the numerous papers that I prepared and submitted to them during my time at Lancaster.

I am also grateful to the other members of the Department of Sociology at Lancaster, especially Nick Abercrombie and Bryan Turner, with whom I had many fruitful discussions. More generally, I should like to thank the Department collectively for its support and for its democratic practices, which integrated students at every level into its decision-making process.

After completing my doctoral work, I returned to New Zealand in order to take up a postdoctoral Fellowship at Massey University, in Palmerston North. This enabled me to modify, shorten, and rewrite substantially my thesis into a form appropriate for publication. During my year at Massey University, I received every assistance from the members of the Department of Sociology, especially Professor Graeme Fraser, who has been extremely helpful, and Helen Harker, who typed the manuscript immaculately.

Finally, I should like to thank Susan Shipley, who has helped me considerably at every stage of both my thesis and book with incisive comment, endless proof-reading, and constant encouragement and support. Her contribution has been invaluable.

March 1981   J. E. M.

Some corrections have been made in the 1986 reprint.

J. E. M.

Introduction

Since the publication of Althusser's work, there has been considerable and renewed interest in the development of a more refined and articulated Marxist analysis of contemporary and historical societies. Although the work of Althusser itself is more philosophical in nature and lacks systematic provision of concepts for analysis, those who have followed on have attempted to remedy this lacuna. Most importantly, we can instance the work of those such as Poulantzas, Balibar, Bettelheim, Godelier, Terray, Meillassoux and Rey in France, that of Hindess and Hirst, Tribe and Taylor in England, and the work of Wright, for example, in the USA.

Recent Marxist theory has also had considerable input from André Gunder Frank and those influenced by him, such as Wallerstein and Emmanuel. These currents of thought have largely coalesced into three streams: theories of the advanced capitalist economy and state; theories of modern forms of the interdependence of capitalism and the third world; and theories of 'primitive' societies involving a Marxist anthropology. With the outstanding exceptions of Wallerstein and Anderson, little attention has been paid to the historical problems and theoretical issues associated with the emergence of capitalism itself from within Western Europe. Even taking into account the more immediate relevance of the first two streams of theorising mentioned above, it is rather odd that so little energy has been directed into study of the transition from feudalism to capitalism in Western Europe. After all, it was one of the most important historical problems for Marx himself and has remained a key issue of theory within modern-day sociology. As a result, Marxist thinking on this problem has largely remained within the confines of the debate engendered in the pages of *Science and Society* in the early 1950s.

This lack of development has surely had detrimental effects on Marxist theory in other areas. Comparison between the initial emergence of capitalism in the West (and its effects on the pre-capitalist economies) and the impact of capitalism on underdeveloped economies in the world today must be beneficial. Additionally, Marxist theory of the modern capitalist economy and state is to a considerable extent predicated upon an understanding of the origins and development of this form of economic and political structure.

This book proposes to analyse the development of feudalism and the transition to capitalism in the hope that a more adequate understanding of the emergence of capitalism in the West might arise. Of central concern are the transformations which occurred in the relationship of peasant and landlord – that is, of agrarian structural change leading to capitalism. My discussion centres on two components of analysis: (1) the concepts by which structural analysis of feudalism and the transition to capitalism may be achieved; and (2) a consideration of the significance of class struggle between peasant and landlord in engendering the changes which occurred. I shall attempt to unify these two components – an urgent undertaking. At present a yawning gulf exists between recent 'structuralist' analyses of the problem, in which formal and abstract structures are applied to the historical problem in question, and work by Marxist historians such as Hilton, Hill, Thompson and Hobsbawm, who emphasise the creative impulse given to historical development by class struggle.

I have chosen to focus upon England for several reasons. There is unparalleled source material and documentation for the medieval period in England, which has been widely studied, and there is considerable Marxist work on English agrarian history. Furthermore, England was the first country in which industrial capitalism became a dominant force. More and more, the reasons for England's development are sought in prior crucial changes in agrarian structure, upon which her industrial supremacy could be constructed. In spite of this, there is a lack of work combining detailed historical studies of agrarian transformation with theoretically informed discussion of the development of feudalism and the process of transition. On the one hand, seminal authors in the field of agrarian history, such as Vinogradoff, Postan, Kerridge, Beresford and Thirsk, and to a lesser extent Tawney, have not linked their findings systematically into a view of the transformation of England by the emergence of capitalism. On the other hand, theoretical discussions of the transition from feudalism to capitalism such as that conducted by Marxists in the 1950s have failed, as Hilton points out, to link up with detailed studies. In combining these two components, I hope to remedy some of these failings.

The development of argument in this book is complex, since I am combining the theoretical movement entailed in critique and revision of theory with a specific analysis of English development in which there is a movement in time. Moreover, the structure of argument is unified by a detailed study of particular peasant communities in the county of Warwickshire, through which the revised theoretical categories may be employed, the role of class struggle indicated, and the place of these communities in England's agrarian development made explicit. The revolt I have chosen as a case-study draws many of these considerations together, since it offers an excellent example of the struggle between peasant and landlord and was central in agrarian development, as well as involving those very peasant communities in Warwickshire whose feudal structure was analysed previously. In consequence, it is important that the reader keep in mind the relevance of these aspects of the overall argument for later sections of the book.

In Chapter 1, I examine critically various Marxist theories of feudalism and indicate three crucial areas of inadequacy. One such area is that of feudal economic structure. On the one hand, 'economic' theorists provide conflicting analyses of economic structure: for example, whereas Sweezy's theory is non-specific, so that feudalism is subsumed beneath a general category of pre-capitalist economy, Banaji, in contrast, fails to include forms of economy which are properly feudal. On the other hand, 'political' theorists adopt Marx's own ill-formulated conception of the pre-capitalist economy in which the producer is united with his means of production. This leads them to posit the distinctiveness of feudalism solely on the basis of its political structure, a conclusion which fails to comprehend the basis of this political structure in a specifiable and distinctive feudal economy.

Secondly, both 'political' and 'economic' theorists fail to provide adequate accounts of feudal political structure. The former fail to anchor feudal political structure in the economy. Such superstructural components themselves then assume the character of relations of production, as occurs in Anderson's work. By contrast, 'economic' theorists fail even to consider what political components might be required by their proposed economic analysis.

Thirdly, neither type of theory comprehends the place of commodity relationships within feudalism. The three responses evident – that commodity relationships are external to feudalism (Sweezy); that they are definitional (Banaji); or that their place remains unspecified – are inadequate resolutions of the problem.

I attempt to resolve these problems by revision of the concept of the feudal mode of production (FMP) through a summary and critique of this concept as put forward by Hindess and Hirst. As iconoclasts in the

Marxist world they have proposed a novel means of reconceptualising this mode of production. This section of their book *Pre-Capitalist Modes of Production* is probably the most productive and positive example of their work to date. Crucial to their revision of the FMP is the concept of separation of the producer from the means of production, a concept which allows the extraction of rent as an *economic mechanism* rather than one based upon extra-economic coercion, as 'political' theorists of feudalism would have it.

In spite of this important advance, Hindess and Hirst's analysis of the economic structure of feudalism is deficient, and this is reflected in their analysis both of political structure and of commodity relationships. I shall reformulate the concept of the FMP taking these considerations into account by the introduction of (a) a revised conception of separation from the means of production; (b) the specification of further political conditions of existence; and (c) analysis of specifiable types of enterprise for which commodity relationships are present or absent.

Chapter 2 provides detailed illustration and discussion of my revised theory of feudalism by reference to medieval England. Of concern here is an understanding of the relationship between the peasant community and the feudal enterprise (the manor), and the character of the latter as it was found in England. I examine the economic subsumption of the community by the enterprise through ownership of means of production (such as the manorial watermill), the constitution of feudal tenancies, and the organisation of production. This subsumption was paralleled by the political domination of the peasantry by their lord through the servile condition of villeinage, which is analysed in detail and related to the concept of political conditions of existence.

Having provided a theoretical and structural analysis of feudalism in England, in Chapter 3 I consider the development of feudalism in terms of Marxist theory. This involves distinguishing between theories of the 'internal dissolution' of the FMP, in which internal contradictions bring about its development and eventual destruction, and theories of 'external dissolution', in which feudalism itself as a static entity is destroyed from without by capitalism. These two types of theory are, in fact, antithetical forms of the same (auto-effective) mode of explanation of historical change. This mode of explanation ignores the role of class struggle and relies upon the self-generated movement either within or between the modes of production concerned. In contrast, I propose a form of analysis which takes account both of struggle between classes (peasant and landlord), and of the structural constraints within which this struggle occurs.

With these theoretical issues clarified, I examine in Chapter 4 the trajectory of feudal development in England from the eleventh to the fifteenth century, by way of a critical discussion of the work of two central non-Marxist historians, Vinogradoff and Postan, in relation to themes introduced earlier. The development of English feudalism is linked empirically to the role of class struggle via an examination of the changing relationship between peasant and landlord. I argue that there were two turning-points – the late twelfth century and the latter half of the fourteenth century – during which time this class struggle played a crucial role. Then, I introduce in Chapter 5, as a detailed study to be pursued throughout the book, the example of certain felden Warwickshire peasant communities, their feudal structure and development, and the place of concrete struggles between peasants and their landlords in the determination of different lines of development. As a result, I distinguish between two distinctive types of peasant community – 'open' and 'freehold' communities.

In Chapter 6, which opens Part II, I examine theories of the transition from feudalism to capitalism, a necessary step if we are to understand transformations beyond the feudal period. I reject theories which propose an auto-effective 'linear' conception of the succession of feudalism by capitalism, in favour of an approach which stresses the combined coexistence or articulation of the two modes concerned. I suggest that the articulation of agrarian capitalism with feudalism was specific to England at that time and cannot be compared directly with more modern forms of this relationship. Additionally, the role of the state is crucial: it is analysed by reference to the concept of absolutism. Much abstract Marxist analysis of this political form has resulted only in contradictory conclusions and in little detailed understanding of the historical role of absolutism. Anderson's work is a notable exception to these comments, but even he fails to reconcile his conception of absolutism with its historical place. Linking this form of state into feudal political conditions of existence enables a resolution of the contradictions apparent in analyses such as those of Dobb and Anderson. I propose certain revisions to the Marxist conception of feudal political structure so that absolutism may be integrated within it as a centralised form of feudal state. Having clarified the role of the state, I proceed to outline the theoretical relationship between absolutism, the transitional economy and class struggle.

The following chapter (7), which is concerned with the fifteenth century, acts as a link between Chapters 4 and 5, which end with the fourteenth century, and Chapter 8, which focuses upon the period

1485–1640. In Chapter 7, changes in agrarian structure after the feudal crisis but before the intervention of the absolutist state, are examined in general and also related to peasant communities in the Warwickshire felden. Crucial for the peasantry at this time was security of tenure in land; the question of secure tenure was itself dependent upon the resolution of struggles by peasant communities against their landlords.

In Chapter 8, I relate the theoretical structure of state, economy, and class struggle to England in the period 1485–1640 in terms of agrarian transformation, the role played by the Tudor and early Stuart state, and peasant revolt. I argue, contrary to the accepted view, that capitalist agrarian transformation (as manifest in enclosure) had a devastating impact on the peasantry, especially in the Midlands, throughout the entire period, and that these changes in the long term led to the destruction of the peasant economy. During this time, the state was concerned consistently to prevent or at least to hinder these detrimental agrarian changes, because of its own close structural links with the peasantry. Its survival required the continued existence of a strong and prosperous peasantry. However, the peasantry, having largely lost the battle for secure tenure, was now forced to take its demands for an amelioration of its condition to the absolutist state. Often these demands took the form of revolt, but were largely aimed at securing a mitigation of the effects of the agrarian changes rather than attacking their causes.

We may consider the Midlands Revolt of 1607, discussed in Part III, as an integral part of the final attempts by a weakened peasantry to change the course of agrarian development by enlisting the state's aid in its cause. However, even though the peasantry partially succeeded in its goal, English absolutism itself was insufficiently strong to counter the long-term developments in agrarian structure. By the mid seventeenth century, its own existence and that of the peasantry hung in the balance. Chapter 9 offers a study of the causes of the revolt, its events and development.

This particular revolt was chosen for detailed study for the following reasons. It was the last large-scale outburst by the peasantry and it was concerned with changes which lay at the heart of agrarian development – the enclosure movement. Other peasant revolts, which have been more fully researched and analysed, do not bear such a close relationship to enclosure. As a result of this strategic location, it is all the more surprising that there have been no previous efforts to study the Midlands Revolt in detail. It would seem that attention has been diverted from the revolt by an interpretation of agrarian change in the late sixteenth and early seventeenth century which detracts from its importance. In the last few decades this interpretation has consolidated into an orthodoxy which stresses the emergence of a new form of enclosure which did not give rise to effects harmful to the peasantry. The Midlands Revolt is thereby seen as anachronistic, as is state activity in preventing enclosure at that time. In order to assert the importance of this revolt, I have challenged this interpretation of the enclosure movement and of the state's policy on the agrarian problem. In this respect, I have intruded into the realm of specialists in agrarian history in order to reopen the issue.

In Chapter 10, I analyse participation in the revolt by the peasantry and their allies, and their choice of centres of protest. Participation is explained in terms of the location, with respect to the economic structure of the Midlands region, of the local county towns, and different types of peasant community in the felden ('open' and 'freehold' communities) and in the wooded–pastoral areas. In particular, I look at the involvement of the felden Warwickshire peasant communities examined earlier and relate this to their development from the medieval period. In this way, I provide a close and grounded application of the theoretical categories introduced earlier, since the structure of these communities at the time of the revolt in 1607 is explained with reference to their feudal structure, combined with the effects of the particular struggles between peasant and landlord within those communities. The involvement of these communities in the revolt of 1607 emphatically unites the Midlands Revolt with my wider argument established in the book as a whole.

There remains a notable gap between the work of Marxist historians and that of Marxist theoreticians. Some progress has been made in the form of the work of Anderson and the neo-Marxist Barrington Moore, and there are promising developments in the USA under the influence of Wallerstein's seminal work. However, all these people rely upon historical research done by others. No attempt is made to confront primary historical sources, even in the printed form. This neglect is understandable given the breadth of enterprise of these authors, but it does leave them vulnerable to the uncritical reproduction of interpretations which are not easily reconcilable with a Marxist view of history, but which filter through to influence their work.

I hope to have avoided these problems to some extent. I have been fortunate to have had eminent Marxist historians such as Kosminsky and Hilton to do much of the spade-work for me with regard to the medieval period. However, Tudor and Stuart agrarian history, by contrast, urgently requires detailed work within a Marxist perspective. In this field, it has been a crucial concern of mine to question accepted analyses and to consult original sources where possible, so that both analyses and sources could be assessed with respect to the wider parameters of a Marxist history.

In order to treat satisfactorily the themes now introduced, we must begin with the question of feudal structure, so that we may grasp the changing relationship between peasant and landlord and the agrarian transformations which were thereby induced in England in the period 1100–1640.

PART I

Feudalism

1 Feudal Structure: Theoretical Issues

Prior to considering the development of feudalism and the transition towards capitalism, it is essential to be able to specify theoretically the structural character of feudalism itself. We shall see later that in-adequate analyses of feudalism have given rise to many problems in understanding this historical process. Throughout this chapter, I shall relate various Marxist theories of feudalism to three key themes – economic structure, political domination and commodity relations. The issues posed lead me to propose a revised theory of feudalism which is able to take account of the problems involved. Before doing so, I shall consider two groups of theorists: those who place primary emphasis upon the political features of feudalism, and those who base their theories upon its economic structure.

POLITICAL THEORIES

We shall begin our examination of theories of feudalism with Marx's own observations, which have been used by the vast majority of Marxists as a basis for a 'political' theory of feudalism. The term 'political' is used here to connote a fundamental emphasis on political structure in the definition of this mode of production. Marx, it has been generally accepted, adopts the following view of feudalism. In his words,

> *The direct producer*, according to our assumption, *is to be found here in possession of his own means of production*, the necessary material labour conditions required for the realisation of his labour and the production of his means of subsistence. He conducts his agricultural activity . . . independently.[1] [Emphasis added]

This economic structure requires that surplus labour be extracted by coercion, since, in contrast to capitalism, there is no direct economic mechanism which would ensure the appropriation of surplus labour by the exploiting class. In Marx's words,

> In all forms in which the direct labourer remains the 'possessor' of the means of production and labour conditions necessary for the production of his own means of subsistence, the property relationship must simultaneously appear as a direct relation of lordship and servitude, so that the direct producer is not free . . . under such conditions the *surplus-labour* for the nominal owner of the land *can only be extorted from them* [the serfs] *by other than economic pressure.*[2] [Emphasis added]

This is the common starting-point for 'political' theorists: they deduce the necessity for extra-economic coercion on the part of the exploiting class so that this class may extract surplus labour from producers who possess their means of production. Dobb, in his work *Studies in the Development of Capitalism*, defines feudalism in terms of the 'social–economic' relationship of serfdom that existed between the direct producer and his landlord. This relationship was underpinned by coercion and enabled the extraction of surplus in the form of rent from the producer. All the contributors (apart from Sweezy) to the debate of the 1950s on the transition from feudalism to capitalism – which arose in the context of the publication of Dobb's book – adopt a similar definition of feudalism. Hilton, in the introduction to this recently republished debate, concludes that

> Serfdom is the existence-form of labour in the feudal mode of production. . . . Given the effective possession of the subsistence-producing holding by the peasant family, the transfer of the surplus must be forced, since the peasant, as contrasted with the wage labourer, does not need to alienate his labour power in order to live.[3]

Furthermore, recent 'structuralist' Marxists have adopted this starting-point in attempts to systematise Marx's above-cited comments.[4] For example, Balibar suggests that one may make structural distinctions between modes of production on the basis of the producers' possession or non-possession of the means of production. He defines modes of production by the combination of three elements – the labourer, the non-labourer and the means of production – into two relationships, the relation of real appropriation or possession, and the property relation. The expropriation of surplus labour requires extra-economic coercion if there is a non-correspondence between these two relationships, as is the case in class-based pre-capitalist modes of production in which the producer possesses the means of production. The economic structural non-correspondence of such pre-capitalist modes requires or determines the dominance of politics. In this way, structuralists use their analysis of pre-capitalist modes to illustrate the workings of the mechanism of 'determination in the last instance by the economy' (a notion which has gained considerable currency through Althusser's writings).

By contrast, Anderson denies any such 'determination by the economy' since he argues that class-based pre-capitalist modes of production may be defined only in terms of their superstructures. Here the logic of the political approach is taken to its limit.

All modes of production in class societies prior to capitalism extract surplus labour from the immediate producers by means of extra-economic coercion . . . [they] operate through *extra-economic* sanctions – kin, customary, religious, legal, or political. It is therefore on principle always impossible to read them off from economic relations as such. The 'superstructures' . . . necessarily enter into the constitutive structure of the mode of production in pre-capitalist social formations. They *intervene* directly in the 'internal' nexus of surplus-extraction.[5] [Emphasis in the original]

For Anderson, the character of the mode of production does not correspond with its economic relationships, since the superstructure is constitutive of the mode.

In consequence, pre-capitalist modes of production cannot be defined *except* via their political, legal and ideological superstructures, since these are what determine the type of extra-economic coercion that specifies them.[6] [Emphasis in the original]

In other words, Anderson suggests that coercion entails a direct intervention in the extraction of surplus labour, and thus is integral to the relations of production rather than merely being a necessary condition for their existence, as is the case for Dobb and the structuralists.[7]

This analysis is exemplified in Anderson's discussion of the FMP in terms of the political structure of parcellised sovereignty. This structure was encapsulated in the 'fief' which emerged through the fusion of vassalage, involving military service and other obligations, and the benefice, a grant of land. In exchange for providing military services and being bonded, the holder of a fief could expect military protection from his liege lord and had rights of usage over his liege's land. These politico-legal units were combined into a hierarchy, at the vertex of which was the suzerain monarch, and at its base the serf. Within this structure, political functions tended to become dispersed, particularistic and overlapping — hence the term 'parcellised sovereignty'. According to Anderson, the key structural characteristics and contradictions which defined feudal-ism are to be derived from this political structure. From this emerges his emphasis on explanation through a comparative history of the state.

In this context, we should consider the premise upon which all such political theories are based. Can or indeed *should* Marx's writings be used in such fashion? We must remember that Marx wrote on the subject of pre-capitalist historical forms largely in order to highlight their distinctiveness from capitalism itself, so that the rise of capitalism and its structure might be more adequately understood. Marx did not analyse pre-capitalist economies at the same level of abstraction as he achieved for capitalism. When examining capitalism as a theoretical object, he referred only to a broad capitalist/pre-capitalist distinction. This is indicated by the common lack of differentiation between various pre-capitalist relations of domination, such as slavery and serfdom.[8] Similarly, Lenin's analysis of the historical development of capitalism in Russia did not necessitate any rigorous distinctions between pre-capitalist economies. He was able to characterise Russian development by using the same broad dichotomous distinction as did Marx.[9]

Therefore, we must ask whether it is valid to follow Marx's fragmentary and allusive comments in order to construct concepts of pre-capitalist modes of production. Above, I have indicated the marked variation in the conclusion which may be drawn from them. In practice, whereas Dobb focuses upon an economic analysis of feudalism and its dynamic, in spite of his commitment to a political definition of feudalism, Balibar, Poulantzas and Anderson attempt to solve the problem primarily at the political level.[10] Nevertheless, Balibar and Poulantzas assert that the political superstructure is dominant for reasons of *economic* structural determination. By contrast, Anderson concludes that feudalism is to be defined wholly in terms of its *political superstructure*.

We must conclude that reliance upon Marx's brief comments fails to provide us with an adequate basis from which to generate a political theory of feudalism (or of other pre-capitalist modes). Indeed, there is some doubt that such an interpretation of Marx is correct. Marx states that 'the property relationship must simultaneously *appear* as a direct relation of lordship and servitude, so that the direct producer is not free'[11] (emphasis added). This passage is usually taken to indicate that feudal relations of production are to be *defined* by political relations of domination. However, the word 'appears' may well indicate that the property relation (relations of production), economically defined, necessarily requires political relations to enforce it. As a result, the economic foundation to the property relation is acknowledged, while the political component may be determined by the economic structure, in much the same way as ideological forms defined by commodity fetishism are determined by the economic structure of capitalism as an 'appearance'.[12]

These comments on interpretation emphasise the problems associated with political theories of feudalism and render the extreme position in this spectrum adopted by Anderson untenable. (I shall examine these problems further in Chapter 3, which is concerned with the development of feudalism.) The foundation for such a theory in Marx's own work is insubstantial, while the considerable difficulties which arise derive from its fundamental economic premise – that the producer *possesses* the means of production. In order to examine this premise, I now turn to consider economic theories of feudalism.

ECONOMIC THEORIES

Sweezy's discussion of feudalism, in response to Dobb, is founded on Marx's observations on the broad economic distinctions between pre-capitalist economies and capitalism.[13] Sweezy argues that Dobb's definition of feudalism is defective because it centres on serfdom – a political category – rather than being defined economically in terms of a system of production for use. This does not imply that feudalism is based on 'natural economy', or that there is no money-based exchange, but that the 'use value' of the product dominates over its 'exchange value' and production is limited to the satisfaction of needs defined by use values. Therefore, there is no pressure for improvement in feudal production methods in order to extract ever-higher amounts of surplus labour. The growth of trade alongside this system gave rise to production for exchange (which for Sweezy equals capitalism), the expansion of production, and the raising of the level of technology, and acted as an external dissolving force upon feudalism.

However, Sweezy's definition of feudalism tells us little about the structural character of the production process (productive forces), or about social classes and property relations (relations of production). In his argument, there is no indication of how a specifically *feudal* economic structure gives rise to production for use. Sweezy operates with a general capitalist/pre-capitalist distinction based not on the structural character of production itself, but on the resultant form of calculation which may arise in any pre-capitalist economy.

As Dobb points out, Sweezy chooses to focus on the sphere of exchange rather than on the relations of production in his analysis of feudalism and the transition to capitalism.[14] Although Sweezy denies adherence to the concept of 'natural economy', he considers that production for exchange is totally incompatible with feudalism, while he defines money rent as a transitional form. This reflects Sweezy's adoption of Marx's undeveloped comments concerning the impact of trade in the transition to capitalism. Like the political theorists, he is influenced by certain observations made by Marx on the character of pre-capitalist forms. Both Sweezy and the political theorists incorrectly interpret these remarks as indicative of a rigorous analysis of the character of pre-capitalist modes of production. Thus, Sweezy proposes that a universalistic distinction be made in the sphere of exchange just as Dobb and others argue for a universalistic distinction in the sphere of production between the unity and the separation of the producer from the means of production. Both Sweezy and the political theorists fail to analyse feudalism in terms of a specific economic structure which would distinguish it both from capitalism and from other pre-capitalist economies.

In contrast to Sweezy, Banaji proposes such a specific definition of feudalism that most of Western European history is excluded from it.[15] Banaji's model – based on Kula's work on Poland – is a response to the traditional political definition discussed above, which he suggests obscures the function of rent and neglects the place of the landlord in the labour process. This approach has considerable promise, especially since Banaji locates the political superior – the lord – within the economic structure.

Through high levels of labour rent, says Banaji, the peasant sector is reduced to the level of simple reproduction and merely serves as a source of labour services for the demesne-dominated enterprise. Its labour process and reproduction are controlled by the landlord; only the organisation of necessary consumption remains autonomous. As a result, through labour services the peasant sector and its labour process are integrated into feudalism. Other forms of rent allow the peasant sector a 'higher elasticity of surplus' and a more favourable distribution of land, which enables it to become autonomous. Thus, for Banaji the pure feudal mode consists of enterprises with large demesnes and heavy labour services. This structure, while not widespread in Western Europe, dominated Eastern Europe from the sixteenth to the eighteenth century.

Banaji also argues that the feudal enterprise was necessarily linked with the market. The landlords' goal of increased consumption became the 'motor-force of expansion' of the feudal economy and drew landlords into production for the market. In this situation, the specific form of calculation (in which labour power had no price) caused expansion of the volume of production via expansion both in demesne area and in labour services. This reduced the peasant sector to a level of simple reproduction, required for the pure enterprise. Hence, highly developed feudalism involved commodity production, a conclusion completely opposed to Sweezy's analysis.

The core of Banaji's argument is that *labour rent* defines the pure form of the FMP as it is the only effective form of landlord control over the labour process, which occurs through reduction of the peasant sector to simple reproduction. However, Banaji gives no reason why extensive rent in other forms cannot give rise to similar effects. Extraction of surplus in the form of produce or money may also reduce the peasant household to simple reproduction. The *form* of rent itself neither necessarily limits nor increases the autonomy of the peasant sector. Here, Banaji conflates the mode of appropriation of surplus labour (rent) and the labour process. For him, the only means of control over the latter is *direct* control through the appropriation of labour in rent. In fact, there is no reason why other forms of rent cannot give the lord indirect but equivalent control over the labour process.

Secondly, we may question the assertion that, as a necessary condition of the FMP, there is a drive for increasing consumption which results in the expansion of the economy through the market. The extraction of rent does not function primarily for consumption purposes but serves to reproduce feudal relations of production, ensuring the position of the landlord class, in analogous fashion to the extraction of surplus value in capitalism. The role of consumption must be analysed in terms of its place within feudal production.

These problems derive from the lack, in Banaji's work, of a conception of feudal *relations of production*. This obscures the nature and function of rent and gives us no understanding of the basis upon which it is extracted. Without specification of the relations of production, the peasant sector may retain control over its own reproduction even in the pure form of enterprise; its continued existence is secured without payment of any rent. Here, Banaji faces the same dilemma as do the political theorists.

Here I have implicitly referred to Hindess and Hirst's theory of feudalism. Working from this basis, I shall construct a theory which comprehends serfdom, commodity relations and different forms of rent and is able to analyse the landlord class as integral to feudal economic structure. In other words, this theory is able to solve problems associated with the three themes identified in this chapter. This is achieved by a reconsideration of feudal relations of production, the crucial component of which is the proposition that *the producer is separated from the means of production*. This formulation both removes the necessity for extra-economic coercion and resolves problems in the economic theories examined thus far.

Hindess and Hirst's Theory of Feudalism

Hindess and Hirst's theory of feudalism is a product of their concern to construct concepts of pre-capitalist modes of production in structurally analogous terms to those which Marx used in the construction of the capitalist mode of production.[16] To this end, they recast the concept of the FMP at the economic level in terms of their conception of a mode of production as a structured combination of relations of production and productive forces. They interpret Marx's comments on pre-capitalist modes to indicate that the economic form in which surplus labour is extracted determines the political relations rather than, as Anderson suggests, that political relations *constitute* the relations of production. Hindess and Hirst endorse the following words of Marx:

> The specific economic form in which unpaid surplus labour is pumped out of the direct producers, determines the relationship of rulers and ruled, as it grows directly out of production itself and, in turn, reacts upon it as a determining element.[17]

They examine the prevailing political definition of the FMP within Marxism, and level the same criticisms at the concept of feudal rent as they level at the concept of tax in the Asiatic mode of production: both the feudal lord and the Asiatic despot extract surplus labour by virtue of extra-economic coercion so that no *economic* mechanism of surplus-extraction upon which classes may be based is specified. As a result, the rehabilitation of the concept of the FMP necessitates demonstration that the landlord is integrated into the FMP by means of an *economic* mechanism of rent-extraction, so that the concept of the FMP involves economically generated classes.

Economic structure

Hindess and Hirst suggest that the producer is *not* in possession of the land in the FMP so that the producer is *separated* from, rather than united with the means of production. This opens the way for the reconceptualisation of the FMP in which rent is not a forced political exaction. In the FMP, land is monopolised by a few landlords, while many 'landless labourers' are forced to pay rent to these landlords for the right to cultivate the land and produce their means of subsistence. The mode of appropriation of surplus labour (rent) acts to ensure the separation of the peasant producer from the means of production (land). The landlord is directly involved in the production process and has economic control over his tenants through his extraction of rent, whilst the payment of rent by tenants is dependent upon their pre-existing separation from the land. In all forms of rent, landlord control is based upon land-tenure and control over ancillary means of production. The landlord may control the size of tenants' holdings, so that their land is insufficient to produce, support and reproduce all the necessary means of production, and other means of production outside the individual holdings, such as pasture, water rights and corn-mills.

In the case of labour rent, the landlord controls the labour process on the demesne, upon which the tenants discharge their labour services. By alteration of the area of the demesne and the extent of labour services (which changes in turn the ratio of surplus labour to necessary labour), the landlord is able to determine the labour input on tenants' holdings and, indirectly, the size of holdings. Furthermore, the landlord may require tenants to bring their own instruments of production (oxen, ploughs, carts, tools, and so forth) for the cultivation of the demesne, during which time these instruments are under the landlord's direct control. Of all forms of control, that which is exercised over tenants' labour on the demesne is the most effective, since the landlord both has a direct functional involvement in production and is able to control the division between surplus and necessary labour.

However, the landlord also exerts control through extraction of rent-in-kind or money rent, even though his relationship with producers is less direct and largely concerns control over the *reproduction* of tenants' means of production. Here, extraction of rent leaves tenants with insufficient produce or money to support all the means of production necessary to cultivate their holdings.

Hindess and Hirst must also establish in their own terms that a set of productive forces corresponds to these relations of production. They argue that feudal relations of production determine the productive forces in the form of independent peasant production. Here, they paradoxically invert Banaji's analysis of the labour process by stressing its independence from, rather than subsumption within, a feudal economy. The link between the forces and relations of production is made by rent, which divides. labour into its surplus and necessary components. In the case of labour rent, tenants bring to the demesne their own methods of working and, often, their own instruments of production so that the landlord's co-ordination and supervision of the labour process on the demesne is constrained by the limits set by independent peasant production. In the case of other forms of rent, the landlord's control over the means of production enables him to exert control over the organisation of production and the labour process on tenants' holdings, which is comparable to that exerted through labour services.

Feudal political relations

Although Hindess and Hirst place primary emphasis upon an economic analysis of feudalism, they also consider that certain political–legal conditions are necessary: this distinguishes their theory from the economic theories of Sweezy and Banaji. None the less, Hindess and Hirst discuss political relations in terms which contrast strongly with the political theorists, as a result of their conception of the economic structure of the FMP.

They argue that specifiable political–legal conditions must be met in order for the FMP to remain in existence; these they term the 'conditions of existence' of the mode. These conditions are based on the *political– legal* separation of the producer from the means of production, upon which an *economic* separation may be maintained. In other words, the economic land monopoly is supported by the political–legal title to land – the 'right of exclusion' – through which the landlord may enforce his rights over land. The extraction of rent is dependent upon this condition of existence, while rent, in turn, provides the basis for the economic separation.

The implications of this approach are far-reaching. No longer is there any necessity for the producer to be legally and personally bound to the landlord; Hindess and Hirst suggest that serfdom as a *personal legal unfree status* is not a necessary component of the definition of the FMP. The FMP requires only the conditions protecting the landlord class's monopoly in land for its maintenance.

The problem of commodity relations

Hindess and Hirst suggest that there is nothing in the concept of the FMP either necessarily to prohibit or necessarily to include commodity relations: all forms of rent effect a separation of the producer from the means of production. Moreover, analysis of whether demesne production is for immediate consumption or for sale is outside the bounds of the concept of the FMP.

None the less, they analyse the different forms of feudalism which may arise, given the presence or absence of commodity relations, by introducing the notion of *variant forms* of the FMP as 'modes of existence' of the FMP. Hindess and Hirst analyse variation in both the degree of economic consolidation of the FMP and the extent to which political conditions of existence support this consolidation. These two variants give rise to a 'set', which is composed of a 'complex unity' of variations in the form of rent, the productive forces, and the relationships borne by the agents of production to the productive process, the elements of which are structured in a 'hierarchy of dominance'. In addition, Hindess and Hirst focus upon commodity relations (external to the concept of the FMP) and associate their absence or presence with high and low levels of combined economic subsumption and political control. The elements of these sets are structured into a hierarchy of dominance. For example, their subset I(a) is characterised by the predominance of labour rent, the expansion of demesne production, an increase in the level of exploitation, the conversion of demesne production to wage labour, and the differentiation of the peasantry into two groups – labourers/cottars and independent tenants paying money rent. However, on smaller estates demesnes shrink, labour rents are replaced by money rents, and rich peasants begin to hire wage labour. Other sets are delineated by variation in the same elements.

CRITIQUE AND REVISION

I shall argue first that Hindess and Hirst's inadequate concept of productive forces poses problems for their constitution of the relations of production. Secondly, I shall suggest that their political conditions of existence are inadequate for the reproduction of the economic structure. My revision of the concept of productive forces allows us to introduce further political conditions of the mode's existence which resolves this inadequacy. Thirdly, their concepts of variants and sets are not theoretically derived. In order to remedy this deficiency, I shall introduce a revised conception of the specific forms of the FMP which is able to take account of commodity relations.

Economic Structure

Hindess and Hirst's specification of feudal forces of production is in contradiction with their own premises concerning the economic structure of modes of production.[18] They assert, as a matter of principle, that the productive forces are structured by the dominance of that mode's relations of production. Nevertheless, they derive feudal productive forces which bear no relationship to feudal relations of production. 'The development of the forces of production in the FMP is therefore limited to developing the productivity of the labour of the tenant *within the limits set by independent peasant production*'[19] (emphasis in original). The labour process on both the demesne and tenants' holdings is defined by peasant producers who are *independent* of feudal relations of production. Omission of the landlord from the productive forces means that the relations of production cannot determine such forces structurally. Moreover, the specific form defined by independent peasant production is itself never clearly defined.

Hindess and Hirst's deficient conception of feudal productive forces arises from their inordinate focus upon *land* as a means of production, so that they neglect to examine sufficiently the impact of the landlord's ownership and control of means of production *other* than land. The root of the problem lies in their inadequate conception of the producers' separation from the means of production.

If these other forms of ownership and control are not acknowledged fully, the extent of separation attainable does not necessarily preclude producers from gaining autonomy from their landlords. The extent of rent is defined only by the landlord's control over land, and is insufficient to reproduce feudal relations of production because tenants may own and control other means of production and thereby may gain control over the labour process. When rent is based upon the separation from both land and other means of production, it is sufficient to reproduce the relations of production and to give the landlord control over the labour process. Separation still depends *primarily* on control over land but the producers are also separated from other means of production in a *secondary* sense, upon the basis of their separation from land.

The extraction of rent over and above that for land by the landlord achieves this secondary separation in two distinct ways.[20] First, it allows the landlord access to larger sources of labour or funds than are available to tenants for investment in means of production beyond the capacity of tenants. The manorial water-powered corn-mill is a good example in this respect, since it may be built and maintained by the discharge of labour services, or by money which is accumulated from rent revenue, and is too advanced technologically and too large to be built and maintained by individual tenants.

Secondly, extraction of surplus may result in a reduction of the productive forces below the level of independent peasant production: tenants do not have the resources to produce and reproduce certain means of production, given a limited land area and high rents. For example, the average feudal tenant was unable to maintain a full plough-team, which required a considerable grazing area and labour time in order to support it. These resources were not available to feudal tenants even though independent producers may have been able to maintain a team. Both examples of separation from ancillary means of production are discussed in detail in Chapter 2.

In this manner, the landlord gains control over the labour process and is thereby constituted as an agent of production so that the productive forces are structurally determined by the relations of production in a specifically feudal form. Feudal forces shape peasant production in two directions. First, the landlord's ownership and control of ancillary means of production may *raise* the level of productivity above that possible in independent peasant production – for instance, by the ownership of a water-powered corn-mill. Secondly, the landlord's ownership and control may *lower* the level of productivity below that of independent peasant production – for example, through the inability of the tenant to maintain a plough-team. In both cases, tenants do not possess the resources to participate in the labour process other than under the landlord's direction and control.

Therefore, feudal productive forces are structurally determined by the landlord's ownership and control of land and other means of production, and are distinctive to the FMP. The limits of these productive forces are defined by the *combination of the agents in the labour process*, as structured by feudal relations of production, rather than by independent peasant production as Hindess and Hirst suggest.

Feudal Political Relations

Hindess and Hirst argue that the separation of the producer and the constitution of feudal relations of production is dependent upon the extraction of sufficient rent to prevent tenants from becoming autonomous producers. However, a level of rent defined *only* by the right of exclusion is insufficient to reproduce feudal relations of production, because it can only guarantee a partial separation based upon land. We require a broader definition of feudal conditions of existence relative to the relations of production and the productive forces in their entirety, so that the separation of the producer in both its primary and secondary sense may be taken into account. These additional political conditions – 'denial of possession' – allow the landlord to extract more rent than is possible by the right of exclusion alone, in order that the landlord may separate tenants from means of production other than land. 'Denial of possession' ensures that tenants are unable to achieve autonomy from the landlord by control over the labour process and effective possession of their tenancies, which would follow from their ownership of ancillary means of production. This condition is a secondary condition of existence which rests upon the right of exclusion, upon which the basic separation of the producer from the land is made. The two conditions differ in their sphere of impact, since, whereas the right of exclusion relates to land-tenure and regulation of the size of holdings, denial of possession relates to the labour process on the demesne and tenancies, and to the means of production used within these labour processes.

Historically, the divison between these two conditions is clearly indicated by the forms of payment due to the landlord. The right of exclusion allows the landlord to exact payment of direct rent for the tenants' right to cultivate their holdings. Payments unrelated to land are made possible by the denial of possession. Some of these levies specifically relate to use of instruments and means of production beyond the tenants' control and/or capacity – for example, 'multure', or payment for the use of the corn-mill. Others explicitly remove tenants' accumulated surplus, such as money payments of 'recognition' and 'tallage', and the levy of the tenant's best beast, in the 'heriot'. I shall examine these payments in more detail in Chapter 2.

This introduction of further political conditions of existence strengthens considerably our conceptualisation of feudalism in terms of economic structure. Without them, our theory would be vulnerable to criticism by 'political' theorists, who would be able to point to the prevalence in Western Europe, in the later medieval period, of seigneurial revenue outside of payments of rent for the holding itself.[21] However, I have analysed the economic foundation for these apparently extra-economic payments in the separation from ancillary means of production and established the political conditions required for such payments.

Commodity Relations and Feudalism

Hindess and Hirst's discussion of variants and sets is a useful starting-point for tackling the problem of the conceptualisation of commodity relations within feudalism. However, they fail to specify the basis for the association of variants and for the construction of sets, with the result that it is unclear why the sets form a 'complex unity' which structures the elements into a 'hierarchy of dominance'. Hindess and Hirst do not provide a discussion of the relationships between the elements of the sets beyond that established by their more general analysis of the FMP; they give no reasons for the inclusion of particular elements, and no indication of the way in which the important structuring components – the level of commodity relations, the level of economic subsumption, and the level of political control – organise the elements of the sets.

For example, in subset I(a) discussed above (p. 13), the dominance of labour rent is not explained. Indeed, the list of elements would lead one to the opposite conclusion, that money rent is dominant, in that Hindess and Hirst suggest that landlords cultivate their demesnes by wage labour, and that the peasantry is differentiated and pays mainly money rent. They fail to make it clear that they are attempting to describe *alternative paths of development* on different types of estate, given a certain combination of important structuring conditions. In the case of subset I(a), on *large estates* powerful landlords may be able to retain labour services, expand demesne production, and intensify exploitation in conditions of extensive commodity relations even though it is impossible for less powerful landlords with *small estates* to retain labour services. On the latter, the way is opened for the disintegration of the feudal economy through commutation and differentiation. I shall discuss this point further in following chapters.

Similar problems arising in the structuring of elements of the other

subsets result from the inadequate conceptualisation of the conditions
of existence of the FMP, the relationship borne by these conditions to
forms of feudal enterprise, and the relationship of commodity relations
to the FMP. I shall now consider these questions by discussion of three
forms of feudal enterprise – the non-commodity, integrated and dislocated enterprise – each of which has specifiable political conditions of
existence for its reproduction.

The non-commodity enterprise

In this form, the feudal enterprise, which consists of demesne and
tenancies, neither produces nor buys any commodities and is not located
within exchange relationships of any form, even barter.[22] These
conditions suggest that all economic activity is contained within the
manorial unit. Assuming that there is no internal division of labour
between tenancies, each holding is a self-contained economic unit apart
from the extraction of rent and must provide the means of subsistence,
means of production, and the raw materials necessary for each cycle of
production. Moreover, the tenant household must provide all the labour
required to cultivate the land. The landlord's source of subsistence is
confined to the produce from the demesne, which is worked only by
labour services. Both production and consumption are predicated on the
internal organisation of the manorial economy; any additional labour
required for the production and maintenance of the means of production used on the demesne must be supplied by labour services, unless
tenants bring their own means of production to the demesne.

These conditions imply that tenant organisation within the feudal
enterprise is an identical cellular aggregation in which there is a strict
uniformity of holdings so that all tenants hold or have rights of access to
approximately the same area of land. There must also be an equality of
distribution of draught animals, livestock, and other means of production, so that equivalent forms of productive activity may take place on
all tenancies. Additionally, the level of rent must be similar for all
holdings, since variation in rent would cause differentiation of tenants in
terms of holdings and means of production, a process which forces the
disintegration of the non-commodity enterprise. Clearly, in our terms it
is the similarity in size of holdings which underlies and reinforces an
equality of distribution of both means of production and rent. Hence
control of the distribution of land underpins the distribution of other
means of production and the general level of rent, and is thus the crucial
factor to examine.

In this form of economy, the 'middle' peasant, who holds land sufficient only for marginal subsistence, is the typical tenant.[23] Such an extent of land was ideal from the landlord's point of view, since his source of labour services was reproduced effectively without tenants being able to retain surplus from which to accumulate 'funds' and become autonomous. Thus, the landlord's interests were to maintain this size of unit, complete with its means of production and necessary livestock.

In this enterprise, labour rent is the predominant form, for several reasons. First, there are inherent difficulties in the definition, collection and co-ordination of rent-in-kind which are virtually insuperable when the landlord's household is totally self-sufficient, as is assumed here. By contrast, when products are marketed widely produce rent may play a relatively important role. However, in the non-commodity enterprise the extraction of produce rent would require specification of a range of produce sufficient to support the landlord's household and the co-ordination of these demands with the production process and products of individual tenants. Furthermore, the produce must be collected and transported to the household regularly throughout the year.[24] In contrast, labour services facilitate flexibility in production on the demesne in that labour may be easily tailored to the immediate needs of the household. Secondly, labour services, especially 'week work', entail regular and continual labour on the demesne, and a quantity of labour which is related to the size of the holding. This relationship induces a stable pattern in the linkage of rent to the units of subsistence. Produce rent, however, is extracted in discrete and discontinuous payments, which does not allow this link to be forged. Thirdly, labour services allow more direct control over the tenant's own labour process than produce rent allows, so that the landlord may control the timing, phases and duration of labour on holdings through his demands. Week work is particularly important in this respect, as it facilitates continuous control. Lastly, the organisation, co-ordination, and supervision of labour services demands and ensures the subordination of tenants to the manorial economy and its discipline, and reinforces the indivisibility of holdings, a condition required by this enterprise. In order to provide labour services, tenants must, by definition, have at minimum a subsistence holding while accumulation of land with attendant labour-service obligations gives rise to an intolerable burden of rent in the absence of wage labour.[25] Hence, labour rent acts as an efficient levelling device in landholding and is instrumental in the maintenance of an equal distribution of land and resources.

I now turn to examine the political conditions of existence associated with this form of economy. The crucial condition for reproduction of this enterprise is the prevention of a differential distribution of land and other resources among tenants, which, in the absence of commodity relations, may occur only as a result of family labour-force size, marriage, and inheritance.[26] The size of the labour force is crucial in defining the area of land that the tenant family is able to cultivate effectively, and the numbers of plough beasts and other livestock that it is able to maintain. Marriage and inheritance are both the means by which the family labour force may be expanded or contracted, and the means of accumulation of land and resources. The political conditions of this enterprise concern the terms of land-tenure, marriage, inheritance, and transmission of land and other property. In the case of tenure, the holding and the tenant must be identified one with the other, so that the holding may not be alienated, added to or subdivided. Additionally, inheritance must be controlled, so that the holding is not subdivided and the new tenant has the capacity to render the labour services attached to the land. The allocation of pasture, meadow and wastes must be controlled, so that tenants have equality of access to these resources. In order for the landlord to extract equivalent rents from all holdings, tenants must be of uniform political status. Marriage requires regulation, especially when the husband is outside the jurisdiction of the manor or of a different political status, so that the tenant population and the number of holdings is held in balance and maintained in uniformity.

In sum, these conditions ensure a *correlation* between land and the means of production allotted to the land, and an *equality of distribution* of these components between the holdings. In order to analyse these conditions further, it is necessary to examine the concrete forms which they take in a particular feudal society such as England. This I do in Chapter 2.

The commodity enterprise

In conditions of commodity production and exchange, we may analyse feudal production in terms of a specific form of calculation. Within this form of economy, reproduction of the FMP requires that extensive tenant differentiation is prevented by political conditions of existence specified by an analysis of the two possible forms of feudal enterprise – the 'integrated' and 'dislocated' enterprise – in which the money and labour forms of rent respectively are to be found. The feudal enterprise is no longer a self-sustaining entity in that its internal division of labour is linked into a wider network of exchange relationships and division of labour within the feudal economy. None the less, feudal production for exchange differs from that within capitalism because exchange is predicated upon the *necessity* for the producer and consumer *to obtain use values* over and above those which may be produced by themselves, rather than for the expansion of exchange value itself, as within capitalism. Hence, the use value of the commodity *dominates* its exchange value. What makes this exchange specifically feudal rather than merely pre-capitalist is the insertion of this form of exchange into a feudal economic structure of production which then determines the place of these exchanges.

The circuit of feudal commodity exchange may be represented as follows:

$$C - M - C'$$

By contrast, capitalist exchange involves the circuit:

$$M - C - M'$$

In Marx's words, the first circuit concerns 'selling in order to buy', while the second concerns 'buying in order to sell' – feudal commodity exchange represents the 'simple circulation' of money, rather than the circulation of money as capital.[27] The dominance of use value shapes the relationship of landlord and tenants with the market and the specifically feudal form of economic calculation.

By contrast with a capitalist form of calculation, Kula suggests that feudal calculation is made solely by reference to the monetary 'costs' borne by the enterprise, as weighed against the monetary 'gains'. In following Kula, Banaji summarises this argument thus:

A specifically feudal structure of accounting crystallised, in which 'costs' were defined mainly as those items of expenditure which required an outlay of cash, and 'profits' as all items of monetary receipt. As items of expenditure, the elements of consumption and production were merged into a single category, the 'sum of all expenses', which was then deducted from receipts to obtain [a] . . . net balance.[28]

This form of calculation implies that all non-monetary components bear no cost to the enterprise, so that it becomes a unit with external monetary relationships of 'costs' and 'gains'. Costs are defined as commodities which are necessary use values for the enterprise that cannot be produced internally, while gains are seen as being made when the enterprise can supply a commodity (in exchange for money) which another agent requires as a necessary use value. Non-monetary components, such as the means of production produced and maintained on the enterprise and labour services provided for the demesne, have no place in this form of calculation.

This form of calculation results in a tendency for the enterprise to become as self-sufficient as possible in essential production and consumption requirements because this favourably alters the balance of costs to gains, so that the enterprise is able to retain a larger proportion of the money involved in its exchange transactions. The enterprise reduces its dependence upon the market for goods, while at the same time increasing the sale of its own commodities. The tendency of feudal enterprises to consume their 'profits' in luxury goods results from the prohibition of investment for the improvement of production by purchase of necessary use values, because this use of accumulated funds is seen as a debit from a favourable balance. However, expenditure on luxury items is not accounted for in this manner because it is external to and follows the cycle of production and realisation of commodities. In effect, the level of consumption of luxury goods is an *index* of the success or profitability of the enterprise.[29]

Having analysed the external relationship borne by the feudal enterprise to the market, I now consider its internal structure with respect to reproduction, forms of rent, and political conditions of existence. The feudal enterprise in a commodity economy faces severe problems of reproduction posed by the differentiation of tenants: contact with the market by tenants opens the way for a more rapid accumulation or loss of land, funds, and means of production than is possible under non-commodity conditions. Tenants able to accumulate land and property will develop the strength to resist the landlord's demands for feudal rent and become autonomous commodity-producers, while other tenants may have to obtain their means of subsistence by wage labour. If there is no demand for wage labour, tenants whose holdings are depressed below subsistence level will be forced to leave in search of larger holdings, new lands, lower rents, or areas where there is demand for wage labour.

Differentiation of this magnitude clearly undermines the feudal economy and occurs in conditions of commodity production and exchange when tenants have access to the market. So that the feudal economy may be reproduced, this access must be controlled by specifiable political conditions of existence in the following areas:

(a) the sale and purchase of wage labour;
(b) the sale and purchase of subsistence commodities;
(c) the sale and purchase of means of production; and
(d) the sale and purchase of land.

Kula and Banaji analyse the feudal form of calculation on the basis of labour services. However, all three forms of rent are possible in commodity enterprises: this conception of feudal calculation is not invalidated by the inclusion of forms of rent other than labour services. In the case of produce rent, the production of the landlord's commodity crop takes place on tenants' holdings and will be treated by the landlord as a commodity for sale as if it were produced on the demesne. In the case of money rent, the tenant has already completed the first half of the circuit of feudal commodity exchange through his sale of commodities for money in order to pay the rent. In both instances, the calculation of gains and costs for the landlord is unaltered, even though part of the circuit of exchange is removed from him. However, *analytically*, produce rent is a transitional form between labour services and money rent.[30] As a result, we must consider only two forms of rent – money rent and labour services – which give rise to two distinct forms of feudal enterprise: the integrated and the dislocated enterprise.

(i) The integrated enterprise. In the form of enterprise in which money rent predominates, both the landlord and tenants are necessarily involved in the market. For the sake of clarity, it will be assumed that the landlord does not also have demesnes which are worked by wage labour, in which case his sole source of income is rent.[31] The phrase 'integrated enterprise' is used to indicate that tenants are *integrated* into the commodity economy of the enterprise. The landlord must exchange the money received from rents for the commodities necessary for his consumption requirements. For the landlord, commodities are necessary use vales for consumption, while, for the tenant, money itself is a necessary use value in order to pay the rent.

$$\text{(rent)} \quad M_1 - C_3 \quad \text{(consumption)}$$

Tenants are required to give money rent; they must produce commodities to exchange against money in order to pay rent:

$$C_1 - M_1 \quad \text{(rent)}$$

However, tenants will attempt to extend contact with the market beyond the necessity to obtain money for rent for two reasons:

(1) they may not have access to all the use values necessary for production and consumption; and
(2) they may use their contact with the market to gain autonomy from the landlord.

The landlord must limit tenants' contact with the market to that necessary for the conversion of produce into money for rent, while tenants struggle to extend their involvement with the market. Their degree of success defines the extent of their autonomy from the landlord. The circuit involved in this contact with the market over and above rent is as follows:

$$C_1 - M_2 - C_2 \quad \text{(use value for autonomous tenants' production)}$$

Overall, the landlord will figure largely as the consumer and tenants as the producers of commodities. The pattern of exchange is represented in Figure 1.1.

Through a variety of strategies the landlord may limit accumulation of money by tenants. He may either raise rents sufficiently so that $M = M_1$, or channel this money (M_2) away in conditions subject to his control.[32] Nevertheless, a certain degree of differentiation and accumulation will tend to occur in this form of enterprise. For the landlord, it is preferable that this differentiation results from family labour-force size, marriage and inheritance (non-commodity sources), rather than from tenants' involvement with the market, since the former is markedly

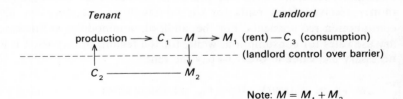

FIGURE 1.1 Economic structure of the integrated enterprise

slower and is more controllable. If the landlord retains the demesne, and thus requires smallholder wage labour to work it, differentiation may be allowed to a certain extent. Moreover, middle tenants find it particularly difficult to render money rent, so some differentiation of this group would not be problematic.[33] In conclusion, we cannot expect to find the uniformity which is characteristic of both the non-commodity enterprise and the enterprise persisting with labour-services in a commodity economy – the dislocated enterprise, which requires minimal differentiation. None the less, differentiation must remain under the landlord's control in order for the integrated enterprise to be reproduced.

(ii) The dislocated enterprise. By contrast with the non-commodity enterprise, in the dislocated enterprise the landlord's economy is strongly oriented towards the market, even though rent is extracted in the form of labour. Products from the labour-service worked demesne are sold for money, which buys commodities for the landlord's consumption. The reproduction of this form of enterprise requires within it a separation of tenant production and demesne production for the market; hence, the enterprise is 'dislocated' in that the landlord must erect a barrier between tenant production and the market. Tenants must remain in a state of artificial self-subsistence, since the combination of labour services and production for exchange upon their holdings is an extremely unstable situation which leads rapidly to commutation and differentiation. Therefore, the more general necessity in commodity forms of enterprise for the landlord to reduce costs through his minimal dependence upon the market is extended here as a forcible measure which prevents tenants' contact with the market. The landlord both turns away from the market for commodities which might be considered necessary for production and forcibly maintains his tenants in a state of artificial self-subsistence. The landlord, through labour services (L_2), attempts to lower the tenants' own labour time (L_1) to the minimum which is necessary for reproduction on holdings. Tenants in this form of enterprise participate in production for the market only through their contribution of labour services on the demesne (see Figure 1.2).

The retention of labour services in the dislocated enterprise requires that conditions analogous to those discussed for the non-commodity enterprise are secured. Differentiation due to family labour-force size, marriage and inheritance must be prevented if the supply of labour services is to be maintained. In short, political conditions are required to ensure that a middle peasantry is retained. These requirements are additional to those required more generally for the reproduction of the

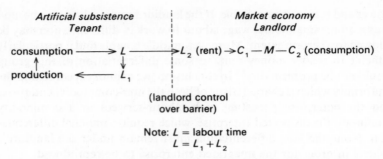

Note: L = labour time
$$L = L_1 + L_2$$

FIGURE 1.2   Economic structure of the dislocated enterprise

commodity enterprises and those required for the maintenance of artificial self-subsistence.

This particular combination of form of rent and commodity production has provided theorists of feudalism with a very tricky problem of analysis. Some, such as Wallerstein, conclude that this form – manifest in East European 'second serfdom' – represents a 'proto-capitalism', because of its production for the market.[34] Others, such as Banaji, take the opposite view and suggest that the dislocated enterprise represents the pure form of the FMP. Neither view is correct, since commodity production may be integral to the FMP, while the dislocated enterprise is only one among several forms of feudalism and thus does not represent the pure feudal mode. Each of the three forms of enterprise dominated parts of Europe at particular times: eleventh-century England was dominated by the non-commodity enterprise, while in the later medieval period this was replaced by the integrated enterprise; by contrast, Eastern Europe from the sixteenth to the eighteenth century was dominated by the dislocated enterprise.

I have analysed the FMP above in a manner which begins to answer problems raised by various theorists, both 'political' and 'economic'. Primarily, this has been founded upon a reconceptualisation of feudal economic structure such that the producer is separated from the means of production. I have also argued that political conditions of existence are a means of reinterpreting the political component of feudalism and are necessary for the reproduction of that economic structure. Moreover, I have analysed feudalism in terms of different forms of feudal enterprise and their specific political conditions of existence in order to take account of the presence or absence of commodity relations and of the various forms of rent.

2 Feudal England: Economic and Political Structure

I shall now provide detailed illustration of my revised theory via analysis of English feudalism. Of crucial concern here are the separation of producers from ancillary means of production, the relationship of the peasant community to the feudal economy, variation in manorial structure, and the constitution of the manor and villeinage as political categories appropriate to the feudal economy.

ECONOMIC STRUCTURE

The Manorial Corn-mill

The water-powered corn-mill was a considerable advance over the domestic hand quern, which used only human muscle-power.[1] The widespread adoption of this new technology did not occur until the Middle Ages, even though the principle was known from 100 B.C. The establishment of a watermill required legal rights over the water supply and a sufficiently large source of grain to make its operation worthwhile, since there were considerable construction and operation costs. As a result, watermills were largely found in the hands of lords or in sizable urban centres where there was sufficient demand for their full utilisation. From the ninth century onwards, lords who operated watermills began to demand of peasants obligatory use of the mill as a part of their jurisdictional rights or 'ban'. By the tenth century, the consolidation of seigneurial authority enabled lords to extend the 'ban' to embrace many other forms of monopoly, such as the use of the baking-oven, the wine-press, and the sale and production of alcohol.

In England, more than 6000 watermills are recorded in the Domesday

Survey of 1086. The expansion of manorialism under the Normans had led to the introduction of milling monopolies (milling-sokes) throughout England. The soke reflected the lord's individual capacity to assert and maintain the jurisdictional rights of monopoly, and resulted directly from the more general expansion in lords' powers from the late eleventh to the late thirteenth century. Peasants within the soke – the boundaries of which were at least coincident with the manor but often extended further afield – were forced to have their corn ground at the lord's mill. They were charged a 'toll' or 'multure', a payment which originally was a proportion of the flour itself, but later was commuted for money at the will of the lord. The toll hit those of basest tenure hardest; villeins paid one-twelfth of their grain, whereas wealthy freeholders paid only one-twenty-fourth. Peasants within the jurisdiction of the manor were not permitted to retain their handmills. Throughout the medieval period there were constant clashes, struggles, and lawsuits over handmills.[2] Tenants were forbidden to remove corn from the manor for it to be ground elsewhere, and were forced to grind corn purchased outside the manor at their lord's mill.

Thus, the lord's watermill was a feature of the manorial economy and played an important part in his separation of the peasant producers from ancillary means of production. This means of production in the lord's hands raised the level of productivity, gave rise to a heightened division of labour with the emergence of a full-time miller, and released tenants' labour time for the cultivation of their holdings and for the demesne. By his ownership and control of the watermill, the landlord became directly involved in the labour process.[3]

The Shared Plough-team and Communal Agriculture

It is well-known that the organisation of Western European feudalism took the form of co-operation between tenants. Cultivation was based upon a systematic rotation of the community's land divided into 'fields', so that a certain proportion could gain 'heart' each year by lying fallow. This fallow land was opened up to the community's livestock for rough grazing. Outside the arable fields were common pastures, meadowland, wastes, woodland, and so forth, whose use was regulated by the community. Production upon strips in the open fields required the co-operation of tenants, who contributed oxen to form a full eight-oxen plough-team. However, collective organisation of agriculture allowed considerable scope for elements of individual production within it. Apart from the shared plough-team, tenants by and large brought their own instruments of production to their land, which consisted of many long thin strips held individually within the community's fields. Medieval peasant agriculture contained elements of both communal *and* individual organisation of production.

In spite of the empirical coexistence of such elements, Hindess and Hirst insist that individual land-tenure and individual payment of rent sufficed to destroy any collective basis for agriculture and to define independent peasant productive forces.[4] However, I have demonstrated that their analysis of feudal productive forces is incorrect, since in their scheme the landlord is not constituted as an agent of the labour process. As a result, their dismissal of collective elements of agricultural production is too hasty. The redefinition of feudal productive forces so that the place of the landlord is recognised necessarily integrates elements of both individual and collective organisation of agriculture within feudalism. Individual elements are brought within feudalism by relations of land-tenure and rent, as indeed Hindess and Hirst suggest. What they fail to recognise is that the landlord was inserted into the collective elements of the labour process by the imposition of manorial structure on the peasant community.

In order to delineate how communal organisation of production was subsumed within feudal production, I shall examine the place of the shared plough-team. The heavy eight-oxen wheeled plough marked a significant advance in agriculture.[5] The light 'scratch' plough pulled by only two oxen was not suited to many parts of Northern Europe, since it could not deal with heavy and wet soils. Its use was largely confined to well-drained uplands, which left much of the richer alluvial lowlands uncultivated. By contrast, the eight-oxen plough, with coulter, ploughshare and mouldboard, was able to work these soils, and had additional advantages in that cross-ploughing was no longer required. Its use automatically produced the 'ridge and furrow' profile, which aided drainage.

The eight-oxen plough-team was introduced into England in the ninth and tenth centuries.[6] Such a team was associated with the Anglo-Saxon 'hide', a peasant unit of land of approximately 120 acres, which it was considered capable of ploughing. However, the consolidation of feudalism resulted in a drastic reduction in the size of peasants' holdings, so that they were no longer able to maintain a full team. They lacked pasture for year-round grazing and held insufficient meadowland to produce winter fodder for the eight oxen. In any case, the team would have been hopelessly under-utilised on such small tenancies. Consequently, peasants were forced to share teams and contributed only one or two oxen towards the full team. Units of land appropriate to the new circumstances emerged. The 'virgate' – approximately 25 acres – supported two oxen, whereas the 'bovate' – half that area – supported one ox. There were 4 virgates and 8 bovates to the 'hide' or similar Norman 'carucate'. In this way, the *individual* peasant producer no longer controlled the plough-team – a crucial instrument of production.

Thus far, it might appear that the peasant community collectively controlled the plough-team, rather than the landlord. However, if the landlord through the economic unit of the manor was able to subordinate the entire peasant community, potential collective control was transformed into landlord control. When the manor subsumed the community, forms of peasant collective organisation of agriculture were integrated into the feudal economy and became part of feudal productive forces. In this example, the landlord, through the *mediation* of the community, was able to separate *individual* tenants from the plough-team. More generally, the system of equal holdings distributed among the community's open fields was absorbed into the manor. Holdings calculated in terms of a given number of oxen became manorial administrative units used to calculate labour services and other dues.[7] The identity of units of feudal rent and units of co-operative landholding cemented the penetration of the community by the landlord through the manor. Through the subsumption of the community by the manor, individual tenants were separated from the land and other means of production, and a specific feudal labour process was constituted from elements of both individual and co-operative forms of organisation of production.

Coincidence of Manor and Community

The subsumption of the community by the manor is expressed in the *geographical coincidence* of both entities. The community was defined by the extent of its common open fields and common rights over pasture, meadow, wood and wastes. It almost always coincided with the parish, the basic unit of ecclesiastical authority. The manor was the geographically circumscribed economic unit which comprised part of a landlord's estate. Besides being a unit of property and administration, the manor was a unit of public law, policing, fiscal law, and of the landlord's jurisdiction; it was defined in both political and economic terms. The lands of a manor might be scattered throughout several adjacent communities or consolidated in a unit which coincided with the community. The coincidence of the community/parish and the manor provides an excellent index of the degree of feudalisation of that community. If the two coincided, the organisation and administration of the manor might be successfully imposed upon the community so that the framework of distribution of land between the demesne and tenancies was identical with the communal regulation of land. Furthermore, the manorial court would subsume indigenous community forms of administration and justice, while the co-operatively defined units of landholding would become administrative units for the extraction of rent.

However, the coincidence of manor and community was not typical in medieval England.[8] More than half the peasant communities were not totally dominated by any one manorial organisation. In such 'multi-manorial' villages, 'the unit of economic administration and social organisation was not the manor but the vill . . . the strength of manorial power and its economic burdens were [here] found to be much lighter'.[9] Large feudal estates were better able to impose manorial organisation upon communities: their manors were usually coincident with the community/parish, and were larger than those forced to coexist with other manors in one parish. Kosminsky notes that 'the typical large manor coincides, as a rule, with the village. It makes up one whole with the village community, and by virtue of this is also an administrative and fiscal unit.'[10] In sum, there was a strong association of large estates, the coincidence of manor and community, and large manors. I shall now examine the consequences of this association for feudal economic structure.

Manorial Size and Economic Structure

For this, I shall use Kosminsky's analysis of the Hundred Rolls of 1279, which provide us with a comprehensive survey of the English late medieval economy.[11] We may compare the distribution of land in manors of different size presented in Table 2.1.[12]

First, whereas large manors had relatively small desmesnes (25 per cent of the total land), small manors had large desmesnes (41 per cent). Large manors were formed by the external imposition of the manorial structure on the community so that the demesne lands existed in close correspondence with the provision of labour services for them. By contrast, small manors were often formed by the internal decomposition and differentiation of the peasant community, through which larger landholders were gradually transformed into lords of the manor. Their considerable land-ownership was reflected in relatively large desmesnes,

TABLE 2.1 Manorial size and land distribution

Manors	Land (% of total)			
	Demesne	Villein	Free	Total
Large	25	52	23	100
Medium	35	39	26	100
Small	41	32	27	100
Average (Hundred Rolls)	32	40	28	100

which were only infrequently worked by labour services. Other distinguishing features of small manors were the scattered nature of the manorial lands with respect to village communities, and the small size of tenants' holdings.

For a demesne of a given area to be worked wholly by labour services, the land must command labour-service providing tenancies of approximately twice that area.[13] In England the provision of labour services was associated only with villein tenancies. Large manors had such a relationship of demesne to villein land (25/52), but small and medium-sized manors did not. This reinforces our conclusion that, on the former, the demesnes were closely associated with labour services. Demesnes on the latter were largely cultivated by wage labour. Moreover, rent played a secondary role upon small manors, since it largely consisted of small money payments. Thus, small manors were, by the end of the thirteenth century, already markedly divergent from typical feudal enterprises because tenancies and rents were not central to manorial organisation. The dominant aspect of their economy was large demesnes cultivated by wage labour. These manors had already begun the process of transformation towards capitalist agriculture.[14]

Secondly, Table 2.1 indicates that there was a high percentage of villein land on large manors and a low percentage on small manors and that this relationship is inverted with respect to free tenants. The high percentage of villein land was the result of the establishment of feudal political conditions of existence on large manors. The ability to impose villein tenure and status was closely linked to the size of the manor, and thus to estate size and to the extent of feudal political power of the landlord. I shall consider these questions in greater detail below.

The ability of more powerful landlords to maintain feudal political conditions of existence on large manors is indicated by the low extent of differentiation on their manors.[15] Table 2.2 clearly indicates that

TABLE 2.2   Manorial size and tenant differentiation

Manors	Tenant holdings (% of total)			
	Rich peasants: more than one virgate	Middle peasants: half to one virgate	Poor peasants: fardels and smallholdings	Total
Large	2	71	27	100
Medium	0	63	37	100
Small	0	44	56	100
Very small	0	30	70	100
Average	1	61	38	100

differentiation *decreases* considerably as the size of the manor *increases*. On very small manors, the percentage of poor peasants is very high and that of middle peasants low. In contrast, large manors retain a solid core (71 per cent) of middle peasants and thus display the characteristics typical of the feudal enterprise. The successful prevention of differentiation on large manors indicates that larger landlords were able to enforce the conditions required for the dislocated enterprise in the late thirteenth century, a period when there was considerable penetration of commodity relationships. A further indication of the preservation of a large percentage of middle peasants is the proportion of tenancies with adequate land (half a virgate or more).[16] On large manors almost three-quarters of the tenant population was adequately provided for, while on very small manors the same proportion had land inadequate for subsistence.

I shall demonstrate below that villeinage and high exploitation were closely correlated. Kosminsky estimates that villeins holding one or half a virgate paid three to four times as much rent as did freeholders.[17] We have also noted the association of villein landholding with large manors: Table 2.1 indicates that the ratio of villein to free land is twice as high on large manors as it is on small manors. If we combine these correlations, it is clear that the degree of exploitation increases dramatically as manorial size increases. This association indicates that the landholding monopoly and feudal political conditions were most successfully imposed and maintained on large manors.

We have already noted implicitly the predominance of labour rent in large manors.[18] However, Kosminsky fails to substantiate this correlation with figures. We may circumvent this difficulty by analysing a set of data in which large manors predominated: rent ratios for (a) the

Eastern group of counties; and (b) the Earl of Gloucester's estate. This group of counties, in which fully-formed large manors predominated, had the most extensive labour services at that time. On the manors of the Earl of Gloucester – one of the greatest and most powerful feudal lords – the preponderance of labour services was even more marked. Thus, there is a correlation between large manors and the extent of labour rent. Here see Table 2.3.

TABLE 2.3   Large manors and labour services

Rent: per cent of total	Eastern Group	Gloucester	Average (Hundred Rolls)
Freehold money rent	28	23	19
Villein money rent	33	30	57
Villein labour rent	39	47	24
Total	100	100	100

We may summarise the above relationships between manorial size and economic structure: as the size of the manor increased, the proportion of villeins increased, the proportion of free tenants decreased, labour rent as a proportion of the total increased, and money rent decreased. Differentiation was lower in large manors, where the level of exploitation was higher. All of these characteristics are explicable in terms of the relationship of manorial size to estate size and to political power. The extent of political power determines whether the landlord is able to structure the manor into a feudal form. On large manors, the landlord was able to impose the political conditions required for the maintenance of feudalism.

Villeinage and Tenant Economic Structure

Below, I shall examine villeinage in the context of feudal political conditions of existence. Here, I shall delineate the economic structure of villein tenancies. My analysis of manorial structure has indicated certain features of villein tenancies: their association with labour rent, that such tenancies were predominant on large manors, and that the level of exploitation of such tenants was far higher than for free tenants. So complete was the association of labour services and villeinage that proof of the performance of services became sufficient grounds to establish villein status. The emerging picture indicates that villeins were closely integrated into the feudal economy. This is reinforced by the much lower differentiation of such tenancies than was the case for free tenancies, as shown in Table 2.4.

TABLE 2.4 Differentiation of free and villein tenants (per cent)

	Villein	Free
Rich peasants	1	8
Middle peasants	61	33
Poor peasants	38	59
Total	100	100

This table shows that there were very few rich villeins and a significant number of rich free tenants. Nearly two-thirds of all villeins were middle peasants, compared with only one-third of free tenants, while well over half the free tenants were poor peasants but only a little over one-third of villeins came into that category. Furthermore, a much larger proportion of villeins than free tenants was adequately provided with land.[19] Thus, villeinage was associated with the preservation of a core group of middle peasants essential for the feudal economy, especially in the non-commodity and dislocated enterprises. Free tenant differentiation was much more advanced: indeed 37 per cent of free tenants held less than 3 acres.[20] Moreover, as villein holdings increased in size, the proportion of labour to money rent also increased. Labour services were largely associated with holdings of half to one virgate – i.e. those of middle peasants.[21]

I have now analysed the economic structure of the manor, its subsumption of the peasant community, and villein tenancies, with respect to the theoretical categories established in the previous chapter. Through the imposition of the manor upon communities, landlords were able to establish the feudal economy. Landlords with large estates were able to consolidate their position: their large manors were characteristic of feudal enterprises in terms of landholding structure, low differentiation, and high rents. On such manors, tenants were predominantly villeins whose tenancies were constituted into a form appropriate for the feudal enterprise. I now turn to examine the form that feudal political conditions of existence took in medieval England.

FEUDAL POLITICAL CONDITIONS OF EXISTENCE

I shall argue that villeinage provides the basis for the establishment of these conditions of existence upon tenancies, while the manor as a political unit combines, subsumes, and controls tenancies so that the feudal economy is established. In contrast to 'political' theorists, I shall examine the *content* of the political relationship between lord and tenant rather than merely register the fact of its existence. Initially, this requires understanding of the means whereby landlords subordinated their tenants.

Legal Doctrine and the Custom of the Manor

By emphasising the disparity between medieval legal doctrine regarding dependent tenants within the manor (villeins) and their actual position, historians such as Postan seek to minimise the impact of their legal status upon their economic position. Here, I examine the *actual conditions* of villeinage in the 'custom of the manor' as enforced by the manorial courts, in addition to its legal character. Even if not coincident with legal theory, custom as adminstered through the courts was largely in the interests of the landlord class.

Postan suggests that villeins were in large part protected by custom, so that their services, rents and tenure were fixed, rather than – as is implied by their legal status – uncertain.[22] He views the extensive and heavy economic disabilities imposed upon villeins as much more important than legal disabilities. However, while acknowledging the severity of villeins' economic burdens, it is important to consider medieval legal doctrine and its impact upon villeinage.

First, laws pertaining to villeinage reflect the coalescence of the practices, expectations and aspirations of the most powerful feudal landlords, those with large estates. These doctrines did not consist of a formulated system of regulation external to and imposed upon individual manorial jurisdictions, but represented the summation of the actual conditions experienced by villeins on manors of powerful feudal landlords, which formed the leading sector of the feudal economy. Many smaller landlords were unable to impose villeinage so systematically and rigorously. Postan seems unable to understand that differences of *political power*, as related to estate size, determined the actual conditions of villeinage. Secondly, these doctrines could be invoked by landlords in times of need, even though they were not constantly required. Such an occasion occurred in the latter half of the fourteenth century, when landlords attempted to intensify the peasants' servile condition in the wake of the Black Death. Thirdly, effective peasant resistance to the oppression implied by legal theory contributed to a non-realisation of the law. Postan's overly narrow focus upon 'objective' economic factors ignores the role of the class struggle in determining the power relationship between landlord and tenant. I shall have more to say about this later, in Chapter 4.

In general, we must take account of the imposition of political/legal restrictions upon the peasantry for two reasons. First, economic disabilities cannot be considered in isolation. Postan is unable to explain why *villeins* experienced such heavy burdens compared with free tenants. As I have argued, economic exactions require political–legal conditions for their existence. We must examine villeinage in legal terms, in so far as villeinage was framed within and justified by the corpus of medieval law, together with the reality of villeinage, for which the 'custom of the manor' is central. Secondly, the extensively villeinised tenant populations on manors of powerful landlords experienced feudal political conditions of existence in their most developed form. On such manors, the correspondence between legal doctrine and the actual position of villeins was relatively high.

The divergence of law from customary practices is reflected in the place accorded to *de facto* states of affairs in medieval legal theory.[23] *De facto* status was to be protected at law until proven otherwise, *de jure*. The villein had *customary de facto* rights, since lords failed to deny these at law in many cases, even though the villein had no rights at all if and when his lord sought to establish his legal status. It is often assumed that custom protected the peasantry and promoted communal self-government of the manor. However, this role has been exaggerated: custom developed in accordance with the needs of the manor rather than the community, it did not necessarily bind the lord to its dictates, and it was itself subject to the will of the lord.[24]

In England, the locus of custom was the manorial courts.[25] Custom was created and maintained through the operation of the courts and was recorded in their rolls. Behind the courts existed the oppressive legal framework within which the full extent of feudal landlord power could be mobilised. The *economic subsumption* of the community was ensured by its *political subsumption* through the manorial courts.[26] Moreover, although the lord was not himself dependent upon communal by-laws, it was in his interests for the village to establish effective regulations so that order was maintained among tenants.[27] In some instances, lords even forced villages to establish bylaws for the 'common good', while of course the court fines fell into the lord's hands.

The custom of the manor was shaped and enforced in two types of manorial court: the 'hallmote' – used for everyday administrative purposes of the manor; and the 'court leet' – a wider system of policing and jurisdiction.[28]

The hallmote was formally ordered to meet every few weeks but usually met less frequently. It dealt with everyday problems of administration and organisation and with disputes both within the village community and between the lord and tenants. The court probably gave rise to relatively 'neutral' judgements of disputes between villagers by their peers, as Homans suggests, but fundamentally it was an organ of the manor, not of the community. It was presided over by the lord or one of his senior officials, such as the steward, and compulsory attendance (suit of court) was demanded of all villeins and some freeholders. The lord had the right to overturn villagers' assessments and impose higher fines. Moreover, he often became the plaintiff against his tenants, though tenants were unable to bring an action against him: this produced a situation of considerable power over villeins, who could not seek justice outside their lord's jurisdiction. In consequence, the custom of the manor was ultimately subject only to the will of the lord. However, his actions were constrained in the formation of custom by tenant strength relative to his own power.[29]

An important indicator of the lord's wider powers was the 'court leet', which involved the right to hold a private 'view of frankpledge'. From its origins as a royal jurisdiction involving a social network of free men established for the purpose of suppression of crime, frankpledge was both granted to and usurped by many powerful lords and thus was subordinated to their needs. This right was increasingly exercised privately by the lord over all his dependent tenants within the manor. As Bloch comments, 'in their hands it was destined to be a powerful instrument of coercion'.[30] This franchise was the most important and the most common of all royal rights in private hands. Although lords gained considerable revenue in 'amercements' (fines) as a result of their jurisdiction, primarily it was a means of political authority over tenants.[31] The biannual holding of the court became the most fundamental expression of manorial authority in the subsumption of all dependent tenants within the lord's jurisdiction.

The Political Constitution of Tenancies

Vinogradoff distinguishes between three aspects of villeinage, in terms of the lord's power over his tenants: (1) disabilities concerning villein land rather than the landholder; (2) burdens of villeins arising from the exercise of power as feudal lordship; and (3) the personal disabilities of villeins.[32] The first is concerned with the conditions of *land-tenure*, related to the primary political condition of existence – the right of exclusion; the second reflects the lord's ability to enforce payment *over and above* rent for land: and the third concerns *personal servitude*. The latter two dimensions relate to the secondary condition of existence – denial of possession. These three dimensions of villeinage each ensured a necessary element of feudal tenancies: respectively, the holding or tenancy itself, its means of production, and the person of the tenant. The exercise of landlord power in each of these three dimensions enabled the subsumption of tenancies within the feudal economy.

As I have established, control over *inheritance and marriage* in the non-commodity form, and control over tenants' *contact with the market* are crucial for the reproduction of the feudal economy. I shall now examine how feudal political conditions of existence were embodied in villeinage, keeping this in mind.

Tenure

In law, villeins could possess no property – which would seem to make their 'possession' of land precarious indeed.[33] They could be shifted from one plot to another within the manor or be removed from their land altogether. Legally, all land acquired by villeins belonged to their lord. Transfer of land without the mediation of the lord was prohibited. The villein was forced to deal only with his lord by the 'surrender' of land to him; the lord then had the right to 'admit' a new tenant to the holding at his will. However, in practice villein tenure was less precarious than this, even though it was not afforded protection outside the jurisdiction of the manor's courts. A certain protection was given by the customary recognition of possession in this court, which from the thirteenth century was recorded in the court's rolls. This protection was in principle frail; none the less, continuity of possession from generation to generation was usually established. The lord's legal rights were rarely exercised and, if exercised, would have resulted in extensive disruption of the economy. Nevertheless, land-tenure was still controlled by means of records of possession and changes of possession in the manorial courts. This allowed the landlord to maintain the units of landholding in the manor in a form suitable for the feudal economy.

In the non-commodity enterprise, the primary control over land-tenure was the regulation of inheritance. The transmission by inheritance of holdings made them extremely vulnerable to fragmentation by the division of land among the holder's children. The feudal economy, especially in its non-commodity and dislocated forms, required the regulation of inheritance so that holdings were not subdivided: this took the form of impartible inheritance.

In England, impartible inheritance was found in those areas where feudalism was most strongly established and where landlord power was at its height.[34] Such inheritance practices were associated with heavy manorialisation, large demesnes, heavy labour services, the coincidence of manor and community, and hence with strong landlord control over peasant communities. Impartible inheritance was also closely associated with villeinage – indeed, it became a test of villein status.[35]

Inheritance customs provide an excellent example of how custom rather than the law provided the framework for the feudal economy. In law, villeins were unable to inherit land. None the less villein land was inherited, but the land remained under the lord's control. Inheritance was recorded in the court's rolls by surrender and admittance, while changes in inheritance practices required the lord's permission. In other words, inheritance was fixed as a custom of the *manor*.

Regulation of inheritance was closely linked into regulation of marriage. It was common practice for a son to delay marriage until the holding was transferred to him. Moreover, the levy of 'merchet' functioned to control land-tenure by the regulation of the woman's share (in the dowry) of the family's inheritance of land. Through merchet, lords were able further to control villein property rights in land.

In commodity forms of enterprise, control over the purchase and sale of land becomes paramount. Legally, villeins were unable to acquire and transfer land other than through the manorial courts. In particular, they were unable to engage in land transactions by the use of 'charters', a specifically freehold form of landownership. However, Postan argues that in the early thirteenth century villeins participated in the active land market by means of charters, and that this indicates a laxity in manorial control.[36] Often landlords allowed these transactions to occur through a system of licensing and fees rather than through surrender and admission. At this time, when labour services were not crucial to the economy as a whole, some *purchase* of land by villeins would not have threatened the feudal economy, other than on dislocated enterprises which required retention of a villeinised subsistence middle-peasant population. Lords were willing to allow purchase as long as they were able to regulate the exchanges and profit from them in their manorial courts. By contrast, the *sale* of villein land to free tenants was much more threatening, since land was thereby removed from the lord's jurisdiction. These transactions were singled out for prohibition.

Additionally, lords were better able to control the villein land market than Postan would allow.[37] Hyams contends that Postan, through his use of the frequency of attempts at prohibition as an indication of the extent of evasion, overestimates the market in land. The prevalence of attempts at prohibition may be interpreted as a reflection of a *major offensive* by landlords, rather than a relaxation of restrictions as Postan argues. Hilton argues that intense legal pressure, involving restrictions on villein land-transfer, was exerted by landlords in order to reduce them to a uniform unfree villein status. Lords were indeed able to regulate the market in land and to prohibit illegal land transfers among villeins. All transfers had to be formally registered in the manorial courts; there was little chance of change in possession going unnoticed by the lord. Furthermore, a major determinant of the market in land was the prior accumulation of resources by peasants through the market in produce. I shall argue below that lords were able to limit villeins' ability to accumulate such resources both through their demands for rent and other levies and through the restrictions placed upon villein transactions in produce and means of production.

Jurisdictional powers

In addition to constituting an economic unit, the manor was a jurisdictional unit.[38] Lords gained important franchises for their manors from the Crown: (a) immunities from royal authority – for example, taxes and military service; and (b) powers exercised within the manor, such as taxation and jurisdictional powers. The most important jurisdictional power gained by lords was the view of frankpledge, in addition to which the lord might be granted powers of 'sake and soke' – generalised jurisdictional rights. One such example of the soke was the milling monopoly.

In England, lords' jurisdictional powers were not as highly developed as in France, since royal central authority was very strong from the Norman Conquest onwards. Bloch suggests that monopolies (*banalités*) were strongest where central authority was weak, and thus where jurisdictional rights could be easily usurped by individual lords. Nevertheless, important monopolies were widely established in England from the eleventh century onwards. In addition to the milling-soke, we may instance the monopoly over the baking-oven, the monopoly over the sale and manufacture of ale and beer, and the manorial rights over the sheepfold. It is not entirely clear whether these jurisdictional rights were applied only to villeins or whether they were coextensive with the manor. In France, it appears that all peasants were subject to the *banalités*. Bennett considers that monopolies were an integral part of servile burdens in England, and Vinogradoff relates them specifically to servile status. It may be expected that lords with sufficient power to obtain such jurisdictional powers would also be able to impose villeinage upon their tenants. Thus, there would have been a rough correspondence between the establishment of monopolies and villeinage.

Another important aspect of the lord's jurisdictional powers was the right to take produce or money from tenants over and above rents due from holdings. This was justified by the legal doctrine that villeins could not own land and property; hence it belonged to the villeins' lord and could be demanded from them when the lord so desired. These rights were expressed in numerous levies and payments.

Tallage was an annual tax which, if at the will of the lord, was considered an index of villeinage.[39] Villeins often paid an amount almost equivalent to the rent paid for holdings. Tallage thus played a crucial part in determining both tenants' standard of living and their ability to invest in land and other means of production – middle peasants were thereby prevented from accumulating surplus. The heriot, entry fine and merchet removed surplus accruing from inheritance and marriage. The heriot – the expropriation of the tenant's best beast on his death was closely identified with villeinage. This removal of the tenants' most important means of production controlled their accumulation of property in the most drastic form possible. Entry fines played a similar role: the new tenant was forced to pay a levy for admission to the holding, the amount of which was at the will of the lord for villeins. Like tallage, entry fines were often at a very high level. Merchet represents an attempt to place upon marriage controls similar to those placed upon inheritance. The marriage of a villein's daughter (and sometimes son) resulted in a fine – a tax on surplus. Next to labour services, merchet was the most important test of villein status in the thirteenth century, and represented strengthened control and exploitation by lords. Other similar exactions which removed tenant surplus were leyrwite – a fine for extra-marital fornication by a female villein; recognition – payment to the new incumbent of a manor by villeins; amercements – jurisdictional fines in the hallmote and court leet; licences to buy and sell stock and grain; monopoly payments for the use of the corn-mill, baking-oven, and so on; chevage – payment for permission to leave the manor; and, pannage, turbary and others – payment for the use of commons, woods, wastes, rivers, and so forth. Hilton highlights the significance of these payments deriving from the 'exercise of lordship' in his study of Staffordshire, a county in which such exactions were extremely heavy in the late thirteenth and early fourteenth centuries, even though rents for land were not particularly high and there were many freeholders.[40] On the manors of the two most important landowners, these exactions accounted for *40 per cent* of all revenue.

The function of all these exactions was to remove surplus from tenants and thereby to prevent their accumulation of land and property. Such accumulation was part and parcel of the tendency towards differentiation, which would undermine the feudal economy.

In the non-commodity enterprise restrictions associated with inheritance and marriage sufficed for control of the transfer of produce and means of production. However, accumulation of property and resultant differentiation were exacerbated in commodity forms of enterprise, in which tenants had access to the market in produce and goods. Indeed, this is perhaps one area in which landlords did not establish effective control over their tenants.

In the thirteenth century, the overwhelming preponderance of money rent indicates that the market in grain was dominated by peasants. Even on large estates whose demesnes were geared to market production of grain, the proceeds from money rent outweighed that of demesne grain sales. There was little necessity for lords to restrict the grain sales of their tenants, especially in integrated enterprises in which peasants needed to obtain money for rent, since these sales did not affect the manorial economy as directly as did the sale of essential livestock.[41] However, abnormal sales of grain by villeins were prohibited and the milling-soke controlled the flow of grain as a commodity across manorial boundaries. Furthermore, peasants faced considerable difficulties in selling grain in town markets owing to the restrictions imposed by urban authorities. Lords took a different position over the sale of livestock which were essential to the cultivation of the demesne and tenancies; the sale of plough and draught animals was prohibited. These restrictions were based on the legal doctrine which made the villein and his goods the property of his lord.

In general, lords were content to tap the accumulated surplus of villeins from sale of produce on the market by the exactions discussed above, rather than attempt to insulate their villeins from the market. By the thirteenth century, the feudal economy was dominated by commodity relationships in which peasants were deeply involved, so that there was little incentive to prevent the contact of tenants with the market. Only in dislocated enterprises would this have been sought.

Personal servitude

Here we must consider villein status, which was of the following character.[42] Villeins and their property were owned by their lord, they might be sold to another lord, transferred from manor to manor or within the manor, and shifted from one plot to another at the will of the lord. This personal dependence was enforced through the territorial unit of the manor and its courts. However, once outside the manor, villeins were also outside their lord's jurisdiction and were regarded as equivalent to free men, as long as their servile status remained unproven. Permanent freedom was gained either by a lengthy absence from their lord's jurisdiction (such as one year and a day in a chartered town – hence the expression 'town air makes a man free'), or by manumission. Those of villein status had no access to courts other than manorial courts. Vinogradoff suggests that their lack of freedom was largely a result of this legal incapacity rather than personal debasement. However, such incapacity was the direct result of the consolidation of landlord power over tenants and itself led to personal debasement.

I have already examined many of the incidents and disabilities which became attached to and eventually were considered indicators of villein status. Tallage, heriot, entry fines, merchet, toll, leyrwite, recognition, chevage, and so forth, were all in principle assessed at the will of the lord, since villein property belonged to him. Chevage forced villeins to seek permission and pay him if they desired the privilege of mobility in and out of the manor. Along with merchet, this gave him control over his tenant populations. Establishment of a view of frankpledge was particularly important here, since lords were thereby able to maintain a check on all tenants within their tithings. Any unexplained absence (or presence) would have been immediately apparent. Thus, villeins' legal status and incapacity, their bond with lord and manor, and the development of considerable powers to constrain them on manors ensured a tenant population tied to the manor and dependent upon its lord.

Regulation of marriage is of crucial importance in the maintenance of a tenant population on the manor and its balance with the number of holdings.[43] The general legal position was that the nature of the *holding*, whether villein or free, determined the *status* of the offspring of a 'mixed' marriage between villein and free persons. This solution neatly side-stepped the problem produced by mixed marriages by recourse to a direct link between status and tenure. However, this was fraught with difficulties, since many free tenants cultivated unfree land but, legally, were not thereby supposed to become villeins. Bastardy caused particular difficulties, since legal theory implied that such children were born free. This problem was dealt with by the prohibition of 'fornication' and the levy of the leyrwite – linked to villein status – if transgressed. The children of married villeins presented few problems: they were born villeins. Birth was by far the most common origin of villein status. Marriage was regulated by merchet and required the lord's permission. If a villein woman married outside the manor, the lord demanded a higher merchet payment as compensation for the loss of her person and progeny. Moreover, tenants could become villeins by prescription and acknowledgement in the manorial court. Throughout the consolidation of feudalism, free tenants under pressure from their lords became villeins in this way.

In commodity forms of enterprise, mobility of wage labour caused major problems for the maintenance of tenant populations. However, there is little indication of much explicit regulation of mobility at the local level before the Black Death.[44] None the less, villein status generally bound tenants to the manor, while the most effective control lay in prevention of differentiation in the first instance, upon which the existence of wage labourers within the manor was premissed. Mobility of wage labour was not a serious problem until after the Black Death, at which time labour became scarce and wage levels rose. At that time, the increasingly centralised state intervened in the form of the Statutes of Labourers, which allowed lords to reclaim villeins who had fled their jurisdiction and contracted to labour for an employer elsewhere.

Having substantiated the theoretical categories appropriate to the feudal economy and its political conditions of existence by reference to England, I am able to consider the development of feudalism, its decline, and the transition to capitalism. I now move from structural considerations to the question of historical development, through which the fourth theme – the role of class struggle – is introduced.

3 Class Struggle and Historical Development

Although there is considerable diversity in Marxist theories of feudal development and the transition from feudalism to capitalism, they have one feature in common: a stress on the determination of historical change by theoretically specified components of modes of production, either internal to the FMP (internal dissolution), or external to this mode and identified with incipient capitalism (external dissolution). In such theories, historical change is seen as the working-out of contradictions either within a mode of production or between modes. These two types of conceptualisation of change represent opposed or antithetical forms of auto-effectivity of the modes concerned.[1] Auto-effectivity entails the *imposition* of the theoretical structure of the mode of production on history, so that the movements of this structure are determinant of change. The role of class struggle in historical change is thereby ignored. This omission is highlighted in the analysis of the process of transition, in which there is wholesale movement from one mode of production to another.

INTERNAL DISSOLUTION THEORIES

The Decline of Feudalism

Authors such as Dobb, Anderson and Kosminsky use a theory of internal dissolution. Dobb suggests that internal structural factors were decisive for the decline of feudalism. For him, the inefficiency of the feudal system of production (productive forces) combined with the growing consumption requirements of the landlord class (relations of production) gave rise to unendurable pressure upon the peasant producers and led to the inability of the system to

46

reproduce itself.[2] These conditions were manifest in a series of crises in the economy in the fourteenth and fifteenth centuries, which reflected the exhaustion of the economy, the mass desertion of serfs to the towns, and so forth. Dobb considers that economic factors such as the price and availability of wage labour and the profitability of demesne production were crucial to the divergent outcomes of the feudal crisis in Eastern and Western Europe, leading to the strengthening of the system in the former and its decay in the latter.

Anderson's position resembles that of Dobb. However, he replaces the traditional Marxist view of historical development, in which the productive forces break through obsolete relations of production, with an analysis which emphasises the leading role of the relations of production.[3] For Anderson the feudal crisis was signalled by the faltering and receding of the productive forces as a consequence of the effect of feudal relations of production, which led to a 'seizure of the mechanisms of reproduction of the system', and to overpopulation, falling grain yields, extension of cultivation to marginal lands, and then to soil deterioration, and the withdrawal of cultivation from marginal lands. When combined with the bad harvests of the early fourteenth century and the Black Death of 1348–9, this caused a demographic collapse. (Here, Anderson relies too much on a demographic conception of the feudal crisis.) The crisis unleashed a 'desperate class struggle' on the land, as landlords sought to immobilise the peasantry, hold down wages and maintain rents. Peasant revolts erupted throughout Western Europe in the fourteenth and fifteenth centuries and had a profound impact on the 'balance of class forces'. Rents declined, wages rose, and the peasantry was emancipated.

The above summary seems to imply, contrary to my introductory remarks, that Anderson incorporates the role of class struggle into his analysis of the decline of feudalism. None the less, he gives overriding emphasis to certain structural features of Western European feudalism which determined such struggles and the direction of development. He argues that the parcellised sovereignty characteristic of Western European feudalism allowed autonomous towns and a free peasantry to exist in the interstices of the political hierarchy.[4] In consequence, the nobility was unable to maintain serfdom after the feudal crisis (in contrast to the Eastern European nobility), because the towns gave peasants a resort for flight from their masters and engendered the conditions for peasant revolt, while the free peasantry provided a basis for successful resistance to landlord pressure. In this manner, the political contradictions inherent in parcellised sovereignty were first heightened and then resolved by its disintegration.

Anderson's analysis of the decline of feudalism depends upon the resolution of contradictions both at the economic and political levels. These contradictions are internal structural components of the FMP which allow little role for the class struggle in historical change. As a result, Anderson's avowal that the resolution of the crisis depended upon the class struggle contradicts his substantive analysis. His approach to history – comparative structural analysis – is not inclined towards a class-based Marxist theory of development. Anderson himself argues that the introduction of class struggle into the analysis would 'change Marx's theory of complex objective contradictions into a simple subjective contest of class wills'.[5] I shall argue below that this position is based upon the false division between, on the one hand, objective contradictions of a mode of production (auto-effectivity), and on the other, class voluntarism. On the basis of this division, Anderson demarcates his own position from that of Dobb, suggesting that Dobb ascribes development to the resolution of class struggles, thereby ignoring the objective contradictions of feudalism. But in fact Dobb, like Anderson, analyses the decline of feudalism in terms of the contradictions between the relations of production and the productive forces. They both ascribe the decline of feudalism to the *internal structural contradictions* of that mode of production.

Like Dobb and Anderson, Kosminsky suggests that the feudal crisis was caused by the internal structural contradictions within feudalism, between its relations of production and the productive forces. The former became a 'brake' upon the development of the latter so that 'the conditions for reproduction of the labour force' were destroyed.[6] However, Kosminsky also draws out the implications of peasant struggles for the development of feudalism, discussing many such examples from English history.[7] He argues that increased exploitation by landlords and increased production for the market led to the intensification of landlord–tenant struggles.

Anderson mistakenly suggests that Kosminsky ascribes the decline of feudalism itself to the class struggle. Although stressing the role of peasant struggles to a greater extent than Anderson, Kosminsky retains an explanation of the crisis in terms of internal structural contradictions, as I have shown above. Kosminsky posits the emergence of serious peasant struggles only as a *reaction* to the increased economic pressure and as an *expression* of the heightened contradictions of the fourteenth century.

This view gives rise to certain difficulties. First, the consolidation of serfdom in Eastern Europe after the feudal crisis was not accompanied by peasant revolts of any significance. In this instance, increased economic and political pressures did not result in a corresponding escalation of peasant resistance. Thus, we may not assume a direct and determinant relationship between heightened contradictions and class struggle. Secondly, as Hilton points out, this view implies an absence of struggle prior to the feudal crisis, a period which is then 'characterised by an organic balance between functional social groups whose members recognised their place and did not seek to step beyond it'.[8] Struggles are detached from their origin in feudal relations of production and are seen as symptomatic only of a pathological state of feudal society, rather than its normal condition. This under-estimation of the fundamental significance of the relations of production casts the feudal crisis in a more overtly demographic mould, an interpretation which Marxist theorists are sometimes inclined to move towards. Anderson, who relies excessively upon the work of Postan, adopts a position which is perilously close to an outright demographic view of development. Hilton argues that conflict is endemic to feudal society and a necessary feature of relations of production. In his terms, 'the struggle for rent was the "prime mover" in feudal society'.[9] Of course, struggles were intensified and widened in scope in the later medieval period as a result of changes which I shall examine below. However, we must not place so much emphasis upon the connection of the class struggle with the structural developments of feudalism that struggle becomes only a reaction to and an expression of its contradictions. In sum, theories which focus upon the internal structural contradictions of the FMP neglect the role of class struggle in change. At most, struggle is introduced only as an expression of the contradictions of feudalism and is therefore without efficacy in determining historical change. These theories are auto-effective because they explain historical change in terms of the movements automatically generated by the theoretical structure of the mode of production, through the *internal dissolution* of that mode by the working out of the contradictions within it.

The Transition from Feudalism to Capitalism

Dobb contends that his analysis of the transition to capitalism is strengthened by the existence of an interregnum in the fifteenth and sixteenth centuries during which capitalism was not yet dominant, even

though feudalism had declined markedly.[10] The emergence of capitalism required this period for feudalism to be broken up internally.
However, although Dobb persists in terming this period feudal, he is
none too clear why. As a result, he vacillates between viewing it as
feudalism in a state of 'advanced disintegration', and suggesting that it
was characterised by the feudal exploitation of the 'petty mode of
production'. Sweezy rightly seizes upon this ambivalence in order to
point out that Dobb contradicts himself by terming this period feudal at
all, because serfdom (at the centre of Dobb's definition of feudalism)
had largely disappeared by this time. When closely examined, Dobb's
position amounts to no more than the negative implication that, if
capitalism was not yet dominant, feudalism in some form or other must
have remained. This argument is extremely weak and results in his
inability to deal with the changes which occurred in the later medieval
period.

For Anderson, the changes crucial to transition were found in the rise
of absolutism – a feudal state which nevertheless fundamentally departed from feudal political structure.[11] This introduces unresolved
contradictions into his analysis. (For my critique of Anderson's view of
absolutism, see Chapter 6.) Like Dobb, Anderson argues for the
presence of feudalism by virtue of the fact of the non-dominance of
capitalism. As long as a free market in land and labour did not exist,
feudalism remained, even though serfdom and parcellised sovereignty
had disappeared.

Dobb and Anderson face similar problems of analysis because their
conception of the FMP is inadequate in two respects; it is defined in
political terms and it is auto-effective. First, their reliance upon a
political definition of the FMP precludes effective analysis of the
intervening centuries crucial to the process of transition. I have already
considered Dobb's and Anderson's theories of the FMP in Chapter 1.
My discussion of the FMP indicates that serfdom was not definitional of
that mode but contributory to its conditions of existence. I shall argue in
Chapter 6 that serfdom and parcellised sovereignty were the forms in
which such conditions of existence were manifest, given localised
control. The decline of this political structure did not result in the
complete destruction of feudalism, as is implied by the theories of the
above two authors. Throughout the period of transition, the *primary*
condition of existence of the FMP, the landed monopoly, was maintained by the centralised political state known as absolutism, whereby
the landlord class could continue to extract rent from peasant
producers.

Secondly, Dobb's and Anderson's emphasis on the decline of feudalism as a process historically separated from the rise of capitalism constitutes capitalism as an external agent. Both trace the independent rise of capitalism – Dobb by focusing upon the emergence of petty commodity production in towns and the role of merchant capital, Anderson by stressing the prefiguration of capitalism in the rise of absolutism. Neither analyses the relationship of feudalism and capitalism systematically. To a considerable extent this results from their inadequate theories of feudalism, which create both a theoretical and chronological gap which cannot be filled. Such problems posed within theories of internal dissolution demand the introduction of an implicit theory of external dissolution – capitalism as an untheorised external agent – if the logic of explanation is to be completed.

EXTERNAL DISSOLUTION THEORIES

Theories of the decline of feudalism and the transition to capitalism which centre upon the contradictions *between* modes of production rather than *within* a particular mode I shall term 'theories of external dissolution'. These theories suffer from two problems. First, they are unable to analyse the relationship between the two modes concerned because the nascent mode, capitalism, is conceived as an untheorised external agent through which transition is induced, while the superseded mode is conceived as a static and self-reproducing entity. Secondly, these conceptions of capitalism and feudalism require the implicit introduction of a notion of internal dissolution for a comprehensive explanation of transition, because the mechanisms of interaction between feudalism and capitalism are not specified. For Sweezy, whose discussion of transition is analytically superficial, these problems remain masked; in the case of Balibar and Poulantzas, they are evident.

Sweezy's theory of transition depends upon the external dissolution of feudalism by the rise of capitalism.[12] The expansion of production for exchange (which for Sweezy is equivalent to capitalism) destroyed feudalism from the outside, because it revealed the deficiency of feudal production for use. Hence, the feudal landed classes, previously only concerned with use values in consumption, turned to production for exchange. The increased consumption which arose from their involvement in commerce led them to seek increased revenue and gave impetus to the ever-expanding production for exchange. The rise of towns as centres for the exchange economy gave the servile agricultural population new opportunities for freedom, and helped destroy the bondage of the cultivator to the land. Sweezy views the FMP as essentially static, self-reproducing, and fixed at a low level of productivity. Change occurred through the external rise of production for exchange and its contradictions with production for use.

Combination of Modes of Production

Recently, attempts have been made to reconceptualise the transition from feudalism to capitalism in terms of the *shift in dominance* from one mode to the other within the social formation concerned. According to this perspective, all social formations consist of a combination of modes of production structured hierarchically, so that one mode dominates over the other(s) and determines the character of the social formation. This move from the more simple traditional Marxist identification of mode of production and social formation was first elaborated by Althusser. Other authors have developed these suggestions further. In particular, Poulantzas attempts to systematise the concepts of mode of production and social formation. He suggests that 'the social formation itself constitutes a complex unity in which a certain mode of production dominates the others which compose it. . . . The dominance of one mode of production over the others in a social formation causes the matrix of this mode of production . . . to mark the whole of the formation.'[13] The transition entails the displacement of dominance from one mode to another in the social formation.

One very important reason for the introduction of this more complex view of societies was Althusser's rejection of 'historicism' – theories of history characterised by a unique and linear conception of time.[14] Such theories view history as 'periodised in evolutionist fashion into self contemporaneous "modes of production", the static or "synchronic" analysis of which has a dynamic or "diachronic" development in time into another mode of production'. Althusser insists that the history of social formations cannot be viewed in terms of unique and linear time, because each mode in the combination has its own rhythm of development.

Althusser's discussion of historicism has similarities with my discussion of theories of internal and external dissolution in so far as these views of history share a conception of transition as the *linear* replacement of one mode by another. However, in spite of the fact that Althusserians such as Balibar and Poulantzas argue for the necessity of analysis of social formations as combinations of modes of production, little detailed analysis in these terms has been achieved.[15] Both authors not only fail to carry out such an analysis, but also rely upon an external agent which functions to dissolve feudalism.

Balibar argues that modes of production have the capacity for indefinite reproduction because their conditions of existence are necessarily secured as an effect of the structure of that mode, which consists of a structural homology or correspondence between the relations of production and the productive forces.[16] In this way, Balibar reproduces the auto-effectivity of internal-dissolution theories (the necessary dissolution of a mode through its internal contradictions) in *inverted* form. Balibar's reaction against historicism takes the form of the removal of any conception of historical change. In order to comprehend the transition, Balibar introduces the concept of the transitional mode of production (the manufacturing mode). Unlike other modes, there is no homology but rather a contradiction between its (capitalist) relations of production and its (feudal) productive forces. In this way, the mode reflects the contradictory coexistence and combination of capitalism and feudalism in the transitional period. The reproduction of this mode results in the transformation of the productive forces by the relations of production so that correspondence is re-established in the emergence of the new mode, capitalism.

As Hindess and Hirst point out, Balibar is forced to introduce the manufacturing mode as a device which facilitates the transition between the two self-reproducing eternal modes – feudalism and capitalism; otherwise there is no possibility of transition.[17] However, Balibar's reaction against historicism is misplaced. There is no need to posit a conception of modes of production as eternities in order to criticise historicism. One may base a critique on historicism's omission of the role of class struggle. Balibar resorts to an intervening transitional mode which generates transition through the mode's *internal dissolution* (the dynamic of manufacturing). However, this augmentation only makes explicit the problems involved in the *external dissolution* of an otherwise eternal mode of production. Balibar makes no analysis of the conditions of emergence of capitalist relations of production within the manufacturing mode, but shifts the problematic point of the transition process from the movement between feudalism and capitalism to that between feudalism and manufacture. Capitalist relations of production are invoked as a *deus ex machina* which enables transition but which also leaves the relationship between feudalism and capitalism entirely untheorised and merely exacerbates the problems discussed above.

In a later chapter, I shall discuss Poulantzas's theory of absolutism and its role in transition. Here, I shall briefly summarise the arguments relevant in this context. Like Balibar, he adopts a conception of transition as the structural non-correspondence of relations of production and productive forces. Poulantzas suggests that both the (capitalist) absolutist state and capitalist relations of production were 'dislocated' from the feudal productive forces in the transitional period. In these conditions, he argues that absolutism was able to act outside the limits of the FMP so as to create the conditions for the emergence of capitalism, because of its 'relative autonomy'. Like Balibar, Poulantzas introduces an agent external to the FMP and untheorised in its historical origins which, through structural non-correspondence, was able to induce transition. Both authors revert to the more simple linear perspective and utilise an auto-effective concept of modes of production.

The reasons for this are twofold. First, the lack of a developed theory of the combination of modes of production precludes such a complex form of analysis. In this respect, the vocabulary employed by Althusserians (which includes such terms as 'combination', 'coexistence', 'dominance' and 'articulation') is indistinct; the precise relationship of one mode with another remains unspecified. Secondly, and more importantly, even if such a theory were developed further, the conceptual pitfalls posed by transition would not be avoided, because of the enduring reliance upon an auto-effective concept of modes of production. Both theories involving linear replacement and those which rest on combinations of modes of production neglect the role of class struggle. This occurs whether transition is explained in terms of the internal contradictions between feudal relations of production and productive forces, the rise of production for exchange, the effect of the manufacturing mode, the rise of absolutism, or the shift in dominance from one mode to the other. All such theories depend upon antithetical and auto-effective but *mutually necessary* conceptions of internal and external dissolution. Theories involving internal dissolution ultimately require the introduction of an external agent to accomplish transition, or, in other words, they invoke external dissolution. Similarly, theories of external dissolution necessarily introduce a conception of internal dissolution at the core of their analysis. Both types of theory introduce their antithetical form because the *only* means of explanation of transition is by way of the contradictory combination of these antitheses, if an auto-effective conception of modes of production is to be retained. Only by the creation of a theoretical space for class struggle can these problems be solved.

CLASS VOLUNTARISM

Hindess and Hirst's major concern is to replace theories of modes of production which invoke 'structural' and 'teleological' forms of causality by a theory in which the effects of class struggle on historical change may be taken into account.[18] For them, in structural causality 'the functioning of the structure [of the mode of production] reproduces the conditions of its existence as effects'. They take as an example of structural causality Balibar's non-transitional modes of production. In teleological causality, 'the functioning of the structure produces the conditions of its dissolution as effects'. Here, Hindess and Hirst use Balibar's transitional mode as an example. These two forms of causality underpin the two forms of theory of the transition which I have examined – theories of external and internal dissolution respectively. Hindess and Hirst attempt to revise a Marxist theory of modes of production with these concerns in mind. Balibar's concept of conditions of existence had allowed no space for class struggle because the mode automatically secured its conditions of existence and thereby ensured its continued existence. However, Hindess and Hirst suggest that the maintenance of such conditions of existence is dependent on the class struggle over them. This constitutes an initial step towards avoiding auto-effectivity, since the reproduction of modes through their conditions of existence is no longer conceived as occurring automatically but depends upon the class struggle.

Hindess and Hirst suggest that such struggles are subject to a 'determinate material causality with real relations producing certain definite effects'. Furthermore, they suggest that

> The particular *political, ideological and economic conditions that determine these forms of struggle ... are never reducible to or deducible from the structure of the dominant mode of production alone.* In that respect the existence or otherwise of a transitional conjuncture, the possibility or otherwise of specific transformations, can only be established by an analysis of the real conditions of the class struggle in the social formation in question.[19] [Emphasis added]

They argue for the severance of the class struggle and thus the locus of historical change from its means of conceptualisation in the mode of production and its conditions of existence. However, they fail to provide any form of analysis of the class struggle in its place, even though, as Asad and Wolpe point out, 'the class struggle and its "determinant conditions" are all important', in both the explanation of the transition from feudalism to capitalism and, more generally, the historical development of modes of production.[20] In other words, Hindess and Hirst argue for *class voluntarism*. They oppose auto-effectivity only with its opposite – 'a simple subjective contest of class wills', in Anderson's words.

THE STRUCTURING OF CLASS STRUGGLE

In order to avoid the problems associated with auto-effectivity and class voluntarism, we require a means of reconciling these apparently opposed positions. We must recognise both the structuring of historical development as conceptualised in terms of modes of production or whatever, and the important contribution to development made by the role of the struggle between classes (categories themselves derived from concepts of modes of production). Hindess and Hirst approach this problem (while at the same time providing contradictory statements such as those discussed above) by suggesting that the mode of production plays an important part in the specification of the 'primary forms and certain general characteristics' of struggles and in the governing of the 'possible effects' of these struggles.[21] These constraints do not determine the *specific outcome* of struggles themselves; rather they structure these struggles and define the range of *possible outcomes*. The specific outcome is explained only by way of the particular resolution of the class struggle. Poulantzas, similarly conscious of this problem, makes a distinction between theoretical structure and class practices in order to clarify the relationship. Class practices have a degree of 'autonomy' from the structure of the mode of production whilst being structured by that mode. The relationship between the two is defined by the 'limits of variation of the class struggle . . . which are the effects of the structure'.[22]

Wright proposes such an analysis by recourse to systems theory.[23] His discussion of various modes of determination – especially structural limitation, selection and transformation – goes to the heart of the problem of the relationship between structure and class struggle. Structural limitation establishes limits of variation and probabilities which structure the class struggle. Selection involves a second-order setting of limits: within the limits set by structural limitation, it concretely determines ranges of outcomes. It is in this sense that we may refer to determination, rather than by way of a rigid auto-effectivity.

Transformation concerns the simultaneous reshaping by the class struggle of those structures which themselves exert the modes of determination discussed above. It is the relationship between structural limitation (together with selection) and transformation which is crucial here. Broadly speaking, through these modes of determination the structure of the mode(s) of production sets the terrain of variation and defines the range of outcomes within which historical transformation through class struggle defines the specific outcome and hence the direction of development. In Chapter 6, I shall develop further such a theoretical analysis in the transitional situation by considering the role of the state.

Thus, historical change is neither totally determined by the self-generated motion of theoretical structures, nor indeterminate as a consequence of the free play of class struggle. The division between these two conceptions – auto-effectivity and class voluntarism – is false and must be discarded. To this end, I have developed the concepts of the FMP, its conditions of existence, and the different forms of feudal enterprise so that the structuring of struggle might be more adequately understood. When these analytic tools are worked into the study of the trajectory of feudalism in a particular social formation and related to the character and effects of landlord – tenant struggles on development, the precise relationship of theoretical structure to class struggle becomes clear. With these points in mind we may now examine English feudal development.

4 The Trajectory of Feudalism and Class Struggle in England

THE RISE OF FEUDALISM

Prior to analysing English development in the terms proposed, I shall briefly outline the two dominant historical schools of the medieval period – which I shall term the 'classical' and 'demographic' perspectives. These two perspectives are introduced because they have influenced Marxist accounts of this period, in the relative absence of detailed Marxist discussions of English development. I shall use these two perspectives as a springboard from which to develop in detail my analysis of the role of class struggle and to illustrate how my revised theory of feudalism is able to deal with the complexity of English development.

In the classical perspective, exemplified in the work of Vinogradoff, the feudal economy comprised self-sufficient manorial estates provided for by the labour services of their villein populations.[1] The development of feudalism itself is seen as a linear and gradual evolution and consolidation of manorial structure. Each element which made up the unity of the feudal economy in the manor – demesnes, labour services and villeinage – is assumed to be interrelated with and dependent for its existence upon the other elements. This conception of feudalism is fundamentally static; change is conceived only as the historical *realisation* of the political and economic unity of manorialism as an *essence*.

As a result of the internal stasis of manorialism, classical theorists had to invoke an external agent of destruction of this essence, hence introducing a conception of external dissolution. This took the form of commodity relations, especially in the guise of the commutation of labour services into money, which was reflected politically in the decline of villeinage. There are certain broad similarities between this perspective and Sweezy's theory of feudalism. Both view feudalism in terms of natural economy, introduce commodity relations as an external agent of change, and measure its impact by the development of money rents. Both conceptions depend upon the realisation and external destruction of an essence. Furthermore, the essential unity of elements of manorialism results in a failure to differentiate between different types of feudal enterprise, such as dislocated and integrated forms, and between the economy and its political conditions of existence, giving rise to a conflation of villeinage and labour services.

In response to this view, Postan suggests that the manor was preeminently a 'quasi-capitalist' enterprise engaged in production for the market.[2] Its profitability determined both the economic fortunes of tenants and the form of rent extracted from them. Whereas, when grain prices were low, demesnes contracted, the economic position of tenants improved and labour services declined, high grain prices encouraged a reversal of this trend. Through connection of secular price-trends with demographic pressure upon land and resources, Postan links the movement of the manorial economy with a more general demographic view of history. Other historians, such as Titow, Kershaw, Miller and Hatcher, have elaborated this perspective.[3] In this way, Postan analyses the development of the feudal economy in terms of its fundamental *internal contradictions* between population and resources, thereby introducing a theory of internal dissolution. I have already noted the influence of this approach upon Anderson's analysis. The demographic perspective has a certain appeal for Marxists, who like Anderson stress a contraction of the feudal economy caused by 'stalled' productive forces.

As with the classical perspective, demographic theorists obtain only a partial view. Postan neglects the non-commodity and integrated enterprises, and accords no place to political relations and landlord—tenant struggles. He assumes that tenants' economic position and form of rent are automatic and unproblematic responses to the movements of the demesne-based economy. Here, the links between his position and that of Banaji are clear, while there are similarities also with Dobb's emphasis on the importance of the availability of wage labour and profitability of demesnes in the determination of development. With this background established, I shall now examine feudal development chronologically.

The Twelfth Century

In Vinogradoff's analysis, the twelfth century was integral to the secular trend of the consolidation of manorialism, labour services and villeinage. There was little to distinguish this period apart from the increasingly clear demarcation of free and villein status. By contrast, Postan argues that the twelfth century saw an important *reversal* of development involving the widespread commutation of labour services and the shrinkage of demesnes. This change was caused by the uncertain market conditions resulting from the political and economic instability of the civil war of Stephen's reign in mid-century, and the consequent breakdown of authority in the countryside. In these circumstances, lords 'farmed out' their demesnes, since they preferred to obtain a fixed income for their manors rather than manage them directly. In addition, grain prices did not favour the direct exploitation of demesnes.

Kominsky concurs with Postan's view that money rents developed in this period, but suggests that they often resulted from conversion of *produce rent* into money, rather than commutation of labour services as Postan suggests. Furthermore, Kosminsky argues that the corn market expanded rather than contracted in this century and that peasants took advantage of this opportunity to trade more extensively with towns. Lords found it easier to profit from peasant trade through rent increases upon commutation than to do so by the extension of demesne production. In this case, conversion to money rents gave rise to an *increase* in exploitation, rather than a decrease as Postan suggests. Furthermore, lords retained the right to change rents back into the labour form.[4] Thus, the contrast between the twelfth century and both the preceding and following centuries is not as great as Postan maintains. Landlords maintained, and in many instances strengthened, their position through commutation. However, this consolidation of the feudal economy did not reflect the simple realisation of manorialism suggested by the classical perspective, as we shall see below.

Kosminsky's view of the twelfth century is reinforced by the character of landlord–tenant struggles in this period – that is, where records of them exist.[5] Unfortunately, sources of such conflicts are rare in England, although better documented on the Continent. Generally Hilton suggests that they were characterised by peasant defensive resistance to landlord advancement: such struggles were similar to those evident in earlier centuries in France and Italy. Hilton concedes to Postan that some tenants may have taken advantage of the breakdown of authority during the Civil War period to obtain commutation on favourable terms. However, these would have been isolated individual cases and did not represent a generalised aggressive stance by tenants. The rearguard action of peasants was maintained into the following century, in response to the continued consolidation of the feudal economy.

The Thirteenth Century

For Vinogradoff, this century represents the full realisation of the manorial system. Here, the manor reached its peak of development: the demesne economy flourished, labour services increased, and villeinage was extended to the majority of the tenant population. However, despite exemplifying the classical view, this period also draws out the contradictions in this perspective. Vinogradoff simultaneously suggests that feudalism was only 'settling itself' in the twelfth and thirteenth centuries, and that this period was characterised by the 'break-up' of feudalism.[6] This contradictory assessment results from the inability of this perspective – which involves a *linear evolution* of manorialism – to comprehend the complexity of feudal development. The Hundred Rolls, which I have examined in Chapter 2, clearly show this complexity. Vinogradoff's contradictory conclusions apply to distinct sectors of the feudal economy. Manorialism was realised to the full on large manors or dislocated enterprises, upon which demesnes were enlarged and labour services increased in this period. On small manors, in the face of the extensive penetration of commodity relations, lords were unable to prevent commutation, differentiation and the emergence of a free tenantry. Here, the disintegration of feudalism had already begun. Moreover, on other manors, a feudal economy had only recently been established as a result of the depression of tenants' status in the late twelfth century and the consequent intensification of labour services. I would argue that, in order to understand the development of manors of different structure, we must consider them as distinct forms of feudal enterprise.

In contrast, Postan focuses upon a specific type of manor – the dislocated enterprise – and concludes that its fortunes were crucial to the development of feudalism. According to Postan, grain prices began to rise dramatically in the mid twelfth century. This trend was maintained until the second decade of the fourteenth century, forming the basis of the resurgence of a manorial economy based upon demesne production for the market. At the same time, population increased, the area under cultivation was expanded, and lords sought the expansion of demesnes and the intensification of labour services. Landlords resumed direct control over demesne production and managed their estates rationally in order to profit from the market. In short, Postan considers that the manorial economy experienced a 'boom' in the thirteenth century.

However, Kosminsky suggests that the rise in grain prices arose from the increasing social division of labour owing to the expansion of the non-agricultural population, the development of the domestic market and the demand for foodstuffs, rather than, as Postan argues, as a simple result of the pressure of population upon land.[7] Also, Kosminsky suggests that the two great famine years of 1315 and 1316 distort Postan's price-series. Kosminsky argues that prices rose rapidly from the mid twelfth century until the mid thirteenth century, from which time up to the late fourteenth century they remained at a consistently high level. Thus, at a time when Postan argues that demographic pressures on land were at their height – the late thirteenth and early fourteenth centuries – grain prices had long been stabilised. It would appear that there is no obvious and direct link between population, land and prices, and that we cannot understand the expansion of the demesne economy simply in terms of grain prices.

Postan's emphasis upon economic factors gives rise to his neglect of the considerable political and legal pressure brought to bear upon the peasantry in the late twelfth and early thirteenth centuries. Such economic changes in themselves would not necessarily have led to the consolidation of the feudal economy. The extensive imposition of villeinage was required so that the feudal economy might be maintained and strengthened and demesnes expanded in the prevailing conditions of extensive commodity relations. The expansion of the market in the thirteenth century could have resulted in the *emancipation* of the peasantry into a class of free petty-commodity producers. In similar economic conditions, French landlords failed to strengthen their position politically and economically, so that such an emancipation occurred at this time.[8] In England, landlords made a determined and successful assault upon the position of their tenants. Thus, a crucial component of the path of development in England was the *resolution and effects of landlord–tenant struggles.* Through this sudden increase in political and legal pressure, the unfree character of villeinage was clarified, sharpened and closely linked with numerous servile obligations and with labour services, so that the landlord class was able to strengthen its control over tenants economically. The consolidation of the manorial economy often took the form of the expansion of commodity-producing demesnes worked by labour services, as Postan suggests. Thus, the political offensive made possible the formation of dislocated enterprises as a significant sector of the feudal economy, as well as the maintenance of integrated enterprises.

Extensive peasant resistance resulted from the sudden reduction of their status and increase in exploitation, and it became a significant force in England in the early thirteenth century.[9] I shall now examine both the form and the effects of landlord–tenant struggles until the fourteenth century, up to which time the parameters of these struggles remained constant.

Peasant Resistance, 1200–1349

Analysis of conflict prior to the fourteenth century suffers both from the nature and the paucity of sources. Indeed, Hilton argues that the impression given of the fourteenth century as the period of open conflict between landlords and tenants is itself partially the result of the adventitious survival of evidence.[10] Furthermore, the nature of the sources severely limits our knowledge of these struggles. Even though most conflicts were local affairs, sources of information are largely confined to the records of the central courts; manorial court rolls are very inadequate for these purposes. As a result, much of the endemic localised conflict – what Hilton terms 'the continuous day-to-day struggle' – is lost to history.[11] We must rely upon sources that tell us only about conflicts which were sufficiently serious and in which tenants had the legal rights, the resources and determination to pursue their claims in the courts of the King. In order to do so, they had to claim either free or 'villein sokemen' status. Such actions at law were undoubtedly the end-products of long and sustained struggles against landlords with reference to a whole host of disabilities, incidents, burdens and obligations that their landlords sought to impose on them.

The lack of both records and historical study gives rise to certain methodological problems. We should not assume that tenants' struggles were in vain even though almost all verdicts of the central courts went against them. Successful struggles were fought *locally*, as is suggested by my analysis of feudal enterprises. However, there is little to indicate the outcome directly, since manorial records such as court rolls, rentals and extents are scattered and, if they exist, have rarely been worked upon with these purposes in mind. It is extremely difficult to match struggles recorded centrally with local records so as to substantiate a strict temporal relationship of cause and effect between tenants' struggle and a change in their position. (We may note that Hilton's work is an outstanding exception in this respect.) Thus, we must be content with establishing a general temporal association between a shift in the incidence, extent, and seriousness of struggles, and change in the general economic and political position of tenants. But we must note that this change does not reflect a sweeping movement identifiable with one

particular cause, but is the summation of a tendential shift within the
localised power relationships of landlords and tenants.

By far the most common form of action within the central courts was
the claim to be 'villein sokemen' of 'ancient demesne'; indeed, more than
half the documented cases of conflict in the period 1200–1349 explicitly
concerned this issue. Villeins who held 'ancient demesne' lands of the
King possessed a privileged tenure compared with villeins on land
subject only to their lord's jurisdiction.[12] The former were 'villein
sokemen', who had the protection of royal law and were personally free.
They could not be deprived of their lands; their services, rents, and terms
of tenure were fixed; and they enjoyed certain immunities from taxation
and from the jurisdiction of the hundreds. They were not subject to the
arbitrary will of their lord unlike other villeins, even though they often
held land from a lord, rather than from the Crown directly. In sum,
villein sokemen were exempt from the aspects of villeinage associated
with *jurisdictional powers* and *personal servitude*; lords could maintain
only the political conditions of existence related to the landed monopoly, or villein *tenure*. They were unable to maintain the conditions of
existence related to the denial of possession. As such, this status was
similar to that of free tenants, since both were subject only to the
primary condition of existence of the FMP, the right of exclusion.

Courts of law could establish lands as part of ancient demesne by a
search of the Domesday Book. Villeins – who felt the increasingly
oppressive weight of exactions and disabilities – focused much of their
energy on attempts to prove that they were protected by this tenure,
especially since the increasingly clear-cut definition of villeinage in the
thirteenth century precluded other forms of legal argument.[13] Needless
to say, villeins had minimal success with this strategy. The difficulties
involved in proving such status were immense, and it is clear that the
King's courts largely supported the interests of lords. Even if it were
established that villeins held ancient demesne land, the fact that they
were termed 'villani' in the Domesday Book was sufficient to confirm
their status as villeins outright. It was conveniently forgotten that in the
eleventh century this term had none of the servile connotations it was to
gain later. Villeins had to prove their direct descent from those explicitly
recorded as villein sokemen in the Domesday Book. Thus, it was
sufficient for the lord to argue that the ancestors of his villeins had taken
up their tenancies after Domesday. Technically, this sophistry was
beside the point, because villein socage was a form of tenure, not a
personal status; anyone who held such land should also have enjoyed the
privileges which pertained to it. In other instances, villeins did not have

an obvious case to plead according to the Domesday Book. None the less, they tried this course of action as it was the only one open to them.

There is a steady stream of instances of tenants' resistance to lords' attempts to depress their political and econqmic position through villeinage. This resistance was largely defensive, often taking the form of the claim of ancient demesne. There were two peaks in resistance: (1) in the late thirteenth century, as a result of political intervention by the King, and (2) in the early fourteenth century, in difficult agrarian conditions.[14] In the former, enquiries made by the Crown in the 1270s (chiefly known for the Hundred Rolls of 1279), raised the hopes of villeins in many parts of the country. These enquiries were made in order to re-establish and assess the rights of the Crown over its ancient demesne lands in the face of the appropriation of these rights by lords. Tenants often obtained writs based on villein-sokeman tenure which suspended their lords' increases of services, rents and other exactions. In the period 1270–99, of forty-three documented instances of conflict, twenty-eight concerned the issue of ancient demesne status explicitly. Such conflict was largely located in the South and Midlands and was prevalent on monastic estates – more than half the recorded instances occurred on such manors.

In the latter period, the 1320s, the increased incidence and severity of disturbances may well have been based upon the hardships caused by the agrarian crisis which engulfed England from 1315 to 1322 and gave rise to difficulties for both lord and peasant for some time afterwards. Monastic landlords were again at the centre of conflict. There was a series of small revolts in 1327, the focus of which were monasteries such as St Albans. In the same year, 'ten thousand' villeins and townspeople led by two clerics who bore the rebel banners marched against the monastery of Bury St Edmunds. This year was also one of upheavals on the manor of Ogbourne, Wiltshire, which belonged to the Abbey of Bec. There had been trouble on this manor for a long time, for in 1277 and 1309 villeins had laid claim to ancient demesne in the courts. Discontent continued to exist at least until 1341, when the tenants obtained letters patent against their abbot. Moreover, in 1328–9 the villeins of the Abbot of Vale Royal on his manors of Darnhall and Over in Cheshire rebelled.

In spite of widespread resistance over the period 1200–1349, tenants met with little success. The possibility of successful resistance had largely been eliminated by the mid thirteenth century. At most, actions had been aimed at limiting landlords' efforts to depress their position. As Hilton observes,

The small-scale actions of English villagers in the 13th century were usually defeated. Supported by the greatest of feudal landowners, the King, the lords normally won in the royal courts, for the tide was running too strongly against peasant interests. This does not seem to have been the case in parts of France, Italy and other European countries. The period was, for some peasants in these countries, an era of stabilisation, marked precisely by gains which the English peasants failed to achieve, namely the fixing of customary rights at an acceptable level.[15]

We may conclude that the failure of peasant resistance allowed the landlord class to consolidate the feudal economy at a time of extensive commodity relations through the widespread imposition and deepening of villeinage. This represented the decisive turning-point in English agrarian development which was to prove crucial in determining the insecurity of peasant land-tenure in later centuries.

Regions of England at the End of the Thirteenth Century

At this point, since we have available the comprehensive survey of the feudal economy known as the Hundred Rolls, I shall analyse the different regional economic structures in England.[16] This enables us to understand the structural determinants of later struggles and development, having now established that the state of development manifest at the end of the thirteenth century followed from the successful struggle of landlords against their tenants. The fundamental distinctions between Southern and Eastern, and Northern and Western England lie in the different extent of the consolidation of both the feudal economy and the political power of the landlord class: feudalism was more fully formed in the South and East than in the North and West. The greater penetration of commodity relations in the former regions was superimposed upon these differences. Relatively speaking, the percentage of villeins to free tenants, the percentage of labour services to money rent, the extent of differentiation, and the level of exploitation was high in the South and East and low in the North and West. The extensive penetration of commodity relations in the former regions caused considerable differentiation on many small manors, upon which lords were unable to secure the political conditions of existence of feudalism. This more than counterbalanced the lack of differentiation on large manors upon which powerful landlords were able to secure these political conditions and to maintain a uniform villeinised tenant population, which suffered heavy exploitation. In dislocated enterprises, labour services were retained and the demesnes were turned towards the production of grain for the market, while in integrated enterprises powerful landlords took high money rents. The combined effect of considerable landlord power and extensive commodity relations in the South and East thus produced strong contrasts in manorial structure between large manors, in which labour-services remained dominant, and small manors, which had begun to disintegrate. We may thereby understand the contradictory developments of the period which were crucial in the revolt of 1381, examined below.

In the North and West, feudalism was not fully established, landlords were generally less powerful and the penetration of commodity relations less extensive. However, this last characteristic also reduced tenants' capacity for resistance to landlord pressure; feudal political conditions of existence were easier to maintain. In small manors there was not the same tendency towards extensive differentiation and disintegration of the manor as in the South and East. In any case, given the relative absence of demesnes and labour services, prevention of differentiation was not an urgent matter. The weak imposition of manorial structure is indicated by the widespread lack of coincidence of manor and community. Extensive upland and pastoral areas inhibited the formation of manors which dominated communities and made it difficult to maintain labour services. In these circumstances, landlords allowed and encouraged the commutation of the extensive produce rents and of the few existing labour services. In sum, the manorial structure of Northern and Western England was generally characterised by weak forms of development of the non-commodity and integrated enterprises; there was little possibility of the formation of dislocated enterprises.

Both Kent and East Anglia were exceptions to the broad trends established for Southern and Eastern England. Kent lay across the major trade route to France and the Continent; here the early development of commodity relations enabled the peasantry to resist the consolidation of feudalism. The Kentish peasantry were free, able to alienate and subdivide land between heirs (the inheritance custom known as gavelkind), and gave only minimal labour services. Manors were not centralised and had little impact upon agrarian structure, and produce rents were from an early time commuted for money. Gavelkind and free alienation of land caused rapid and early differentiation of the peasantry. By the thirteenth century, there were many landless or near-landless labourers alongside the wealthy secure freeholders. In sum, Kent's unique geographical position allowed its peasantry to defend its freedom and extend its privileges from an early date, but at the cost of increasing fragmentation.

East Anglia had certain similarities with Kent. As part of the southern Danelaw, its social structure was based upon a free peasantry and incomplete manorialisation. As a result, the manor and community rarely coincided, and there developed an extensive peasant land market and partible inheritance customs.[17] From the twelfth century onwards, greater manorialisation resulted in the introduction of labour services and a partial loss of freedom. Peasants in East Anglia were partially assimilated into the feudal economy, since they lacked the resources of the Kentish peasants, based upon strong integration into the market. (This structure was to be an important factor in Ket's Rebellion of 1549, which will be analysed later.)

The Midlands was intermediate in structure between the highly feudalised South and East and the incompletely feudalised North and West.[18] Within the Midlands, there were differences based upon the broad geographical distinctions discussed above. Generally, the East Midlands was more highly feudalised than the West Midlands; this is clearly apparent from the Hundred Rolls. Additionally, specific counties had distinctive economic structures. The considerable labour services in Northamptonshire placed it more with Southern and Eastern counties than with the Midlands, while in Leicestershire (part of the northern Danelaw) there were many free peasants, manorialisation was incomplete, the manor rarely coincided with the community, demesnes were relatively small, labour services were low, and villeinage less prevalent than elsewhere in the Midlands. Leicestershire's social structure was more akin to that of a more westerly county, such as Warwickshire. I shall examine the structure of Warwickshire in Chapter 5.

We may conclude that the geographical pattern of feudal development was complex and dependent upon specific factors such as the extent of commodity relations, the availability of land reserves for a pastoral economy, and the earlier establishment of a free peasant social structure. Given these considerations, we may analyse the development of feudalism in terms of the theoretical categories which I have established above.

CRISIS

The place of the fourteenth century in development has been even more hotly disputed than that of previous centuries. To a large extent, the timing of the onset of the decline of feudalism has been measured against one of three landmarks. First, classical medievalists consider the *timing of commutation* of labour services with reference to the Black Death of 1348–9. Secondly, Postan and those of the demographic school refer to a more generalised conception of demographic crisis which extends the onset of decline back to the famines of 1315–17. The crucial question is that of the *chronology of population decline* and of indicators for such changes. Thirdly, Marxist historians tend to emphasise the *political role* of the Peasants' Revolt of 1381, even though they also recognise the importance of economic changes which preceded the revolt. Here I shall outline the first two positions before examining the Marxist interpretation in the context of late-fourteenth-century struggles.

The classical view of development in feudal England takes as its point of reference the Black Death and its effects upon the manorial economy in terms of the commutation of labour services. Initially, Thorold Rogers argued that commutation had begun before the Black Death and that the plagues, in decreasing the labouring and tenant populations, led to the reimposition of services. This 'feudal reaction' gave rise to the explosive outburst of the peasantry in 1381 against such harsh exploitation, and this in turn resulted in the final abandonment of labour services and villeinage. In response to this view, Page argued inversely that commutation was initiated by the Black Death, since villeins were then able to flee their landlords and seek high wages in the prevailing conditions of labour scarcity. As a result, landlords were forced to concede to tenants' demands for the commutation of services. However, Gray criticises Page for an over-generalised view of the process of commutation and argues that it developed unevenly; whereas in the North and West commutation preceded the Black Death, in the South and East services remained until after the plagues. Gray neatly resolved previous arguments by demonstrating their geographically specific sources. For example, Page relied upon data from conservative ecclesiastical estates in the South and East of England. In conclusion to her summary of the debate, Power admits the probable futility of this controversy.[19] She argues that no one such event may be seen as determinant of commutation and of the decline of feudalism and that the manorial economy contained the seeds of decay within itself, so that it was destroyed slowly over three centuries. None the less, her analysis adheres to the classical approach in that a money economy is seen as the agent of decline.

This debate is clearly located within the classical perspective: all participants assume that commutation is always of labour services.

However, the existence of money rents does not imply prior commutation of labour services. In Northern and Western England, many rents had always been in the money form, and if commutation had occurred it was likely to have been of produce rent and not labour services. Furthermore, the money economy failed to act as the solvent of feudalism, as the classical theorists would have us believe, because commutation and money rents were most prevalent in regions where there was less extensive penetration of commodity relations, in the North and West. [20] The classicists are wrong to assume that the spread of a money economy *per se* engenders commutation and the dissolution of feudalism.

Like Page, Postan minimises any feudal reaction after the Black Death and suggests that the revolt of 1381 gave no impetus to change. The crucial difference between Postan and classical theorists lies in his relegation of the political and economic position of tenants to the status of effects of movements of the manorial economy. For Postan, the faltering and contraction of demesne production is the key to dating the decline of feudalism. One might imagine that for those of the demographic school the Black Death would have played an important role in this process, through the decimation of the ranks of tenants upon which the demesnes relied for labour. However, for his argument Postan relies more upon the trend in grain prices than upon the Black Death. He argues that prices sagged and demesne profits declined from the early fourteenth century onwards. The famines of 1315–17 are seen as the first indication of the underlying imbalance of population and resources. The Black Death is thus seen as a tardy manifestation of a demographic crisis apparent some time earlier.

Postan's argument concerning a declining population is dependent upon indirect indicators, among which are high wage-levels, low rents, tenancy vacancies, and contraction of the cultivated area. Population decline was caused by the very expansion of the feudal economy and population which pushed the limits of cultivation on to marginal lands and tended to exhaust the soil. Given a precarious balance of population and resources, the series of bad harvests in the second decade of the fourteenth century was sufficient to reverse all trends in wages, prices, rents, population and demesne production.

As I have argued above, though Postan tends to neglect the role of tenants' political and economic position these components of feudalism are crucial to the determination of development. In this respect, the debate on commutation is of some importance. The differential timing of commutation in regions of England indicates that commutation proceeded unevenly and in inverse relationship to the extent of penetration of commodity relations, in the face of which dislocated enterprises in Southern and Eastern England required the successful assertion of landlord power. In spite of this, Postan assumes that the political and economic position of tenants resulted automatically from the dynamics of the demesne economy. In addition, there is some doubt whether the limits of the demesne economy were reached in the early fourteenth century. Kershaw argues that large grain-producing estates, or dislocated enterprises, profited from the prevailing conditions of the market after the famines of 1315–17, because the rise in grain prices outweighed by a factor of two the decrease in production.[21] In general, he suggests that the agrarian crisis hit hardest the poor, sparsely populated regions, rather than wealthy and densely populated regions such as South Eastern England, where the economy merely stagnated. Indeed, until the 1370s on large estates, labour services were intensified and *relative* exploitation was increased. Income on such estates was then only 10 per cent lower than it had been before the Black Death, even though population had declined by one-third in the intervening period. For a considerable time after the famines of the early fourteenth century and plagues of the mid fourteenth century, large landlords marketing grain from their demesnes were able to maintain their position, especially in the South and East of England.[22]

The resilience of the demesne economy until the late fourteenth century poses problems for the demographic perspective. It is also questionable whether there was further population decline after the plagues of 1348 to the 1360s.[23] If not, in Postan's terms the basis for continued economic decline from the early fourteenth century would be removed. Moreover, the extent of population decline in the early fourteenth century itself has been challenged. Also, Kosminsky's revised price-series does not indicate a decline in grain prices until 1380, rather than the early fourteenth century, as Postan argues. If prices are important, the turning-point would seem to coincide with the final disintegration of the dislocated enterprises and the revolt of 1381, rather than with the famines earlier in the century. As a result, in the terms of the demographic perspective, there are considerable problems of analysis: the onset of feudal decline seems to have occurred in the late fourteenth century.

The underpinnings of the demographic approach may also be attacked. Kosminsky argues that 'overpopulation' or the imbalance of population and resources was a result of the feudal mode of production – a specific set of economic and social relationships – rather than a natural and inevitable consequence of population growth.[24] The monopoly of landownership by landlords resulted in artificial over-population caused by various factors such as the binding of tenants to the manor, the maintenance of such a level of exploitation that peasant land could not be effectively cultivated and kept in 'good heart', and the seizure of commons and wastes, with the result that the peasant economy was exhausted. These conditions were reflected in the extension of cultivation to marginal lands, and the rise in rents, land values and grain prices. Thus, the effects of the crisis of feudalism in the fourteenth century are those outlined in the demographic perspective, but the causes must be seen as a *social* consequence of the feudal mode of production rather than as a natural and inevitable consequence of population expansion.

I have now returned to the crucial theme of the last chapter – the role of class struggle in the decline of feudalism. I have indicated that the pivotal point of the trajectory of feudalism lay in the late fourteenth century – at the time of the Peasants' Revolt of 1381 – rather than in either of the two landmarks signified by the classical and demographic perspectives. This requires examination of the role of landlord–tenant struggles in the latter half of the fourteenth century.

1350–81: the Shift onto the Offensive

After the Black Death, discontent and conflict became more frequent and widespread: tenants began to move onto the offensive against their landlords. Unrest was particularly common in Southern and Midland counties – the areas in which feudalism was most advanced, population density highest, and market production best established. Here feudal contradictions were at their sharpest.[25] Moreover, struggles were concentrated in monastic estates, which were renowned for their conservative management and were among the most powerful in England. In the period concerned, there were more than forty instances of conflict in fourteen Southern and Midland counties, many of them on ecclesiastical manors.[26] In many Southern counties, discontent increasingly took the form of widespread refusal of services, mounting arrears of rent, and outright flight from manors, as well as continued lawsuits over the issue of ancient demesne status. Claims of ancient demesne were now seen by villeins as a basis for complete emancipation, both of personal status and tenure, and these claims were increasingly expressed forcibly.

By the 1370s, much of the South and the Midlands was in a state of unrest.[27] In 1377, in twenty parishes in counties such as Hampshire, Wiltshire, Surrey and Berkshire, villeins laid claim to ancient demesne status. At the same time there was trouble in Dorset, Devon and Somerset. This unrest caused the House of Commons in October 1377 to petition the King to act to prevent a peasant rising on the scale of the Jacquerie. In response, the King issued an ordinance reaffirming the *status quo* and supporting landlords' efforts to suppress unrest and enforce services, through commissions of Oyer and Terminer. Such commissions were issued for Wiltshire, Hampshire, Surrey, Dorset, Somerset and Oxfordshire in 1377–8, and for Northamptonshire in 1380, while in Devon the Sheriff was ordered to suppress rebellious assemblies.

All facets of villeinage became the subject of struggles between tenants and landlords. The most common and central disputed incident was the existence and/or level of labour services. In most instances villeins refused to perform such services, as part and parcel of their claims regarding status. Tenants almost invariably focused upon this aspect of villeinage, which was a primary indicator of servile status. Other components of villeinage also featured in disputes. Tallage-at-will and merchet – particularly common incidents of villeinage – were often singled out. Other manifestations of feudal political conditions of existence were also fought over: villeins attempted to remove restrictions regarding sale, purchase and accumulation of land; disputed entry fines; attacked mill monopolies; refused to accept regulation of marriage; and denied their subjection to manorial courts.

THE PEASANTS' REVOLT OF 1381

Ever since Thorold Roger's statement that the revolt of 1381 effected the final abandonment of villeinage, the dominant view has been to deny the revolt a prominent role in historical change.[28] Postan, for example, argues that the revolt was not a reaction to intensified oppression and gave no impetus to change, since it occurred at a time of improved economic conditions for the peasantry. Power concludes that the economic changes contingent upon the impact of a money economy were neither inhibited nor hastened by the revolt, while other historians, such as Lipson, Oman, Dobson and McKisack, adopt a similar position. What are these conclusions based upon? Postan forms his conclusions on the basis of the demographic perspective, while the other authors mentioned rely upon the classical perspective: they measure the effects (or lack of them) in terms of the progress of commutation. Inevitably, the revolt fails to come up to their expectations as an obvious landmark in commutation. Villeinage only gradually withered away, over a long period. Thus, it is deduced that the revolt had little effect. In association with this, Oman argues that the multitude of landlord–tenant conflicts both before and after the revolt diminishes the impact of the revolt itself: it cannot be seen as a singular, unique and transformative event which shaped development.

However, this argument is based on the assumption that, if the revolt was to have any impact at all, it would take the form of a pervasive transformation of the condition of the peasantry at a stroke. Such an expectation derives from the classical view of development, in which change is seen as a linear and generalised process. However, paradoxically, the additional stress on the evolutionary nature of change within this perspective entirely rules out the possibility of any radical transformation. Thus, authors within the classical perspective are unable even to pose the question, let alone answer it in the affirmative. A transformative role for the revolt is denied as a logical necessity. But the denial of an immediate and generalised transformative role for the revolt does not imply that it was insignificant. We may appreciate the revolt's true importance as a dramatic summation of the endemic *localised* landlord–tenant conflicts of the period.[29] Villeins sought to improve their condition by the attainment of personal freedom, which implied that their lord's power over them – expressed in jurisdictional powers and personal servitude – would be destroyed. Such struggles could be resolved at the local level in relation to the particular landlord concerned. By contrast, the destruction of the *landed monopoly* required the overthrow of the landlord class as a whole, whose political interests were increasingly expressed and unified in the central state, and thus could be realised only by the destruction of central authority. The revolt of 1381, in spite of its wider scope and larger scale, remained within this local framework. Its greater unity was gained as a result of the extension of the sphere of activities of the central state, rather than by a fundamental attack on feudalism.[30]

Hilton suggests that, throughout Western Europe in the later Middle Ages, peasant revolts were transformed from localised movements limited in scope and aimed at altering only the balance of the relationship of community and lord to regional and large-scale revolts concerned more with the transformation of social relationships. This change was associated with the emergence of a strengthened central state complete with fiscal and judicial powers, and with the expansion of trade, commodity relations and communications.

In England, the incidence and weight of the state's fiscal demands increased dramatically in the fourteenth century, leading peasants to associate grievances deriving from both private and public exactions, and producing attacks on royal tax-collectors. Central authority was extended over manorial powers through the justices of the peace (JPs), members of the local nobility and gentry, and was increasingly required because lords found that they were unable to impose authority in their courts. This was reflected in legislation in two spheres: (1) wage labour – the Statutes of Labourers, 1349–51; and (2) the extraction of rent – the 1377 ordinance regarding claims of ancient demesne and refusal of services. The wage-freeze and restrictions upon mobility inherent in the Statutes of Labourers hit hard both poor peasants and labourers as the source of wage labour, and rich peasants as employers of labour. Justices charged with the administration of these statutes were often also landlords concerned to secure a cheap and stable labour force for their demesnes. Through these means, lords' existing seigneurial rights were protected nationally. As a result of this intervention, peasants increasingly identified the power of the landlord with that of the central state. Attacks were made upon the sessions of justices of labourers in Middlesex in 1351, in Lincolnshire in 1352, and in Northamptonshire in 1359.[31] The ordinance of 1377 and subsequent commissions of Oyer and Terminer in the period 1377–80 constituted centralised controls over an increasingly assertive peasantry. Both interventions by the state indicate the inability of individual lords to assert control over tenants. After the Black Death manorial authority was breaking down under the combined weights of economic changes and tenant resistance.

In this period, the conflicts inherent in feudal society were intensified, especially in the South and East, where commodity exchange was most fully developed and landlord power was strongest. In this part of England, dislocated enterprises were juxtaposed with smaller manors upon which the conditions of existence of feudalism could not be maintained. In other words, peasant communities which experienced severe conditions of servitude existed alongside other communities which had gained sufficient strength from their early contact with the market to be able to resist a depression of their status, and those which had largely escaped from their servile condition earlier in the fourteenth century. Moreover, in manors where differentiation had advanced rapidly because political conditions of existence could not be enforced, wage labourers formed a significant proportion of the population. The legislation against labourers further exacerbated the tensions which underpinned the revolt of 1381. Here, the contradictions associated with the development of feudalism were pushed to their limits. Thus, the weight of the state in the freezing of wages, restrictions on labourers' mobility and repression of peasant discontent was felt with heightened effect in South Eastern England, a region in which tensions had reached breaking-point. In these conditions, the tax demands of the 1370s and 1380–1 provided the necessary catalyst for the revolt.

There is little point in describing the revolt in detail; this has been done adequately elsewhere by authors such as Oman, Dobson and Hilton. Here I shall briefly comment upon the relevant characteristics of the revolt for my analysis.[32] The revolt centred on South Eastern England – in Essex, Kent, Middlesex, Hertfordshire, Cambridgeshire, Norfolk and Suffolk. In these counties, differentiation of the peasantry was very marked. The occupational structure of the rebels broadly reflected that of the counties involved. Hilton concludes that 'the rising was one of the whole people below the ranks of those who exercised lordship in the countryside and established authority in the towns'.[33] Organisation was based on village communities' extant organisation from which support was widened by recourse to the hundredal units. The considerable localism gave strength to rebel organisation and derived from the most important source of conflict, the constraints and exactions associated with villeinage. In order to emancipate themselves, villeins had to attack the locus of servility in their landlord's power over them. As a result, manorial court rolls were burnt and charters of freedom forcibly extracted in many places from landlords.

The rebels' most important demands, as articulated within the 'Mile End' programme, involved the destruction of serfdom, fixed rents at four pence an acre, and freedom of access to markets. This was to be realised in the fifteenth century. The Mile End programme reflected the interests of the upper and middle layers of the peasantry, who were increasingly becoming petty-commodity producers. If these demands had been met, they would have effectively ended manorial domination and secured tenancies at a reasonable rent, without questioning the basis of landholding itself. Further demands made included an end to feudal lordship, the removal of existing laws, and the abolition of the ecclesiastical hierarchy. More concrete and immediate issues were reflected in demands for the execution of the King's 'evil' advisers – considered to be responsible for the poll taxes and the maladministration of justice; revision of the Statutes of Labourers, and an end to outlawry (an important means of control of labourers and peasants); and the throwing open of private game-reserves for common use. This latter set of demands largely reflected the interests of poor peasants and was articulated in the 'Smithfield' programme of the Kentish rebels. Generally, the rebels appealed to the King as the leader of a putative 'people's monarchy' with no intervening administrative structure, lay or ecclesiastical, between the peasantry and the King. The King, under duress, granted the rebels charters of freedom which were, none the less, immediately revoked when the revolt was over.

However, the extraction of charters from the King was largely irrelevant to the landlord–tenant conflicts of this period, including the revolt of 1381 itself. Such charters were not an appropriate means of gaining emancipation. This battle had to be won in the struggles between lords and tenants. The revolt of 1381 and the conflicts in which it was immersed assisted in hastening the end of manorial authority. By the fifteenth century, the peasantry had largely won for itself the demands articulated in the revolt. In other words, the importance of the revolt lies in the transformation of the *conditions and efficacy of localised struggles* rather than in its supposed immediate, general and radical effects. Localised struggles themselves became more fundamental in nature and more widespread than before. The transformation of such widespread conflicts into a peasants' revolt was largely due to the impact of the centralisation of the state. But this is not to disguise the fact that the fundamental issues both existed and were to be resolved at the local level.

After the revolt, unrest was endemic in Southern and Midland counties.[34] In July 1381, after hearing of the revolt, Worcester Priory tenants in Worcestershire and Warwickshire withheld labour services and prepared for an insurrection. In 1382 and 1384, there were plots in Norfolk for a renewed rising. In 1383, Lewes Castle in Sussex, which belonged to the Earl of Arundel, was stormed and all rolls, rentals and charters burnt. The same situation of ferment is indicated in the pages of the Calendar of Patent Rolls. In the period 1385–1400, there were nineteen Commissions of Oyer and Terminer issued for twenty-five places in twelve Southern and Midland counties – Berkshire, Devon, Essex, Huntingdonshire, Northamptonshire, Shropshire, Somerset, Staffordshire, Sussex, Warwickshire and Wiltshire. Thus, the same pattern of disturbances occurred after the revolt as before it. This indicates that we should interpret the revolt itself not as a unique and generally transformative event, but as a peak in a period of half a century of intense local landlord–tenant struggles, in which such struggles became fused with issues of a more centralised nature. The full measure of the impact of the revolt of 1381 is to be found in the cumulative effects of a myriad of struggles in that period.

By the end of the fourteenth century, it had become clear that the Statutes of Labourers could not be made to work, that manors with large commodity-producing demesnes reliant upon labour services had no future, and that manorial authority was disintegrating. Before that time, it remained possible that landlord power might be tightened up in the wake of the Black Death and that the dislocated enterprise might become the dominant feature of the economy. In similar economic conditions in Eastern Europe, precisely these changes took place in the rise of 'second serfdom'. In the West, however, landlord power disintegrated and dislocated enterprises disappeared. A significant contribution to the divergent development of Eastern and Western Europe was made by the sustained struggles of tenants against their landlords, struggles which culminated in the revolt of 1381. This contribution has largely gone unrecognised. Although the development of feudalism provided the structuring conditions of the struggle between landlords and tenants in the feudal crisis, the specific direction of development was dependent upon the resolution of these struggles.

I have now traced the development of landlord–tenant conflicts in the thirteenth and fourteenth centuries. This development was marked by a shift from defensive resistance to the landlord offensive of the thirteenth and early fourteenth centuries, to offensive struggles against local landlord power in the late fourteenth century. In these two centuries, there were two decisive turning-points in feudal development. First, the failure of peasant resistance in the thirteenth century allowed the landlord class to consolidate the feudal economy. Secondly, the turn of tenants' resistance onto the offensive in the late fourteenth century contributed to the inability of the landlord class to maintain a highly consolidated economy in the form of dislocated enterprises, and to the ultimate decline of feudalism. In this way, the importance of landlord–tenant struggles for the development of feudalism is evident.

5 Development in Warwickshire

In this final chapter in Part I, many of the threads discussed thus far will be drawn together by means of a detailed analysis of certain peasant communities in the county of Warwickshire. Their different lines of development may be highlighted and linked into the major themes of the remainder of the book: the impact of agrarian change (particularly enclosure) on the peasantry, and the place of peasant revolts in the period of transition towards agrarian capitalism. These very peasant communities were central in the revolt considered in Part III.

In the medieval period, the Midland region as a whole displayed only incomplete feudalisation, but this hid the fact that there were areas within the Midlands in which feudalism was strongly established and other areas where it had little impact. Often the latter comprised areas of late-settled forest in which density of population was low. The distinctive nature of these two types of economy was accentuated by the fact that such areas often lay adjacent to one another. In Warwickshire, two such adjacent areas were known as the 'felden' and the 'Arden'. The former was characterised by so-called 'champion' country in which large nucleated peasant communities cultivated the land co-operatively in the form of arable open fields. This was typical of much of feudalised Southern and Midland England. By contrast, in the Arden communities were smaller and fewer and there was more emphasis on pastoral farming from enclosed assarts taken from the forest. The differences between the felden and the Arden were largely reflected in the contrasts which may be drawn between Kineton and Stoneleigh hundreds respectively (see Map 2). Using such units of county administration as a basis for comparison, we may draw conclusions regarding manorial structure and development in Warwickshire. Initially, however, we must understand some of the broader factors which shaped the feudal character of the county.

79

MANORIAL STRUCTURE

At the time of the Domesday survey of 1086, the three largest landowners in the county were Turchil of Warwick with sixty-nine manors, the Count of Meulan with sixty-seven, and Coventry Priory with eighteen.[1] (The two large lay estates later united to form the estate of the first Earl of Warwick.) In spite of these three large estates, feudal landlords did not exert a strong influence generally on the economic structure of the county. Very few manors were held 'in demesne', so that control which might be established by virtue of immediate ownership and supervision often was not possible. Of Turchil's manors, sixty-three were 'enfeoffed' or subtenanted, while forty-three of Meulan's manors were subtenanted. Both estates were widely dispersed geographically. Other smaller estates were similarly fragmented and exerted little influence. Although Coventry Priory was much smaller than these two lay estates, it exercised considerable control, as the estate was consolidated and only one of its eighteen manors was subtenanted. Other ecclesiastical landlords had little impact, because their estates were assembled piecemeal. They consequently were forced to adapt to existing peasant communities instead of imposing a highly manorialised form.

By the end of the thirteenth century, many lay estates had partially disintegrated through fragmentation and subinfeudation. By this time, the numbers of manors in the county had increased from 111 (in 1086) to 179, an increase of over 50 per cent. Small non-manorial estates also expanded and the extent of coincidence of manor and community fell from 62 to 42 per cent of total manors. Only the Earl of Warwick's massive estate retained a stable nucleus of demesnes and functioned as an organised unit of production. Even here, subinfeudation was extensive; by 1315 only ten manors were still held in demesne, while others were held by fifty-eight tenants holding a total of ninety-seven knight's fees in 110 parishes. By contrast, the old ecclesiastical estates remained unified and extended their landownership throughout the county. In 1086, the Church was the major owner in only twenty-five parishes; by 1300, this was extended to sixty parishes, one-quarter of the total in Warwickshire. Both Coventry and Kenilworth priories developed and consolidated their estates, though neither was sufficiently large to affect the manorial structure of the county as a whole. In 1279, over 60 per cent of Coventry Priory tenants were villeins. The Priory was particularly important in shaping the manorial structure of parishes within which it held land. In contrast to the large lay landowners, it continued to hold most manors in immediate possession, there was no tendency towards fragmentation, and strong continuity of ownership was maintained.

Unlike other religious houses, the Priory did not adopt large-scale sheep-farming in the later medieval period but concentrated on traditional feudal means by extracting surplus from the peasantry through production for the market by labour services on large demesnes. Coventry Priory's strength as a landlord was maintained until the period of the Black Death. In Warwickshire, it was granted a view of frankpledge in Prior's Hardwick, Prior's Marston, Southam and Bishop's Itchington, in addition to markets in Southam, Bishop's Itchington and Coventry. Its manors continued to be based upon large labour-service worked demesnes.[2]

Regionally, we may distinguish between the two Warwickshire hundreds of Kineton and Stoneleigh, which reflect the difference between a highly manorialised, densely populated 'felden' region and an only partially manorialised, sparsely populated, and wooded region. Although estates experienced considerable fragmentation in both hundreds, this was more marked in the former. In 1086, 69 per cent of manors coincided with parishes, compared with only 50 per cent in the latter; by 1279, in the former it had fallen to 40 per cent, while in the latter there was only a minor decrease, to 43 per cent. This closing of the gap between the two hundreds reflects the emergence in Kineton of large numbers of small manors without demesnes (forty-seven manors out of a total of ninety-six), a development less apparent in Stoneleigh (only thirty-two out of eighty-two).[3] In Kineton hundred, in addition to the many small manors, there were also many large ones (49 per cent of the total compared with an average of 35 per cent throughout the Hundred Rolls). Some of these large manors were under strong and direct control by their lords, such as Coventry Priory, while others experienced little control, because of the divorce of overlords from direct supervision of manors.[4] In these marked contrasts between large and small manors and the extent of coincidence of manor and community, we have the key to understanding later divergent developments within the felden Kineton hundred. In Stoneleigh hundred, however, medium-sized manors predominated, largely as a result of the late formation of ecclesiastical estates in this area, which meant that they were unable to unify their manors into a geographically consolidated unit.

THE PEASANTRY

Overall in Warwickshire, the period 1086–1279 saw a decline in gross numbers of villeins while at the same time villeinage was made more servile. In 1086, 57 per cent of households were villeins, 30 per cent bordars and 13 per cent serfs. By 1279, villeins formed only between one-quarter and one-half of the households in the two hundreds of Kineton and Stoneleigh. At the same time, the numbers of freeholders increased and the peasantry as a whole paid a higher-than-average proportion of their rents in money, this being 70 per cent of all rents. Moreover, both villein and free stratification profiles, when compared with those of other counties covered by the Hundred Rolls (apart from Oxfordshire), show a weighting towards the upper levels of the peasantry. This was due to the relative lack of manorialisation, combined with a low penetration of commodity relations characteristic of the West Midlands. Both Warwickshire and Oxfordshire in the West Midlands had more rich and middle peasants and fewer smallholders than more easterly counties such as Huntingdonshire, Cambridgeshire, Bedfordshire and Buckinghamshire. Powerful landlords maintained a tight grip over local and regional trade. Chartered markets were dominated by the Earl of Warwick, Coventry Priory and the Earl of Stafford – the very landlords who held estates dominated by labour-service worked demesnes.[5] As a result, even though trade was fairly well developed, it was not dominated by peasants producing independently for the market.

The two hundreds of Kineton and Stoneleigh provide strongly contrasting patterns of development in the medieval period. In 1086, Stoneleigh hundred was sparsely populated and not very prosperous, owing to its late colonisation. By contrast, Kineton hundred was even then intensively cultivated and densely populated. From Domesday onwards, the Arden experienced a rapid expansion of population and cultivation through colonisation, while the felden remained relatively static, having reached an equilibrium between land and population in the prevailing conditions of strong manorial control.[6] In 1279, the population density was the same in both hundreds, but their economic structures remained very different. Stoneleigh was noted for freehold tenure, while Kineton was markedly villeinised (see Table 5.1).[7] Also, the gap in peasant wealth between the two hundreds was maintained. In 1279, the half-virgate was the predominant holding in Stoneleigh and the full virgate in Kineton.

Lords sought to attract peasants in Stoneleigh by offering freehold

TABLE 5.1   Tenant structure in 1279 in Stoneleigh and Kineton
hundreds (per cent)

	Free	Villein	Smallholder	Total
Stoneleigh	52	23	25	100
Kineton	21	57	22	100

Source: R. H. Hilton, *The English Peasantry in the Later Middle Ages*
(Oxford: Clarendon Press, 1975) table, pp. 126–7.

tenure. Even in Kineton, freeholders comprised over one-fifth of the
total population, indicating the uneasy coexistence of large manors held
by powerful lords and small manors held by weaker lords. In Stoneleigh
hundred, labour services were rare and where demanded were not heavy.
Services were found in only twenty-seven of the forty-five parishes, while
in eighteen manors containing demesnes there was no villein land at all.
Thus, where demesnes existed, they were normally worked by wage
labour. In Kineton, manors in thirty-eight of the forty-eight parishes
demanded labour services – eight demanded week work and twenty-two
demanded seasonal work – while only nine manors containing demesnes were without villein land. Thus, labour services were more
prevalent and heavier than in Stoneleigh, even though they were
relatively low compared with more southern and eastern parts of
England. These differences between the two hundreds were reflected in
the relative proportion of money to labour rent – in Stoneleigh 77:23
and in Kineton, 67:33 – and in the extent of provision of labour services
for demesnes: in Stoneleigh this was minimal, while in Kineton some 35
per cent of demesne land was provided for. As one might expect, both
villein and free holdings were more differentiated in the former than in
the latter.

OPEN AND FREEHOLD COMMUNITIES

I shall now trace the development of two types of peasant community in
felden Warwickshire – open and freehold communities. These are
introduced here (even though their structural character was not
apparent until the sixteenth century) because their structure may be
explained by recourse to their development from the medieval period
onwards. In Chapter 10, I shall expand upon their characteristics.
Suffice it here to say that both open and freehold communities were

noted for peasant control over land in the sixteenth century. This feature explains both their capacity to resist enclosure from outside and their antagonism towards enclosure, which was expressed in involvement in the Midlands Revolt of 1607. The transformations experienced by such peasant communities from the medieval period, especially the freehold type, were remarkable. Peasants in freehold communities were able, in the face of all odds, to transform highly insecure villein tenure into freehold, at a time when other communities were being decimated because of such insecure tenure. For this reason, it is important to establish the precise causes for such a radical change. In so doing, we are able to contrast the fortunes of freehold communities with the more usual path followed which ultimately led to the extinction of communities.

The medieval origins of open and freehold communities contrasted strongly. Whereas the former experienced little feudal control, reflected in a *lack of coincidence* of manor and community, the latter suffered considerable control manifest in the *coincidence* of manor and community. I shall examine the open communities of Harbury, Napton-on-the-Hill (Napton), Fenny Compton and Tysoe, and the freehold communities of Prior's Hardwick, Prior's Marston, Southam, Bishop's Itchington, Cubbington, Burton Dassett and Hillmorton.[8] For their geographical location, see Map 2. Their paths of development are depicted in Figure 5.1. In 1086, all but Tysoe of the open parishes contained at least several manors, most of which were subtenanted. By 1279, all the open parishes considered had a highly fragmented manorial structure, which reflected a decline in control by their landlords. By contrast, freehold communities were largely controlled by a single lord through only one manor throughout the period (see Table 5.2). Coventry Priory was particularly important because of its unity of ownership and control in four such parishes – Priors' Hardwick and Marston, Southam and Bishop's Itchington.

These differences of manorial structure were reflected in the economic structure of the peasant communities concerned. Freehold communities contained highly feudalised tenant populations whereas open communities did not. Open communities by and large were characterised by extensive freehold, much differentiation, and money rents. This was certainly true of Harbury. The 1332 Subsidy returns indicate that Napton had experienced considerable differentiation. (We have no information for this parish in 1279.) In Fenny Compton, virtually all tenants were free, highly differentiated and paid money rents, while the demesnes were worked by wage labour. Lastly, Tysoe contained many

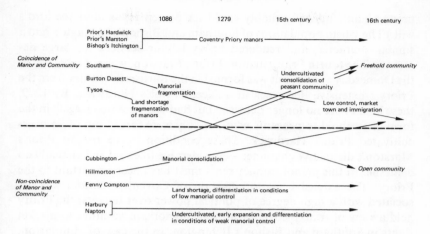

FIGURE 5.1   The development of open and freehold communities

TABLE 5.2   Numbers of manors in open and freehold communities

| | 1086 | | 1279 | |
	Total	Subtenanted	Total	Subtenanted
Freehold				
Prior's Hardwick	1	0	1	0
Prior's Marston	–	–	1	0
Southam	1	0	1	0
Bishop's Itchington	1	0	1	0
Cubbington	3	2	4	2
Burton Dassett	1	1	5	3
Hillmorton	5	4	1	0
Open				
Harbury	5	2	9	5?
Napton	3	3	5	5?
Fenny Compton	3	3	3	3
Tysoe	1	0	5	2?

freeholders who paid money rents and were highly differentiated, while demesne land was entirely absent.

In freehold communities, the influence of Coventry Priory was evident in their extensive manorialisation. In Prior's Hardwick there was a strong core of middle-peasant villeins who would have provided a labour supply for the large demesnes. (In 1279, money rents were predominant, but presumably could have been revoked at the lord's will.) The villein populations of Southam and Bishop's Itchington had a similar character, and rendered heavy labour services for large demesnes. The fourth Priory manor, Prior's Marston, was not recorded in the Domesday survey, but was formed in the thirteenth century from the Priory's extensive demesnes in adjacent Prior's Hardwick. By 1279, these lands were no longer demesne but had been granted largely in the form of freehold to peasants who possibly were forced out of an overcultivated Prior's Hardwick. These conditions gave rise to Prior's Marston's distinctive character – considerable freehold and virtually no demesne. In this manor, money rents must have been important to the Priory. The extensive manorialisation of Coventry manors was associated with a high degree of political power over tenants: the Priory held a view of frankpledge for all four manors, in addition to market rights in Southam and Bishop's Itchington. In the case of Hillmorton, although manorial structure was highly fragmented in the early medieval period, by the twelfth century the lands of the parish were consolidated into one manor in the hands of a resident lord – a development which enabled high manorialisation. These differences in community structure are summarised in Tables 5.3, 5.4, 5.5 and 5.6.

Such is the analysis of manorial structure up to the height of feudal development. However, after this time there is no systematic survey of the feudal economy which we might use. In the circumstances, I shall indicate by means of the role of landlord–tenant struggles in the determination of these two distinctive types of community the position reached at the end of the fourteenth century.

Unfortunately, records of conflicts within these Warwickshire communities are scattered. We may take as an illustrative example for the Coventry manors the experience of other monastic houses in the Midlands which similarly tightened their grip over tenants.[9] Conflict between the tenants and the Abbot of Halesowen in the manor of Halesowen in Shropshire has been particularly well documented. The first indication of trouble occurred in 1234, when all aspects of villeinage came under attack. Tenants fought against the levying of labour services, tallage, merchet, the milling-soke, entry fines, and controls over marriage. A settlement reached in 1243 was broken by the Abbot's increased demands for labour services. After further conflict, a new settlement was made in 1276 on the basis of tenants' claimed ancient demesne status. However, in 1278 tenants experienced a reversal of their position, since no entry regarding their privileged status was found in the Domesday Book and their servile

TABLE 5.3   Domesday structure

	Population					Land				
	Total	Villeins	Bordars	Serfs	Population density per 1000 acres	Demesne ploughs	Peasant ploughs	Density of ploughs	Available land − ploughs	Index of cultivation*
Freehold										
Prior's Hardwick	49	43	2	4	32.1	2	13	39.0	16	+1
Southam	35	20	8	7	10.9	2	8	12.5	12	+2
Bishop's Itchington	43	30	7	6	14.1	2	13	19.6	16	+1
Cubbington	18	7	6	5	8.7	3.5	2	10.6	11	+5.5
Burton Dassett	27	12	5	10	15.1	1	29	24.1	23	−7
Hillmorton	47	26	18	3	14.7	2.5	11	13.7	18	+4.5
Open										
Harbury	41	27	11	3	12.1	3	9	14.1	27	+15
Napton	38	19	15	4	15.3	3.5	8	18.5	16	+4.5
Fenny Compton	33	14	8	11	21.7	5.5	9.5	27.8	14	−1
Tysoe	90	53	28	9	19.0	11	23	28.0	32	−2

* Calculated by subtraction of total ploughs (demesne and peasant) from the available land in ploughs. Positive value equals undercultivation; negative value, overcultivation.

TABLE 5.4 Structure in the Hundred Rolls of 1279

	Population						Land (yardlands)						
	Total	Villeins	Free tenants	Cottars	Population density per 1000 acres	% change in density 1086–1279	Total area	Demesne	Villein	Free	Cottar	% parish cultivated	Maximum % of demesne worked by labour services*
Freehold													
Prior's Hardwick	42	29	10	3	27.5	−14.3	44	20	17	7	0	57.9	42
Prior's Marston	70	43	25	2	19.6	–	41	2.5	25	13.25	0.33	23.0	–
Bishop's Itchington	51	26	8	17	20.0	+41.9	66.25	20	34	12.25	0	34.3	85
Cubbington	37	13	8	16	17.8	+107.0	20.5	5	6.75	8.75	0	19.9	70
Burton Dassett	93	69	24	0	18.7	+23.7	115	40	46.5	28.5	0	46.1	58
Open													
Harbury	115	59	41	15	33.9	+180.0	104.6	38	43	23.6	0	61.4	57
Fenny Compton	34	5	29	0	15.7	−2.8	57	14	3	40	0	52.7	11
Tysoe	123	65	40	18	25.4	+33.7	150.9	27	62.5	61.2	0.25	63.9	96

* This gives us an indication of the extent to which demesnes could be worked by labour services, if services were demanded *in full* from villein tenancies. It is calculated as follows (x = percentage of demesne at maximum which could be worked by labour services):

$$x = 100 \cdot \left(\frac{\text{villein land area}}{2 \cdot (\text{demesne land area})} \right)$$

88

TABLE 5.5   Tenant differentiation in the Hundred Rolls of 1279

		0–8 acres	9–15 acres	16–30 acres	31–60 acres	Over 60 acres	Total
Freehold				No. of holdings			
Prior's Hardwick	villein	3	20	10	0	0	33
	free	3	2	4	0	0	9
	total	6	22	14	0	0	42
Prior's Marston	villein	20	38	10	4	0	72
	free	40	2	4	1	0	47
	total	60	40	14	5	0	119
Bishop's Itchington	villein	0	10	16	0	0	26
	free	0	6	4	2	0	12
	total	0	16	20	2	0	38
Cubbington	villein	0	12	1	0	0	13
	free	12	8	3	0	0	23
	total	12	20	4	0	0	36
Burton Dassett	villein	18	48	28	0	0	94
	free	16	14	12	2	3	47
	total	34	62	40	2	3	141
Open							
Harbury	villein	2	28	30	0	0	60
	free	12	4	2	3	4	25
	total	14	32	32	3	4	85
Fenny Compton	villein	4	1	0	0	0	5
	free	2	10	16	2	3	33
	total	6	11	16	2	3	38
Tysoe	villein	0	4	46	1	0	51
	free	3	4	16	10	3	36
	total	3	8	62	11	3	87

condition was confirmed. At this point, some tenants gave up the unequal struggle and fled the manor. After further litigation, the Abbot's victory was endorsed in 1286, and in 1327 he allowed commutation of labour dues on his own terms.

Conflicts also occurred on manors belonging to the Prior of Worcester in the county of Worcestershire, such as Stoke Prior in 1297 and Teddington in 1336. Later in the fourteenth century, discontent at Halesowen spilled over again in the form of attacks on royal tax-collectors in 1368 and 1374. By 1377, a situation of general

TABLE 5.6 Tenant differentiation and wealth in the Subsidy of 1332

	Total			No. assessed	No. with over ½ virgate in 1279	Median assessment		Average assessment	
	£.	s.	d.			s.	d.	s.	d.
Freehold									
Prior's Hardwick	2	1	0	11	14	2	8	3	8
Prior's Marston	4	16	4	14	19	2	0	6	10
Southam	4	5	5	35	–	2	4	2	5
Bishop's Itchington	5	1	10	44	22	2	5	2	4
Cubbington	1	19	7	19	4	1	8	2	1
Burton Dassett (overall)	12	13	6	81	45	n.a.		3	2
Burton	2	0	8	15	–	2	0	2	4
Southend	2	17	0	24	–	2	0	2	5
Radway		12	0	4	–	3	6	3	0
Hardwick	2	11	5	11	–	4	6	4	8
Knightcote	2	5	0	13	–	4	0	3	3
Northend	2	5	0	14	–	3	4	3	3
Hillmorton	1	10	3	16	–	1	8	1	11
Open									
Harbury	3	16	8	30	39	2	5	2	4
Napton	6	0	10½	29	–	4	0	4	2
Fenny Compton	3	8	9½	20	21	2	6	3	5
Tysoe	8	0	2¼	56	76	2	4	2	10

crisis had arisen on Worcester manors. The Black Death had caused heavy mortality, but, in spite of available land and other conditions favouring relaxation, the Priory refused to budge and maintained tenants' heavy burdens. At Shipston-on-Stour, in Warwickshire, tenants refused both to render services and to recognise their lord. In 1379, the situation of a generalised and co-ordinated refusal of services throughout Worcester manors led the Priory to distrain all goods belonging to tenants—an extraordinary move. This failed to prevent tenants struggling for freedom from services. Having heard of the successful extraction of charters of freedom by the peasant army at Mile End in the South, in July 1381, Worcester Priory tenants again withdrew their services and prepared for an insurrection. This later led to a further distraint of tenants' goods in 1385. Meanwhile in the hamlet of Romsley in Halesowen in 1386–7 tenants refused to perform services and demanded an end to their bondage at a time when the Abbot seemingly had reimposed labour services in place of money rents.

However, this represented the final attempt to reassert a demesne economy. By the fifteenth century, where peasant communities survived these torrid struggles, tenants began to get the upper hand. (This will be pursued further in Chapter 10.) On other manors where the lord faced large numbers of long-standing vacancies and remained intransigent, peasant communities withered away as tenants resorted to the ultimate and irrevocable step in their struggle: they left the manor in a search for land on more favourable terms. This rendered the remnants of such communities and their lands ripe for depopulation and conversion to pasture. (See Chapter 7.)

These conflicts illustrate many of the more general features outlined previously. Struggles first became pronounced in defensive reaction to the landlord onslaught of the late twelfth and early thirteenth centuries. Claims were made to ancient demesne status and were defeated. By the mid fourteenth century, struggle had changed in two important respects. Central exactions and extension of authority by the monarchy were attacked along with local landlord power and exactions, and struggles assumed a more fundamental and general character. The crisis-point coincided with the revolt of 1381, when reimposition of labour services was attempted.

It is likely that similar conflicts occurred on heavily manorialised estates in Warwickshire. The evidence we have for the manors of the Bishop of Coventry in the county (as distinct from Coventry Priory, note) suggests that peasant struggles in the last part of the period led to the consolidation of peasant landholding, in contrast to other estates such as that of the Bishop of Worcester in which peasant communities withered away (see Chapter 7). After the Black Death, in contrast with Worcester manors, the Bishop of Coventry largely managed to retain his tenant populations on Warwickshire manors. Only just over a dozen tenancies, a minimal number, fell vacant in Warwickshire. In particular, the area cultivated in Bishop's Itchington was reduced by only 3¼ virgates over the period 1279–1358. There were two reasons why tenant populations were maintained. Firstly, far fewer tenants died of the plague than was the case in Worcester manors. Secondly, and more importantly, the Bishop was forced into granting substantial concessions in order to retain tenants on his estates as a whole. Servile burdens and labour services were reduced, and terms of tenure were relaxed. Generally, where tenant vacancies remained unfilled this was not caused by economic decline of the communities, but by the Bishop's inability to attract new tenants.

Other less powerful or well-organised landowners in Warwickshire were likely to have fared worse in retaining villein tenants. The limited villeinisation of the peasantry must have rapidly disappeared under the impact of the Black Death, the challenge by tenants, and the general weakness of the landlord class. The small impact of the revolt of 1381 in this area probably can be ascribed to the amelioration of the condition of the peasantry earlier in the century.[10]

Thus, struggles between landlords and tenants took various Warwickshire manors in different directions. This period was crucial for the later fortunes of peasant communities. In some manors, the peasant communities began to take control of the land and increasingly retained their surplus from agriculture; in other manors, communities disappeared altogether.

Turning to look at the incompletely manorialised communities or open communities, we may note the same problem of documentation of landlord–tenant struggles. However, the necessity for conflict was much reduced, because peasants held a relatively privileged position in these communities. In the following discussion, some of the determinants of the character and development of such favourably placed communities are described. Open communities tended to be large – Harbury had 3397 acres, Napton 4027, Fenny Compton 2157 and Tysoe 4800 – and were generally situated in areas of poor soil. Given these characteristics, there were two routes leading to an open community structure in conditions of fragmented manorial structure. Either the parish experienced a considerable expansion in cultivated area in the medieval period itself, leading to fragmentation of holdings and extensive differentiation (as was true of Harbury and Napton), or, if the limits of cultivation had been reached early, a similar process of fragmentation of holdings and differentiation occurred in conditions of weak manorial control. The latter course of development was followed by Fenny Compton and Tysoe.

However, Cubbington had a highly fragmented manorial structure but did not become an open community. Rather, it became a freehold community (see Figure 5.1). In 1279, there were four manors in this parish, much freehold land, and a differentiated tenant population which paid money rents. From then on, the parish developed away from the *open* and towards the *freehold* type of community. This was the result of three factors – its relative smallness (2064 acres), its situation in the Avon river valley (the most fertile area of the felden), and the marked undercultivation of its lands throughout the period. In 1086 the parish contained only half the number of plough-teams that the land was considered able to support, while in 1279 less than 20 per cent of the parish area was in arable, even after the population doubled. Thus, considerable expansion in the cultivated area must have occurred during the period of feudal decline in conditions of relaxed manorial control, so that the freehold community could expand in numbers and landholding without suffering the fragmentation of holdings and further differentiation characteristic of open communities. This suggests that these advantages gave the peasant community sufficient strength to improve its position. The Subsidy returns of 1332 perhaps indicate the beginnings of the emergence of a wealthy freehold community. Some nineteen taxpayers were recorded, compared with only four tenants with half a virgate or more in 1279. Furthermore, the Abbot of Stoneleigh was a resident lord at that time, while Coventry Priory controlled another manor in the parish. From then on, the Abbot consolidated his lands, so that by the sixteenth century he held much of the land in the parish. This development aided in directing the evolution of the community towards the freehold type, since there was the semblance of a unified manorial structure in the later medieval period.

Parts of Burton Dassett followed a similar path to Cubbington, (while other parts were enclosed in the fifteenth century; see Chapter 7). As is clear from the 1332 Subsidy, the parish may be divided into the poor hamlets (Burton, Southend and Radway) and the rich ones (Hardwick, Knightcote and Northend). All the poor hamlets, together with

Hardwick, were depopulated, while the other two wealthy hamlets survived to become freehold communities in the sixteenth century. In this instance, the *overall* fragmentation of manorial structure evident in 1279 masks divergent developments within the parish. When Burton Dassett's development is compared with that of Tysoe, the importance of the availability of land for the expansion of cultivation is clear. Both parishes had a complex manorial structure, many hamlets, and suffered partial depopulation in the fifteenth century. However, throughout the medieval period Tysoe's lands were intensively cultivated. By 1279, the area under arable had reached its limits, 64 per cent of the parish area. By contrast, less than half of Burton Dassett's land (46 per cent) was in arable, and its population density was almost as low as that of Cubbington. As a result, even though Burton Dassett had a fragmented manorial structure, differentiation was not very advanced and there were no cottars. The availability of land inhibited the formation of a highly differentiated open community with many poor tenants, and enhanced the community's struggle for advancement. In 1332, the average assessment was relatively high and the number of households assessed was nearly double the number of tenants with half a virgate or more in 1279. Burton Dassett was more like Cubbington than Tysoe in its development, especially its hamlets of Knightcote and Northend, which survived intact into the seventeenth century. In both cases, the availability of land in the period of feudal decline so aided the peasant communities' struggles that they were able to transform themselves into freehold communities. But these cases were exceptional. More generally, limited manorialisation and extensive freehold in the medieval period led to considerable differentiation, the emergence of wage labour and the formation of open communities. The development of such Warwickshire felden communities as has been outlined above is traced further in later chapters.

We have now reached a point – having examined English agrarian development until the fifteenth century – at which the issues are transformed into those relating to the transition towards capitalism. These are examined in Part II.

PART II

Transition to Capitalism

6   Transition to Capitalism: Theoretical Issues

LINEAR SUCCESSION

In Chapter 3, I raised certain issues pertaining to theories of transition from feudalism to capitalism. I considered this process only in terms of problems arising from neglect of the role of class struggle, rather than confronting head-on questions posed by the emergence of capitalism. At the time I merely observed that the dominant Marxist response has been to introduce capitalism as an untheorised external agent. Traditionally, Marxists have analysed the transition from feudalism to capitalism as a *linear succession*, making no analytic distinction between mode of production and social formation as concepts. This view of transition generated auto-effective conceptions of change, either in the form of internal dissolution (Dobb) or external dissolution (Sweezy), in which a *theoretical linearity* corresponds to a linear chronology in history. In linear conceptions of transition the role of capitalism remains untheorised, as I have shown. This inherent theoretical uncertainty and ambiguity is reflected in Dobb's and Sweezy's writings. Dobb is unable to integrate his otherwise excellent studies of elements of capitalism into his analysis of transition.[1] For him, merchant capital was parasitic upon and integrated within feudalism, its existence was predicated upon feudal extraction of surplus and rested upon the institution of feudal monopolies over trade. Similarly, petty-commodity production was a 'subordinate element' in feudalism, even in the period of interregnum – the fifteenth and sixteenth centuries. Feudal monopolistic control in the form of guilds was implemented over craft production, while in the agrarian sphere petty-commodity production was directly assimilated into the feudal system by the exertion of feudal power.

Eventually, the internal decay of feudalism released these elements of capitalism so that they appeared in a more progressive guise. But from this point on, Dobb reduces the relationship between capitalism and feudalism to an illuminating but theoretically limited historical narrative of the development of these elements until they came together in manufacturing (the putting-out system), and eventually in industrial capitalism. In other words, Dobb fails to analyse the relationship between the two modes of production. This is not possible because he separates feudalism and capitalism in time and integrates pre-seventeenth-century capitalism into feudalism.

Sweezy also adopts a linear scheme of transition. As in Dobb's analysis, the exact status of the period of interregnum – in which Sweezy suggests that 'pre-capitalist commodity production' dominated – is unclear and exists in a theoretical vacuum.[2] Unlike Dobb, Sweezy asserts that merchant capital had complete autonomy from and was dissolvent of feudalism. But their opposed interpretations of the place of merchant capital none the less derive from the same underlying conception of transition as the linear replacement of feudalism by capitalism. Merrington has recently contributed to this debate by suggesting that merchant capital and petty-commodity production, as located within towns, were both internal *and* external to feudalism. However, this approach merely combines both the above interpretations and makes explicit the necessary coexistence of conceptions of internal and external dissolution, rather than resolving the antinomy as Anderson suggests.[3] Unless the role of class struggle is acknowledged, these problems will remain. Moreover, theories of linear replacement are unable to analyse the relationship between the two modes concerned: we must analyse the transitional social formation as an *articulated combination* of feudalism and capitalism.

In spite of their intention to achieve such an analysis, Balibar's and Poulantzas's formulation cannot help us, since they relapse into theories of linear replacement. Anderson similarly makes a plea for analysis by means of combinations of modes of production.[4] However, in practice he makes little attempt to carry it through, but rather, through such terms as 'fusion', 'admixture' and 'concatenation', relies upon uninformative imagery. The only consistent term used is that of 'synthesis', but this refers not to a combination but to a new mode of production – feudalism – the synthesis of the slave mode of antiquity and the distorted primitive communalism of the Germanic tribes. More generally, his analysis of antiquity, Germanic society, and feudalism assumes a one-to-one relationship between the mode of production and the social formation. Anderson's only attempt to investigate the articulation of feudalism and capitalism arises in the context of the absolutist state – a matter I shall consider in detail below. He asserts that absolutism was a feudal state and yet also ensured the 'basic interests of the nascent mercantile and manufacturing classes'.[5] This contradictory role is not explicated and justified by reference to the wider articulation of the two modes.

The above authors place greatest emphasis on aspects of development outside the agrarian sector – such as trade, merchant capital, the towns, manufacturing, and the political assistance given these elements by absolutism. However, it is increasingly being realised that agrarian capitalism was the leading sector of development. Rey's analysis of the articulation of feudalism and capitalism focuses upon this component.[6] For him, the extended reproduction of feudalism through the increased extraction of rent itself created the conditions for the emergence of capitalism in the transitional period, by bringing about a separation of the producers from their means of production. In the first stage of transition, feudal landed property was required for the displacement of the peasantry from the land; then feudal power was used to destroy rural artisan industry and to enforce the reliance of the peasantry on the market. Finally, when agrarian capitalism had attained supremacy, feudal landed property became superfluous. Until then, a *class alliance* existed between the capitalist class and feudal landowners, through which feudal relations of production (rent) were transformed into capitalist relations of distribution. Continuity of landed property effects this transformation in the place of rent.

Rey analyses the articulation of the two modes in terms of the pivotal role of rent and the class alliance. This is a promising start. Unfortunately, his conception of transition introduces a mechanism of the internal dissolution of feudalism: its extended reproduction brings about the transition. As Taylor and Cutler point out, articulation involves the same element (rent) in both modes of production. This introduces at the heart of Rey's analysis a linear conception of transition through the transformation of rent.

THE ARTICULATION OF FEUDALISM AND CAPITALISM

At this point it is pertinent to examine Marxist analyses of the relationship between capitalism and non-capitalist economies outside the transition to capitalism in Western Europe. There are many analyses utilising an approach of articulation with respect to colonialism and the transition to socialism. Recent Marxist work on colonialism, in contrast to Frank's and Wallerstein's image of the universalisation of capitalist market relations, has focused upon the articulation of capitalism with other modes of production. This has also been a key theme in the work of Bettelheim on the transition to socialism.

We may identify two types of theory of the colonial situation. First, there is the type that analyses this context explicitly in terms of combined modes of production – exemplified in the work of Laclau, Amin, Taylor, Wolpe and Bettelheim.[7] Secondly, other theorists posit a new 'colonial' mode of production, social formation or economic system, emergent from the articulation of the two modes of production. Here we may instance Alavi, Banaji, Mandle and Davey.[8] It is not necessary to provide detailed critiques of these means of dealing with the colonial context. The emergence of capitalism from within Western Europe poses questions which are entirely different.

In the first place, capitalism cannot be viewed as constituting a completely formed economic system or mode of production with its own self-contained reproduction cycle until the process of transition was completed by the emergence of industrialism. This may seem an obvious point, but it is one that is crucial to understanding the form that the articulation of capitalism and feudalism may take during transition, especially in England. We cannot directly apply to the transitional period analyses of articulation deriving from the colonial context, in which capitalism itself subordinates, dominates or reproduces other modes or elements of modes of production. This form of articulation requires capitalism to exist as a system experiencing expanded reproduction and dominating other, non-capitalist modes. The specific characteristics of capitalism – its universality, the necessity for expanded reproduction, and its transformative or at least subordinative tendencies – have dominated discussions of articulation. When capitalism itself is not dominant, such conceptions of articulation are misleading.

Secondly, in England, where capitalist development took place earliest, agrarian capitalism for a long period was the leading sector. This represents the inverse of the modern colonial situation, in which the articulation of capitalism in the colonial economy 'underdevelops' or develops in distorted fashion the agricultural sector. But agrarian capitalism in England was not part of an overarching political and economic structure: it was only one sector of a transitional economy still deeply imbued with feudalism. Precisely because it was the leading sector, its relationship with the feudal economy was highly specific and may not be analysed by way of conceptions of articulation deriving from capitalism as a fully fledged system.

Here, I shall not analyse other aspects of emerging capitalism, such as trade, merchant capital and artisan production. To a considerable extent such capitalist elements developed independently and without mutual structural linkages in the period under consideration; thus it is legitimate to consider these sectors apart from one another. Moreover, for the purposes of this book, we need only focus upon the agrarian sector. Here, lines of development can be traced from the medieval period and the place of struggles between peasant and landlord located. The importance of these factors for the general development of capitalism have largely been neglected in Marxist studies of transition.[9] Once we leave the late medieval crisis, Marxists tend to turn their attention elsewhere, mentioning agrarian changes largely in the context of the problem of the 'primitive accumulation' of capital. As a result, there has been no explicitly Marxist historical study of agrarian change in the sixteenth and seventeenth centuries. I shall now trace the parameters of the articulation of agrarian capitalism in England.

England

As Rey argues, continuity of landed property played a crucial role in the emergence of capitalism. The articulation of feudalism and agrarian capitalism in England was unique in that it both penetrated and was embodied in the landed class itself.[10] Rey analysed this relationship as one of class alliance at an abstract level: unfortunately his analysis is vitiated by his conception of internal dissolution. Instead of concentrating on *class alliance*, which implies an already formed capitalist class with clearly defined economic and political interests of its own, we should distinguish *economically* between two sections of the landed class: those who were transforming the function of land under their control, and those who were content to rely upon traditional exploitative means. The political cleavages arising from these different relationships to land did not become fundamental until the English Revolution. Before then, the landlord class was *politically* unified and protected by the absolutist state. There was no political class alliance, since the capitalist section of the landed class formed an integral part of the landed class as a whole in the transitional period up to the mid seventeenth century. After then, the shattering of absolutism allowed a reconstitution of the political unity of the landowning class, now under the aegis of its progressive wing.

This distinctive character of the landed class resulted from its early demilitarisation and turn towards commercial agriculture.[11] In Chapter 2, I indicated the antecedents of capitalist landowning in the later medieval period in the prevalence of small manors without tenancies. Moreover, larger landlords who retained strong control over their land turned it towards market production. The ranks of capitalist landowners were also swollen from below. In small disintegrating manors, richer peasants increasingly controlled wage labour and added to their lands, to emerge in the sixteenth century as yeomen and small gentry farmers. The disintegration of peasant communities through differentiation provided a convenient pool of cottagers and labourers for the demands of the agrarian economy and encouraged an expansion in the home market. To a considerable extent, these developments were set in motion by the disappearance of the political conditions preventing differentiation and accumulation of land and property. Peasant failure to gain secure tenure over land, and landlord retention of control over demesne lands allowed the transfer of much land from the peasant sector to be put to profitable use. Enclosure and the extinction of common rights cut loose the poorer peasants and cottagers from the land and demanded their total reliance upon wages. Reorganisation through enclosure created larger units of landholding and production and allowed the adoption of new methods of cultivation, greater specialisation, and increased investment. This and other factors resulted in expansion in the market in land. Those with capital who wished to invest in land were able to do so. Weakened manorial control allowed the release of the peasant land market from its confines. The emergence of absolute property allowed the detachment of land from traditional obligations and relationships, so that it could be freely bought and sold. The increasing centralisation of the English state, combined with its financial difficulties, resulted in the release of Crown and monastic lands onto the market.

However, we should be careful to note the exact nature of this agrarian capitalism. By and large, it was not associated with a revolution in techniques and technological advance which might constitute a capitalist intervention in order to cheapen commodities and sell at a higher volume to a newly created mass market. At that time, production was a traditional response to *high* prices paid for certain agricultural commodities. In the case of sheep-farming, where market orientation was marked, this form of land-management saw no advance in technique, wool-growers relied upon high prices, and little labour was employed. Moreover, rents – although increasingly dictated by market conditions – were not determined by strictly capitalist criteria, in the sense that they were not amenable to calculation by recourse to concepts of differential and absolute rent.

These comments indicate that we cannot treat agrarian capitalism as one such sector integrated into an overall capitalist mode of production. These agrarian changes were capitalist because through them land was released for the market, absolute property was consolidated, rents became subject to market forces, and the traditional constraints on agricultural development were removed by the destruction of the peasant economy. Land was freed and made available for new forms of management and usage. In sum, these changes concerned the emergence of capitalist forms of *landowning*, rather than of *production*.

The emerging capitalist sector was aided by the low wages and high prices paid for agricultural produce. This gave rise to a 'profit inflation' for those able to take advantage of the conditions. Landlords who transformed their tenancies into market-adjustable leaseholds were able to share in these profits and increase their prosperity. The relatively poorly developed bureaucracy and limited resources of the English state largely denied landowners alternative avenues of self-improvement. Few profits were to be made at court, and the institution of 'sale of offices' in the state developed only tardily and on a small scale. As a consequence, mercantile capital was often deflected into investment in land, rather than purchase of offices. However, this association of merchant capital and agrarian capitalism did not represent a systematic interpenetration of the two spheres which might constitute an emergent capitalist structure. Indeed, precisely because agrarian capitalism developed largely as an autonomous element of capitalism (and as a result transformed the landowning class) it proved to be extraordinarily dynamic and durable. This development was made possible by its articulation into the feudal landed class itself.

A crucial aspect of the articulation of agrarian capitalism with the still predominantly feudal system was its relationship with the absolutist state. Before explicating this, it is necessary to elaborate on the nature of feudal political structure, a discussion which until now has been limited to political conditions of existence.

THEORIES OF ABSOLUTISM

Marxists have largely taken two opposed positions on this form of state. The traditional view is that absolutism remained within the parameters of the feudal state: this is expressed by Hill, Takahashi, Porchnev and, most recently, Anderson and Therborn.[12] In contrast, others, such as Poulantzas, argue for its capitalist character. More recently, in line with one particular strand of Marxist thinking on the state which stresses the autonomy of state structure, authors such as Skocpol sever this political form from both modes of production present in transitional social formations.

I shall take Anderson's analysis as the most systematic setting out of the traditional Marxist view of the absolutist state.[13] Absolutism plays a key role in his more general argument concerning the unique origins of capitalism from within Western Europe. He argues that during the transitional period political power was displaced from the hierarchical structure of parcellised sovereignty and centralised in the hands of the sovereign monarch, as a consequence of widespread commutation of rents, the disappearance of serfdom, and the penetration of commodity relationships. This new political structure of absolutism, although it fundamentally departed from prior feudal state structures, was none the less a 'redeployed and recharged apparatus of feudal domination', which served the interests of the feudal nobility by their incorporation into the state structure through the 'sale of offices'. The revival of Roman Law from antiquity gave juridical expression to the absolute nature of political power and provided the basis for the emergence of absolute property, an essential precondition of capitalism.

Moreover, absolutism was 'secondarily over-determined' by the rise of capitalism itself. This state form ensured the basic interests of the mercantile and manufacturing classes in the process of primitive accumulation: internal barriers to trade were removed, external tariffs enforced, colonial and trading companies promoted, sources of investment provided, and so on. In sum, the rise of absolutism together with the adoption of absolute legal property, although in the interests of the feudal landed class, created the preconditions for the emergence of capitalism.

There are considerable difficulties in Anderson's conceptualisation of the absolutist state. Although he argues both for a political definition of the FMP in terms of parcellised sovereignty and serfdom, and that absolutism represents a decisive break with parcellised sovereignty, he still insists on the feudal character of this state. This is contradictory. As I have argued in Chapter 3, both Anderson and Dobb assert that such social formations were still feudal after the crisis, but are unable to analyse in what form feudalism remained. Moreover, if we assume that this is so, there is little indication of the manner in which absolutism secures such relations of production, other than through incorporation of the landowning class into the state apparatus. Here, Anderson introduces an 'instrumentalist' view of the state: its functioning is defined by the state acting as an instrument of the ruling class through its membership of the state apparatus. In recent Marxist debates on the capitalist state, this form of analysis has been trenchantly criticised and rejected.[14] Anderson is unable to specify a *structural* basis for absolutism's preservation of feudal landed property, precisely because he defines this state in terms which fall outside feudal political structure.

Furthermore, Anderson never analyses transitional social formations explicitly in terms of the interpenetration of feudalism and capitalism: why absolutism is a *transitional* state is not clear. He largely confines his attention to the state's relationship with the manufacturing and mercantile bourgeoisies, rather than analysing its function in relation to feudal domination.

These problems largely derive from Anderson's inadequate theory of feudalism, examined in Chapter 1. His identification of feudalism with parcellised sovereignty makes it impossible to conceptualise the changes following the feudal crisis. These difficulties are also highlighted by his usage of an internal-dissolution theory of transition, which induces an irresolvable tension between, on the one hand, recognition of the dissolution of feudalism and the beginnings of transition in the late fourteenth century, and, on the other, insistence on the persistent feudal character of such social formations through the fifteenth and on to the seventeenth century.

By contrast, Poulantzas, given his 'structuralist' propensities, emphasises the *structural* character of absolutism over and above its *historical origins*, and is thus clearly demarcated from Anderson, for whom the origin of a structure takes precedence over the structure itself.[15] For Poulantzas, the absolutist or transitional state has many of the characteristics of the feudal state, but these are combined with certain crucial structural features of a truly capitalist state which dominate or 'impregnate' the state as a whole.[16] These features involve a centralisation of political power into a form representing the public, political unity of the nation, the emergence of a formal and abstract system of law, and the creation of the institutional means of such power in a bureaucracy and a standing army. In this way, Poulantzas moves away from an instrumentalist view of absolutism.

Consistent with his general emphasis on the autonomy and effectivity of the superstructure (in contrast to 'economistic' Marxism), Poulantzas argues that the absolutist state, which was *dislocated* from and in advance of the economy, acted to bring about the dominance of capitalism. This dislocation allowed the state to contribute to the process of primitive accumulation by, for example, the expropriation of small landowners (the peasantry), the financing of industrialisation, attacks on seigneurial power, and the destruction of internal commercial barriers. Poulantzas asserts that these activities may be carried out only by a state with the 'relative autonomy' of the capitalist state, which allows it to act against the interests of the nobility at a time when the bourgeoisie is itself incapable of advancing capitalism.

Poulantzas's conception of absolutism fulfils the same function as Balibar's manufacturing mode: both act as the mechanism whereby new productive forces homologous with capitalist relations of production are formed outside of the self-perpetuating FMP. Both involve theories of external dissolution. In moving away from an instrumentalist view of politics, Poulantzas excessively emphasises the determinant role of the *structure* of absolutism, and its necessary functioning for capitalism. Below I shall argue that it is incorrect to assume a strict association of structure and function. Moreover, I shall argue that historically absolutism did not function for capitalism, at least not directly.

Trimberger, like Poulantzas, considers that the state's role during transition is transformative towards capitalism.[17] For her also, the state acts as an untheorised external dissolving agent. She suggests that, when there is no one dominant mode of production and class controlling the economy, the state apparatus may attain 'dynamic autonomy' from the economy and act outside the limits of existing modes of production, so as to destroy them and promote a new mode of production. This role for the state is dependent upon its members themselves not having interests in the existing economic structure so that they may hold a 'distinctive class position' and become an 'independent force'. Presumably if members of the state apparatus *were* attached to the dominant class, they would act to preserve its position; the state is then the instrument of the ruling class. Trimberger's discussion relies upon a *negative instrumentalism* – members of the state become an independent force when they do not have interests relating to the dominant class. This discussion is unsatisfactory. The essential problem remains: we must reconceptualise feudal political structure such that absolutism may be integrated within it. This way, the theoretical contradictions and resultant instrumentalism in Anderson's position may be avoided, without our having to treat absolutism as an untheorised external dissolving agent, as do Poulantzas and Trimberger.

The Structure of Absolutism as a Feudal State

In large part, I am able to concur with Anderson's analysis of feudal political structure as the hierarchy of parcellised sovereignty. However, absolutism was not a fundamentally distinct political structure: it was only an extreme form of development of the feudal state which arose in the specific circumstances outlined above. Anderson's argument rests on his understanding that the sovereign monarch ruled with *absolute power*, rather than conditional power; as had suzerain monarchs. However, this conception of power represents only the *ideological* claims made by this form of state, not its real power, which was always related to and dependent upon the landlord class, which it represented centrally. In order to reconceptualise absolutism, I shall briefly reconsider the character of feudal political structure.

The FMP is based upon a landed monopoly in which the landlord class owns and controls land so that tenants are forced to pay rent in order to cultivate it and thereby meet their subsistence needs. This ownership is real, economic and *unconditional*. In England it was based upon the factual control over land established by landlords through their capacity to administer and make decisions taking effect within their manors. In practice, ownership and control usually resided in the hands of the subordinate in the medieval feudal hierarchy (the feoffee), rather than the superior (the feoffor), because the former was more often resident in the manor and able to make decisions concerning its economy.

Within the manor, each unit of landholding or tenancy must be constituted as a political unit as well as an economic unit. The political conditions of existence necessitate enforcement at the level of individual tenancies, especially the '*denial of possession*', primarily through serfdom. Feudal tenants, although *partially* separated in a specific form from the land that they cultivate, perpetually retain a potential effective possession of their land. Political conditions denying such possession prevent this from occurring and must be secured at the level of each tenancy. The reproduction of tenants' separation in the FMP requires the direct intervention of politics in the economic structure of each tenancy, so that the tenancies become feudal in form through the *fusion* of the political and economic structure. This fusion contrasts strongly with the relationship of the economy and politics (the state) in capitalism, in which the state is 'relatively autonomous' from the economic structure and is constituted as a distinct sphere. This characteristic, according to Poulantzas, results from the nature of capitalist relations of production, in which the labourer appears as a 'bare individual' stripped of all means of production (including land), and is thus totally separated from his means of production.

This fusion at the very base of the hierarchy of landowning is replicated throughout the entire structure. At every level, there is a fusion of the economic and political components of feudalism, which is realised in the hierarchy of *juridical–conditional ownership*, i.e. parcellised sovereignty. This hierarchy was comprised of complex sets of vertically defined rights and obligations based both on political and military power and on land. Within it, there was an inevitable parcellisation of power linked to a coincident parcellisation of ownership of land – the distribution of political power was isomorphic with the distribution of economic power. At the vertex of the hierarchy was the suzerain monarch, the largest feudal landholder. The juridical–conditional landownership ties inherent in parcellised sovereignty welded the individual members of the landlord class together into a cohesive hierarchy and a class, and gave them a political unity and cohesion not obtainable from the economic landed monopoly alone. The conditional character of juridical property allowed the formation of vertical linking relationships and networks of landownership embodied in relational categories such as serf, vassal, fief and suzerain.

As I have shown in Chapter 1, Anderson mistakenly identifies parcellised sovereignty with feudal relations of production – that is, with the real economic ownership of land. He fails both to draw a distinction between economic ownership and juridical–conditional ownership and to analyse their relationship. As a result, he equates the destruction of parcellised sovereignty with the destruction of feudalism *in toto*, and is unable to integrate absolutism into feudalism. The distinction drawn above enables us to understand that the dismantling of the juridical property relationships does not necessarily entail destruction of feudal real and economic ownership.

None the less, dissolution of the hierarchy of parcellised sovereignty, based as it was upon serfdom, seriously threatened the landlord class during the feudal crisis. As a result of the erosion of local landlord power over their tenants, the feudal political conditions of existence of 'denial of possession' could not be maintained. But the increasingly centralised state supported the landlord class's claims to landownership and thereby increasingly secured the more fundamental feudal condition of landed monopoly. In this way, the distinction which I have made between the two types of feudal conditions of existence allows us both to explain why villeinage withered away and yet analyse the form in which feudalism remained and was maintained by absolutism.

The destruction of the conditions denying possession eliminated in large part the necessity for strict isomorphic fusion of the economic and political structures. Direct intervention at the level of individual tenancies was no longer necessary nor possible. The right of exclusion from land was now ensured by centralised means outside of tenancies and feudal enterprises. These changes thus caused a *dissociation* of feudal economic and political structures. Political institutions became increasingly separate from economic enterprises and centralised at the apex of the hierarchy and expressed in a bureaucratic form. The political cohesion of the landlord class was no longer given by the hierarchy of parcellised sovereignty itself but by the apex of this hierarchy, the absolute sovereign monarch, who held a royal *monopoly of power and violence* in representing the landlord class centrally. Alongside these changes, juridical property tended to become absolute in nature because of the fracturing of vertical links in the hierarchy, so that the superordinate—subordinate property relationship disappeared. (This was to have disastrous effects on peasant landholding.) In the realm of ideology, these changes were expressed in a clear separation of the political and economic spheres: the sovereign claimed to ensure *absolute* economic property rights over land through his own person (which constituted the political essence of such rights). This was reflected in the monarch's claim to absolute power, and resulted in an ideological 're-fusion' of the political and economic structures in the symbolic image of the absolute monarch.

In spite of an ideological aura of absolute power, the sovereign held only the absolute *monopoly* of political power to be exerted on behalf of the landlord class, rather than unlimited personal power as Anderson suggests. Analytically, the power of the absolutist state is not separable from that of the landed class. The state's partial institutional separation from the class it represented, together with the necessity for it to ensure its own fiscal and military conditions of existence, gave it the appearance of an independent power, while its ideological claims were the sole basis for the absolute nature of this power. (Below, I shall discuss the putative 'autonomy' of absolutism in more detail.) But neither was absolutism simply the instrument of the feudal landed class. Absolutism constantly transgressed individual political interests of members of the landlord class in representing their collective political interests centrally and ensuring its own conditions of existence. I have now indicated how the structure of absolutism is compatible with feudalism. In other words, in terms of the various modes of determination discussed in Chapter 3, absolutism falls within the *limits of structural variation* of the feudal state.

We may contrast this centralised extreme of structural variation of the feudal state with its opposed decentralised feudal political form which developed in Eastern Europe after the feudal crisis.[18] Parcellised sovereignty never existed in the East. None the less, after the feudal crisis the landlord class was able to impose serfdom upon hitherto relatively free peasant populations and consolidate its power in the form of *highly localised and strong control* at the level of individual landlords. Particular landlords subsumed manufacturing within their feudal enterprises, established control over mercantile towns, restricted currency circulation, controlled trade, and prevented the emergence of petty-commodity production. In contrast to the West, the rise of commodity relations and the impact of the feudal crisis in Eastern Europe gave rise to such a strengthening of *localised control* that there was a definite *identification* of the economic and political levels. The landowning nobility virtually dissolved the hierarchy of landownership, so that they individually retained considerable power and the monarch was left relatively powerless. This partial coalescence of the hierarchy prevented the emergence of autonomous towns and a free peasantry (characteristics of the West). In sum, the conclusion of the feudal crisis in the East witnessed the beginnings of a system of localised political structures capable of enforcing both the primary (right of exclusion) and the secondary (denial of possession) conditions of existence of the FMP. This was vital to the formation of an economy dominated by the dislocated enterprise.

The Institutional Structure of Absolutism

The emergence of absolutism in the West caused transformations in the fiscal, military and administrative aspects of the feudal state. Previously, the suzerain monarch, the greatest feudal landowner, at the head of the hierarchy had commanded obedience on the basis of ties of oaths of fealty sworn by vassals who held land from him. The sovereign commanded obedience not as the person residing at the apex of the hierarchy, but as the detached symbolic representative of the unity of the landlord class. Ownership of extensive tracts of land was no longer a key factor in the legitimation of his power, which was extended throughout the realm. As a landowner, the suzerain derived his revenues largely from seigneurial dues from his tenants. As sovereign monarch, the king obtained his largely from taxation, which involved a transmutation of 'feudal' obligations into money, and from custom duties, a levy on the increasing mercantile activity. Both were justified on the basis of the king's extension of authority throughout the realm. Military power also became detached from the traditional obligations of vassalage. If finance were available, the king might command a paid army (the standing army), which owed allegiance to him only as paymaster. This new institutional form, complete with increased fiscal and military powers, required a considerably enlarged administrative structure which carried out increasingly specialised functions – a bureaucracy. Members of the state apparatus were located more on the basis of the 'office' or function performed than on the basis of personal ties of dependence. Often members of the landed class purchased offices, thereby providing a direct connection between this class and the state. However, in no way did this mean that the state itself became the instrument of this class.

This institutional structure brought with it novel problems regarding its continued existence. Its expansion or consolidation was dependent upon its fiscal resources, whilst its strength derived from the size of its bureaucracy and army. These factors we may term the *conditions of existence* of the absolutist state.

These aspects of absolutism have been more closely considered recently by Marxists. Kimmel, following the work of O'Connor on the modern state, argues for the 'fiscal crisis' of absolutism.[19] He suggests that the state had insufficient fiscal resources to pursue the objectives necessary to its continued growth. Restrictions posed by limited taxation capacity led to the sale of offices for revenue, which in turn forced further expansion of the state in order to meet the needs of its members. This contradictory logic impelled the state towards a fiscal crisis.

A focus on the internal structure of the state leads Skocpol to assert its own autonomy and logic of development apart from classes in the social formation.[20] In contrast to Poulantzas and Trimberger, who use conceptions of autonomy to argue for the transformative role of the state towards capitalism, Skocpol excises the state entirely from either mode present in transitional social formations. She clearly states that political structures should be seen as fully autonomous from modes of production and class structures. For her, the absolutist state must be analysed in terms of the conflict between the interests of the state itself in securing its own conditions of existence and the interests of the dominant class. The primary contradiction here lies in the competition between the two 'interest groups' over extraction of surplus from the peasantry.

The constitution of absolutism as an autonomous political form and as a distinct interest group has definite antecedents in the writings of Marx and Engels themselves. Draper systematically sets out their views on absolutism as an 'autonomised' state which in conditions of equilibrium between the feudal and capitalist classes was able to advance its own interests by playing one off against the other.[21] Absolutism first raised the bourgeoisie to prominence in order to counterbalance the power of the nobility and for its own fiscal strength, then increasingly turned towards the nobility as the bourgeoisie's power became a threat.

The danger is that this view of absolutism can so shift emphasis from concerns of class interest to those of sociological 'interest groups' that any claim to remain within Marxist theory is unwarranted. This is in fact what Mousnier achieves in his writings on French absolutism, albeit never having claimed to be Marxist. Lublinskaya criticises Mousnier trenchantly on the basis that the state is severed from class structure and treated as an autonomous interest group.[22] The state, for all its autonomy and own interests (which must be recognised), cannot be detached from the economic and class structure of the social formation. In other words, the interests of absolutism and its logic of development in securing its own conditions of existence must be analysed as *subordinate* to the location of this political form relative to the modes of production present during transition.

STATE, ECONOMY AND CLASS STRUGGLE

At this point, it is apposite to make a more systematic statement of the complex nature of the transitional structure in England. This then will form an organisational basis for following chapters. Returning to certain 'modes of determination' discussed in Chapter 3, we can conceptualise the transitional social formation in these terms (see Figure 6.1).[23]

I have argued that absolutism as a political form falls within the *limits of structural variation* of the feudal state. Moreover, absolutism is *reproductive* of the feudal mode of production to the extent that such a centralised state is able to protect the landed monopoly. Absolutism is not able to secure other feudal political conditions of existence. Thus, this form of state represents a certain non-coincidence of structural

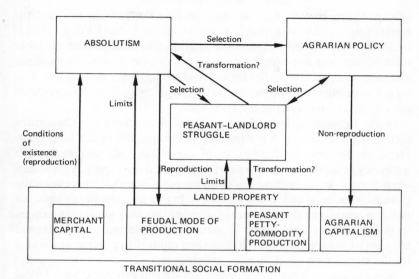

FIGURE 6.1   Relationship of state, economy, and class struggle

limitation and reproduction as modes of determination: there is a discrepancy between structure and function. Absolutism's only partial reproductive capacity for feudalism underpins its character as a *transitional* state, as well as a feudal state. Its inability to secure other feudal political conditions means that it has implicit transformative role in the transitional social formations. It is unable to prevent the expansion of commodity relations and production and the transformation of a feudal tenantry into petty-commodity producers.

This transitional nature is confirmed by its limited and temporary reproductive capacity for emerging capitalism, especially in the mercantile sphere. Such a reproductive capacity arises because of the necessity for absolutism to ensure its own conditions of existence. The reproduction requirements (conditions of existence) of the state structure are to be found in the transitional social formation at large, and thus are defined by various elements of capitalism and peasant petty-commodity production, as well as by feudalism. State policies such as mercantilism and internal trade regulation actually aid mercantile capital, whilst at the same time enhancing the state's fiscal well-being through levies on increased trade, customs and excise duties, and loans.

Absolutism becomes non-reproductive of capitalism when it is no longer useful for the state, thenceforth acting as a barrier to the advance of capitalism. In this way, we may analyse the shifting relationship between state and bourgeoisie in Tudor and early Stuart England, which is clearly documented in the work of Hill. This shifting and unstable relationship does not constitute the state as an essentially autonomous and neutral actor above the classes which struggle for dominance. The state's seemingly autonomous position is derived from its *structural place* in the transitional social formation.

In the agrarian sphere, the conditions of existence for absolutism dictate a policy which is consistently anti-capitalist in the long term. Here, absolutism is reproductive of capitalism only minimally and indirectly in that it generally ensures the landed monopoly. This stance against agrarian capitalism arises because of the state's reliance upon the peasantry for fiscal and military support. In this way, the state's agrarian policy is *selected* by the structure of the state. We may analyse variations in policy and its application in terms of (a) internal organisational changes within the state, and (b) fiscal and military imperatives provided by the state's own conditions of existence.

In ensuring the landed monopoly, absolutism protected both feudal and capitalist landholding in the transitional period. Politically, the landed class was not differentiated into contrasting sectors. However, in order to protect the landed monopoly and its own conditions of existence, the absolutist state was also forced to stifle agrarian capitalism, because of its disastrous effects on the peasantry. The state's protection was extended to guard against peasant revolts which might threaten political order, and to maintain its fragile military and fiscal resources, for which the peasantry was crucial. This will be pursued in Chapter 8.

As a result, there was a *dislocation* between the state and agrarian capitalism. Paradoxically the situation was the inverse of that mapped out by Poulantzas. Absolutism was not dislocated from and in advance of a feudal economy; it was dislocated from, and attempting to prevent the consolidation of, agrarian capitalism. This situation – preserving capitalist landed property politically, yet inhibiting its emergence – introduced contradictions into the state. Absolutism transgressed the *individual economic interests* of an increasingly capitalist landowning class, whilst at the same time it maintained their *collective political interests*. The political articulation of feudalism and agrarian capitalism produced contradictions not only between the functioning of the state and changes in the agrarian economy but also within the state itself. JPs, local landowners and the House of Commons increasingly resisted the state's agrarian policy.

This policy was increasingly necessary while at the same time increasingly difficult for the state to enforce, because of the composition of its administrative membership. The advance of agrarian capitalism undercut the state's fiscal and military capacities, while considerable parliamentary controls negated attempts by the monarch to enlarge taxation and prerogative powers. This situation was to lead to a fiscal and political crisis of the state in the early seventeenth century.

The Role of Class Struggle

The place of class struggle within the transitional social formation, especially that between peasant and landlord, which is our central concern, is particularly complex. Initially, considering other struggles important to agrarian development, representation of an emergent capitalist landowning and farming class was strengthened and played an increasingly important role through the House of Commons. These contradictions within the state apparatus had detrimental effects on agrarian policy.

The articulation of absolutism with agrarian capitalism structured the conditions under which peasant struggles took place. The centralised state structure determined that peasant revolts took an increasingly organised and large-scale form: peasants seeking change necessarily confronted the central state, which held a monopoly of force. Additionally, the institutional separation of landlord class and central state, combined with the state's own need to protect the peasantry, led the peasantry to direct their struggles against landlords and towards influencing the King or Queen on their behalf. A framework for their protests was provided by legislation on the agrarian problem. In consequence, peasant revolts were characterised by 'reformism' and appeals to the legality of their actions – they claimed that the laws were neither being enforced nor heeded by landowners in their locality. However, as a result of the structural constraints on the state, its agrarian policy never went beyond a mitigation of the worst aspects of the advance of agrarian capitalism. Peasant expectations were trapped within a reformist cul-de-sac. In times of revolt, of course, the first priority for the state was to restore order by repression, before it took note of peasant demands and instituted steps to ameliorate their position. In sum, we may suggest that an interactive pattern of *selection* as a mode of determination existed between the absolutist state structure, its agrarian policy, and peasant struggle.

Furthermore, the economic articulation between feudalism and agrarian capitalism itself provided the structural limits of variation of the class struggle between landlord and peasant. In its turn, peasant revolt posed the question of the *transformation* of the economic and political structures of the transitional period. In the remainder of this book, I shall examine whether such transformations occurred. Thus far I have briefly specified the structural conditions for peasant revolts in England in terms of the various modes of determination discussed above. As I have already established, this is insufficient: we must consider the role and effectiveness of class struggle itself. This requires consideration of the nature of the agrarian economy, the role of the state, and the place of peasant struggle in England as a social formation transitional towards capitalism. Prior to doing so, we must follow agrarian transformation in England through into the fifteenth century, so that we are able to comprehend the position reached at the point at which the centralised Tudor monarchy began to extend protection to the peasantry.

7 The Fifteenth Century: Peasant Landholding and Struggles

THE QUESTION OF TENURE

Brenner suggests that the crucial difference between English and French agrarian development after the feudal crisis lay in the fact that, whereas in England peasant landholding was eroded away and land released for capitalist development, in France there was consolidation of peasant proprietorship.[1] In the latter, the state confirmed the heritability of peasant tenure (so that landlords could not appropriate vacant peasant land into their demesnes), and began to organise peasant communities as a tax base. In England, landlords were able to appropriate vacant holdings and thereby transfer much land from the customary to the expanding leasehold sector, preventing the dominance of peasant freehold in the agrarian economy. The increasingly commercially oriented landed class was also often able to transform customary land into leasehold by raising rents and entry fines. Meanwhile peasant land-tenure in the form of copyhold became increasingly insecure, so that overall the peasant sector was of decreasing significance.

Within the peasant sector, the partial collapse of the feudal economy in England allowed considerable changes to occur. The destruction of serfdom severed the previously close interrelationship of the landlord and peasant economy. On dislocated enterprises it was neither possible nor necessary to maintain the equality of tenants' holdings, means of production, and other forms of property. Moreover, the size of demesne was no longer bound by the number of tenants, but was cut loose from the peasant economy and could be expanded and contracted at will. Generally, tenants had relatively free access to the market in land, wage labour, means of production and subsistence commodities. These freedoms allowed the peasantry to gain in autonomy: their rents were

117

reduced or they refused to pay them, and they emerged as petty-commodity producers (none the less still subject to the basic feudal relations of production in the monopoly over land). Increased access to the market accelerated the differentiation of the peasantry; richer peasants emerged as competitors with landlords in the sale of commodities such as grain and in the purchase of wage labour. Demesne land was often leased by these peasants.

Postan argues that the peasantry experienced wholesale *economic promotion* rather than increasing differentiation in this period, contrary to the process outlined above.[2] His argument is based on a suggested decline in the numbers of the labouring poor – which he argues is implied by wage rises and an increase in the average size of holdings. Postan's argument also rests on his assumption that the land market operated to equalise the size of peasant holdings rather than to increase their differences. But Kosminsky argues that wage rises reflected an increase in *demand*, which resulted from the competition for labour between landlords and rich peasants, together with the ability of labourers to defend their interests and to move around for higher wages, rather than merely a decrease in the supply of wage labour. Hilton suggests that the increase in demand itself arose from increasing differentiation which meant that many rich peasants required wage labour. He also points out that the proportion of wage labourers in the population as a whole in this period was not much less than for the early sixteenth century, approximately 30 per cent.[3] We may therefore conclude that in general the peasantry experienced considerable differentiation in the fifteenth century, and that this acted to destroy internally the solidarity of communities. The increased differentiation of the peasantry resulted in an increase in the numbers of wage labourers and of rich peasants or yeomen at the expense of the middle group of peasants, which previously had been so important. (This development is confirmed by analysis of the condition of the peasantry in the sixteenth century.) However, given certain conditions, extensive differentiation did not occur and peasant communities as a whole benefited from the available land. Freehold communities, discussed below, are one such example.

Perhaps more fundamentally, the clarification of an insecure form of peasant land-tenure in copyhold assisted in the destruction of peasant communities from the outside. 'Copyhold' was the recording of tenure by customary possession in the manorial court rolls. Debate over its nature has been dominated by the issue of its *legal* security – whether and at what time this form of tenure received the protection of the law.

Ashley argues that customary practices, for reasons of maintenance of the feudal economy, largely ensured the inheritance of holdings. However, in the fifteenth century, when law-courts were about to take a similar role, the rise of commercial pastoral farming led landlords to deny tenants any legal protection through the courts, in order to gain access to their land.[4] Thus Ashley posits a rather crude and instrumental role for the law. However, he fails to realise that, from the early fifteenth century onwards, cases concerning copyhold came before the court of Chancery; by the Tudor period, copyholders had legal security of tenure. In the light of this evidence, Leadam argues that copyholders had complete legal security in both the courts of Equity and Common Law from 1467 onwards. However, Savine regards the operation of the law courts less sanguinely: he concludes that the central state only took over the existing customary practices and fixed them in law. Tawney largely adopts Savine's perspective in opposition to Leadam, while Gray further refines this viewpoint and documents the emergence of copyhold actions at law. More recently, Kerridge has restated Leadam's position at great length but with no new evidence. Kerridge places heavy reliance upon later discussions of lawyers on the nature of copyhold in the late sixteenth and seventeenth centuries. As in other issues, Kerridge fails to consider wider changes in agrarian structure, and he is content to rest with the deduction that copyholders were secure because they had access to the law courts.

Both Kerridge and Leadam fail to take account of Savine's argument that legal security depend upon *prior customary security*. Remaining within the confines of a legalistic argument, they are unaware that no amount of protection in the courts could benefit a peasantry which *legally* held land insecurely as a result of the definition of custom. As a result, Kerridge wrongly charges Tawney with arguing that the law did not protect the copyholder. In fact, Tawney (following Savine) acknowledges the intervention of the law, especially Chancery, but also suggests that the law could not but follow custom. Interestingly, Kerridge refers to customary practices as 'customary law', as if they existed as a standardised corpus of law-like distinctions which could be made between copyhold of inheritance, copies for life or lives, and tenure at the will of the lord. However, custom was none other than the particular conditions established between tenants and their lord in the manor, and thereby displayed considerable variation according to the resolution of power between the protagonists. After all, the term 'copyhold' was itself a shorthand phrasing of tenure by 'copy of the manorial courts' rolls, according to the custom of the manor and at the will of the lord'. Indeed, the insecurity of tenure incorporated into copyhold was likely to have been considerable, because of its origins in villein tenure, in which the tenant held land at the lord's will.[5] While villeinage largely withered away, insecure copyhold tenure was retained in many instances. In other words, although the secondary conditions of existence of feudalism disappeared, its primary conditions were retained: *Peasant landholding failed to develop into a secure freehold form.* This failure was not an inevitable outcome in English agrarian development; it was determined in large part by the resolution of struggles between peasant and landlord.

PEASANT STRUGGLES

Brenner's account of the divergent developments in England and France in the fifteenth century is inadequate, since he neglects to analyse struggles between peasant and landlord as an important factor in the creation of insecure tenure and the appropriation of land into demesnes. This absence is surprising, given his stress on the 'balance of forces between the contending classes' in determining development.[6] Nevertheless, such struggles had a crucial role to play.

We may initially observe certain similarities between the form that these struggles took and those of the thirteenth century. In both, struggle was largely conducted through the manorial courts and on the terrain of custom, while serious disputes went to the central courts of the King. However, these similarities are superficial. Struggles in the fifteenth century were located in the context of weakening landlord power and of the strengthening of the central state into an absolutist form, while those of the thirteenth century were in the context of the consolidation of local landlord power and private jurisdiction.

The early fifteenth century saw a continuation of tenants' resistance to the imposition of labour services, other levies, and villein disabilities. These struggles still largely focused upon villein status rather than villein tenure, although at the same time terms of tenure tended to improve to some extent. Hilton documents these conflicts on estates in Staffordshire, Shropshire, Warwickshire and Gloucestershire. Dyer's study of tenants' struggles with the Bishop of Worcester exemplifies this type of conflict.[7] From the 1420s until the end of the fifteenth century, tenants refused to pay rents and other levies, such as tallage, recognition, amercements, tax on land transfers, heriots, entry fines, and so forth. Dyer suggests that perhaps one-twelfth of the estate's revenue was withheld in this period. However, he argues that the amount withheld was not as significant as the *effect* of refusal to pay upon the power relationship between the Bishop and his tenants. Their opposition led to the permanent removal of some exactions and to the reduction of others. By the mid fifteenth century, tenant resistance had reached a peak, and involved the co-ordination of many villages in a collective refusal to pay rents and levies. In the forefront of this movement of resistance were the old-established nucleated villages of the Avon and Severn valleys and the Cotswolds, which retained the traditional communal solidarity of a homogeneous customary tenant community. These villages probably bore considerable resemblance to the Warwickshire felden 'freehold' communities, discussed below.

By the late fifteenth century, antagonisms between tenant and landlord over villein status had abated, as a result of tenants' successful struggles, the changed land–labour ratio, and the withering away of villein status. Conflict over rents remained an issue and was increasingly combined with struggle over terms of tenure. Harris cites the example of the Duke of Buckingham's estates, on which rent arrears were 10 per cent of income at the end of the fifteenth century.[8] Tenants were also resisting the Duke's conversion of customary tenures into copyhold. For example, tenants in 'Navisby' (i.e. Naseby) in Northamptonshire refused to pay the increased rents and accept copyholds in 1517–18, while they and tenants on other Buckingham manors refused to pay entry fines. Furthermore, cases of enclosure riots in this period suggest that the peasantry was already experiencing the impact of insecure tenure and the appropriation of land from the customary to the leasehold sector.[9]

The result of such struggles was the formation and hardening of custom in which the 'balance of forces between lord and villein from estate to estate, even from manor to manor, . . . decided how quickly villeins would become free copyholders'.[10] Indeed, the balance of forces not only determined the pace of development of copyhold but also its *form* – whether tenants held copies of inheritance with fixed entry fines, copies for life or lives with arbitrary entry fines, or tenure-at-will. On manors of ancient demesne, villein sokemen held their land on relatively favourable terms, a fact which advantaged them in the struggles involved in transformation into copyhold.[11] Elsewhere, villeinage was transformed into tenure completely at the lord's will and without even the customary protection of villein tenure. Hilton traces the emergence of tenure-at-will from villein tenure in the manors of Leicester Abbey in the fourteenth and fifteenth centuries. By 1477, all holdings apart

from freeholds were held at will, as a result of tenants' incapacity to resist. The instability and fragmentation of holdings through subleasing
and the circulation of land destroyed the community's cohesion. Thus
the development of copyhold out of villeinage was determined by the
specific balance of power between peasant and landlord and the
resolution of struggles over tenure.

The inherent insecurity of much copyhold was compounded by the
emergence of legal conceptions of *absolute property* in land. These
property relations dictated the recasting of customary tenure as an
estate rather than as a *conditional tenure*. Copyhold either became
tenure-at-will and copies for life, in which case the estate was held by the
landlord, or it became copies of inheritance, in which tenure was virtually
equivalent to an estate in freehold.[12] This shift from customary tenure to
absolute legal ownership allowed landlords to evict their tenants when
copies of inheritance were not held. Furthermore the large numbers of
tenants without the security of fixed entry fines were vulnerable to
eviction or exclusion through rack-renting and conversion of the
copyhold into leasehold.[13] The inherent insecurity of copyhold in these
circumstances was reflected in extensive depopulation of peasant
households involving the desertion of entire villages. Here, Beresford's
work and that of the Deserted Medieval Village Group are invaluable in
providing us with concrete evidence of the effects of insecurity of tenure
in the latter half of the fifteenth century.

DESERTED VILLAGES

John Hales, a 'Commonwealth' propagandist and anti-enclosure ad-
vocate, had observed with some exasperation in 1549 that 'the chief
destruction of villages was before the beginning of the reign of King
Henry the seventh'.[14] Beresford takes this as the keystone of his
argument that there was extensive desertion of villages in the period
1450–1520. With respect to the three counties later involved in the
Midlands Revolt of 1607, almost all the 193 villages he documents were
deserted in this period.[15] Beresford argues that relatively small and poor
villages, inhabited largely by customary tenants and tenants-at-will,
were primarily at risk. Moreover, he suggests that 'landlord aggressiveness and [the lack of] tenant's security' were factors explaining
desertion. However, at the height of the feudal economy at the end of the
thirteenth century, such peasant communities *did not* display different
patterns of tenure compared with other communities. Proportions of

freehold were similar. This indicates that from the fourteenth century onwards tenure in these communities became increasingly insecure compared with those that survived. This clearly establishes the centrality of the period after the feudal crisis for insecurity of tenure and the significance of struggles in this period.

As Hilton points out, this weakness of communities was exacerbated by their internal differentiation, which resulted in the disappearance of equality in landholding, accumulation of holdings, and an increasing divergence of the interests of rich and poor peasants and a decline in the cohesion of the community.[16] None the less, desertion still required, on the landlord's side, the power and ability to force through the required changes: this factor should not be ignored. In general, it would appear that desertions resulted from the combination of pressures both from within communities and from without (by their landlords). It was these two aspects which determined the failure of peasant struggles to remain on the land. Outright eviction (stressed by Beresford) and internal disintegration (emphasised by Hilton) were the two faces of a changing agrarian structure.

To some extent Beresford's and Hilton's conflicting interpretations are reconcilable also in terms of a chronological division. In the first half of the fifteenth century, desertions often arose as a consequence of lords' attempted *feudal reaction*, combined with an internal weakening of the community and a drift away from holdings. In the second half of the century, as a result of high wool prices, landlord aggressiveness took a new form: landlords *actively sought to evict* peasant communities in order to convert peasant holdings to pasture. Previously, desertions occurred largely as an unintended consequence of landlords' efforts to maintain heavy exploitation, in which case tenants fled their holdings. I now return to consider an area of England focused upon in Chapter 5 – felden Warwickshire – in order to elaborate upon the above points.

Desertions in Felden Warwickshire

In this part of Warwickshire, as Map 2 indicates, deserted villages were intermingled with the freehold and open surviving peasant communities. There was a high concentration of desertions in this area: one in every four villages suffered this fate and many others were partially depopulated.[17] Table 7.1 indicates that deserted villages in this area were of a type similar to that specified more generally by Beresford. Some 26 per cent of peasants in these villages were free tenants in 1279, compared with 21 per cent in all villages throughout the felden hundred.

TABLE 7.1   Warwickshire deserted villages: extent of freehold and relative size

Deserted village	1279: free tenants, % of total	1332 Subsidy	
		Payment s. d.	No. assessed
Early desertions			
Hodnell (incl. Chapel Ascote, Watergall, and Wills Pastures)	–	28 11	16
Radbourne	–	12 0	7
Chesterton Magna	–	74 6	19
Kingston (in Chesterton)	–	54 11	15
Compton Verney	15	77 6	30
Hatton (in Hampton Lucy)	7(1299)	32 0	17
Burton Dassett (excl. Knightcote and Northend)	27	163 6 (4 hamlets)	51
Late desertions			
Wormleighton	32	69 1	26
Compton Wynyates	64	27 8	13
Charlecote	13	57 0	25
Shuckburgh Superior	–	26 8	8
Shuckburgh Inferior	–	12 10	5
Average	26	40 6	14

Although not quite as low as Beresford's average tax payment for Warwickshire deserted villages overall (in 1334), the average sum paid by the selected deserted villages was considerably lower than for all assessed villages throughout Warwickshire. These villages fitted the general picture of those vulnerable to desertion: they were somewhat smaller than average, yet they retained considerable free tenant populations during the period of the height of the feudal economy.

We may illustrate the two types of desertion referred to above as follows. In support of his argument, Hilton examined the desertions of Chesterton Magna, Kingston and Compton Verney. Dyer, a student of Hilton's, supports this interpretation by citing the case of Hatton.[18] By the early fifteenth century, all these communities were withering away: vacant holdings were left unfilled, and tenants refused to pay rents and left the manor. This allowed others to consolidate and accumulate lands in the manors, and opened the way for pasture farming. As Hilton suggests, 'a vigorous landlord could carry these tendencies to their logical conclusion and become himself the final accumulator of all holdings, which he could then turn to pasture'.[19] In these manors, the precise role played by the landlord in creating the conditions for desertion is not specified: Hilton, for his point, focuses upon the internal structure of the peasant communities concerned. In Hatton, however, the landlord figures more importantly.

Hatton, a hamlet in the parish of Hampton Lucy (then Bishop's Hampton) was part of a manor belonging to the Bishop of Worcester. In the period under discussion the Bishop attempted to maintain heavy rents. When rents were in the form of money, the Bishop leased his demesnes for substantial sums; he did not grant them to the peasant community concerned. Because of these demands, both demesne farmers and peasants alike took action in the form of rent strikes.[20] The Bishop's refusal to yield to tenants led to the partial desertion of some villages, which left them weakened and incapable of resistance to enclosure later. Hatton in the thirteenth century was akin to other 'freehold' communities discussed in Chapter 5. It contained a uniform, highly villeinised tenant population which owed heavy labour services. At the end of the thirteenth century, there was only one freeholder in the village. Because of the Bishop's intransigence, from the end of the fourteenth century Hatton's development was markedly different from the freehold communities under the control of Coventry Priory. In Hatton, vacancies became increasingly common; by 1386 the hamlet was effectively deserted. Dyer suggests that 'there is no evidence that [the Bishop of Worcester] deliberately encouraged the process of desertion'. In fact, given his policy of estate-management, the Bishop's aims would have been to retain his tenants by any means possible in order to exploit them to the full. This attitude was reflected in Hatton rents. The bulk of services had been commuted for very high money rents, while tenants still owed 'boon' services. In these circumstances, the only option left to tenants was to leave. We may surmise that this was also a factor in the desertions of other Worcester manors, such as Upton in Blockley, Gloucestershire, and Craycombe in Fladbury, Worcestershire.

The depopulation and desertion of four of Burton Dassett's hamlets probably followed similar lines.[21] Alcock draws out the similarities between these hamlets and Hatton: there was a lack of tenants for holdings, combined with a decline in seigneurial borough activities. It is probable that Hodnell and Radbourne disappeared for the same reasons: the 1428 Subsidy indicates only four holdings for the former, whilst the latter was extremely small even in the thirteenth century. It is likely that these desertions, which occurred in the early part of the fifteenth century, arose from landlords' continued efforts to exploit their tenants, combined with internal disintegration, rather than from conscious attempts by landlords to evict communities.

The second type of desertion, which largely occurred in the latter half of the century and remained a problem in the early sixteenth century, is that to which Beresford chiefly refers: the conscious and wholesale evictions of entire communities. Here, we may instance Wormleighton, Compton Wynyates, Charlecote and the Shuckburghs. Wormleighton, in fact, had been weakened prior to its final depopulation.[22] By the early thirteenth century, it formed a single manor held from the Crown. The considerable freehold at that time probably reflected privileged conditions of tenure in the manor at large, whilst the peasant community was wealthy and there was much available land. In spite of such favourable conditions, by 1279 Wormleighton's tenant population had shrunk markedly compared with its Domesday population. From that time the number of tenancies halved before final enclosure and depopulation in 1499. The only reason advanced by Thorpe for the decline of the community was that the prevalent changes of overlordship in the late fourteenth and fifteenth centuries resulted in the neglect and decay of the manor. It seems hardly credible that a manor neglected by its lord would lead to the disintegration of the community. Rather, one might expect the reverse, that the peasants would strengthen their grip on the land. Certainly, considerable depopulation was required to extinguish the community finally in 1499.

The other desertions referred to above also involved substantial evictions and immediate conversion to pasture, except in the case of Charlecote, which was emparked. The case of Compton Wynyates, although not documented in detail, poses interesting questions; how was it that a community of which *two-thirds* were free tenants in 1279 could be destroyed two centuries later? Clearly, transformation of land-tenure must have been crucial in this instance.

Peasant communities under the control of Coventry Priory displayed a markedly different development: in them *peasant landholding was strengthened*. In the early fifteenth century, the Priory relinquished control of its demesnes and leased or granted them to the peasants in many Warwickshire manors, in strong contrast to the policy of the Bishop of Worcester.[23] This move seems to have been made because of tenant pessure, rather than for the Priory's advantage. For example, at Packington the demesne was granted to, or perhaps even appropriated by, the tenants, rent-free. In these conditions of relaxed manorial control and abundant land, the peasant communities concerned were transformed by degrees into wealthy freehold communities which paid fixed and increasingly nominal rents. However, elevation of previously highly villeinised communities to freehold communities was the exception not the rule. The high density of deserted villages in this part of Warwickshire bears silent witness to this.

8 English Development, 1485–1640

AGRARIAN DEVELOPMENT

Having traced the development of the English peasantry after the feudal crisis, I shall examine the impact of agrarian change in the sixteenth and early seventeenth centuries on the peasantry. At this point, the relationship of the peasantry with the state becomes of paramount importance. First, we must outline the position in which the peasantry found itself at this time.

The Condition of the Peasantry

For this aspect of agrarian structure, we must rely upon Tawney's masterpiece, *The Agrarian Problem of the Sixteenth Century*, still the only comprehensive and generalised work for this period.[1] In the sixteenth century, peasant land-tenure took two strongly contrasting forms: freehold (20 per cent of the peasant population) and customary tenure (some 80 per cent). The former tenure approached modern freehold in form as outright ownership, whereas the latter was an ill-defined and often insecure form of tenure at a time when conditional property in land was being transformed into absolute property. Customary tenure was defined according to the *custom* of the manor and was almost invariably copyhold (see the previous chapter). Only some 10–20 per cent of customary tenancies comprised tenure entirely at the will of the lord. Most tenancies-at-will had already disappeared, since such tenants were extremely vulnerable to early eviction by their landlords. Of the copyholders, approximately one-half held their lands for life or lives rather than by inheritance, and almost two-thirds faced variable rather than fixed entry fines. This meant that more than half of customary tenants were vulnerable to eviction, either upon the expiry of their term of tenure or through raised entry fines.[2] More generally, we can suggest that *well over half* of the peasant population at large possessed land without security of tenure in the long term.

Tawney's statistical tables indicate that both freehold and customary groups of tenants were highly differentiated. For the former, as the area of land increased, the proportion of peasants represented rapidly declined to a low point at 60 acres. However, as customary tenant land increased there was only a gradual and 'linear' decline as far as 120 acres, indicating a broad spread of these holdings. (See Table 8.1.) Differentiation was more advanced among free tenants as early as the end of the thirteenth century. The free-tenant group became rapidly differentiated from this time; by the sixteenth century some seven-eighths of the total number held less than the 20 acres required for subsistence.[3] The freeholders formed a very heterogeneous group with an overwhelming percentage of smallholders, together with a small group of rich peasants who had accumulated sufficient land to have virtually escaped this category altogether. By contrast, the customary tenant profile confirms that differentiation began later than for free tenants; by the sixteenth century it had not progressed sufficiently for there to have been a complete split between smallholders and rich peasants. Although those without enough land for subsistence formed nearly two-thirds of the total, nearly one-third of customary tenants held 20–39 acres. Thus, we may conclude that the peasantry, dominated

TABLE 8.1   Freehold and customary tenant differentiation in the sixteenth century

Land area (acres)	% of total freehold tenants	% of total customary tenants
0–4	57	35
5–19	26	27
20–39	8	20
40–59	5	9
60–79	1	5
80–99	1	2
100–119	1	1
120 and over	1	1
Total	100	100

Source: reconstructed from R. H. Tawney, *The Agrarian Problem of the Sixteenth Century* (London: Longmans, 1912) table II, pp. 32–3, and table IV, pp. 64–5.

by customary tenants, retained its cohesion based on the interests which derived from a homogeneity of landholding, but also that this cohesion was increasingly threatened. The freehold group was already highly heterogeneous but comprised only a relatively small proportion of the peasantry.

The Rise of Capitalist Agriculture

In any discussion of the emergence of capitalist agriculture in England, we must confront the debate engendered by Tawney.[4] He argued that the middle and lower members of the landowning class (the gentry) rose to economic prominence in this period through their extensive participation in the land market, which had expanded as a result of the sale of Crown and monastic lands, and their introduction of new (capitalist) methods in agriculture. By comparison, the aristocracy declined in importance, as their fixed incomes depreciated rapidly in the face of secular inflation. Trevor-Roper disagrees most strongly with Tawney's view. He suggests that there were no strong differences of estate-management between the two groups, but that the larger size of aristocratic estates may well have given them the edge because of the greater resources available to them. None the less, Trevor-Roper argues that large profits could be made not in agriculture, but rather in the windfalls which a privileged oligarchy reaped from the court. Others denied this opportunity, and those whose only source of income was in land suffered from the effects of inflation and declined in prosperity.

Stone argues that the aristocracy experienced serious financial difficulties from the mid-sixteenth century onwards, and that this was reflected in massive land sales at the turn of the century and in considerable indebtedness. However, from the seventeenth century onwards, this group experienced a partial recovery which resulted both from their adoption of new methods of estate-management and from their closer alliance with the monarchy and the court. Thus, Stone's work, although substantiating Tawney's general argument, also partially incorporates Trevor-Roper's points of difference. The protagonists are largely arguing past each other: evidence may be found for the rise and fall of members of both groups. As Hill argues, both Tawney and Trevor-Roper refer to social and legal groups as if they were economic classes; thus their positions rest upon false premises. If, instead, we examine the changes in terms of the emergence of a capitalist class of landlords and farmers, then the reason why some sections of both the gentry and the aristocracy rose while others fell is clarified.[5]

During the price revolution of the period 1500–1640, in which agricultural prices rose by over 600 per cent, the only way for landlords to protect their income was to introduce new forms of tenure and rent, and to invest in production for the market. Smaller landowners, such as the gentry and yeomanry, adopted these means earlier and on a wider scale than larger landowners, so that more of this group prospered than did aristocrats.[6] The influx of successful yeomen into the ranks of the gentry gave a solid basis to the group from below.[7] The late-medieval pattern of tenancy structure and demesne usage in the manors of smaller landlords encouraged the early adoption of capitalist methods and the employment of wage labour, while extensive involvement of the gentry, especially cadet branches, in the purchase of dissolved monastic lands encouraged the orientation of their lands towards market production. Also, as Stone points out, the result of the extensive social mobility of the period was the *levelling* of the wealth of the upper classes, while at the same time this group as a whole prospered.

This increase in prosperity occurred through the adoption of capitalist forms of management such as raised rents and entry fines; new forms of tenure; demesne production for the market; new agricultural techniques; enclosure and engrossing. It has long been argued that rents fell behind prices in Tudor and early Stuart England. This conclusion underlies Tawney's and Stone's portrayal of the decline of the aristocracy, and is the foundation of Trevor-Roper's belief in the unprofitability of agriculture in this period. However, Kerridge argues that, although rents were slow to rise in the first half of the sixteenth century, after that time they increased at a rate that was far higher than the general level of prices. For Wiltshire, he suggests that rents rose eightfold in the period 1500–1640.[8]

Often, when rents themselves were necessarily fixed, landlords improved their revenue by raising entry fines. More than half the peasantry faced arbitrary entry fines. Other means of increasing rents lay in the conversion of copyhold to outright leasehold, so that rents kept pace with inflation (the practice of racking rents). The rise of leasehold also confirmed landlords' ultimate ownership of the land and tenants' strictly limited rights of temporary usage, which previously had been relatively undefined in customary possession. On demesne land unencumbered by customary tenure leasehold developed early. By the mid sixteenth century most demesne land had been leased or consolidated into landlords' hands and turned towards production for the market.[9] Consolidated demesnes not used by the landlord himself were leased by a few large farmers. Strips on unconsolidated demesnes were often leased by peasants who could be conveniently removed when the landlord wished to reclaim the demesne. Throughout the sixteenth century the number of smaller lessees shrank, while large leaseholding, for which accumulated capital was a prerequisite, became increasingly important. The sixteenth century also saw the rise of the capitalist lessee who was prepared to invest capital in land and stock. The increasing divergence of agricultural prices and wages resulted in a 'profit inflation' for capitalist farmers prepared and able to respond to market trends and who hired agricultural labour. Even though rents increased at a faster rate than prices in the latter part of the period, the capitalist lessee could still increase his profits.

Agriculture in this period was associated with important changes in technique, which Kerridge suggests constituted a veritable agricultural revolution from 1560 to 1760.[10] The introduction of rotating arable and ley pastures, or up-and-down husbandry; the floating of water-meadows; new fallow crops and selected grasses; marsh drainage; fertilisers and stock-breeding – all required a considerable investment of capital and revolutionised the productivity of the land, doubling or tripling it. However, the increasing prosperity of capitalist landlords and farmers was not matched by that of the peasantry overall. In areas such as the Midlands, the interests of capitalist farming and the peasantry met head-on over the issue of enclosure and conversion of land to pasture for the purposes of commercial sheep-grazing.

Enclosure and the Midlands

It is vital to assess the extent and pace of the enclosure movement. First, we cannot understand the state's agrarian policy without also clarifying the extent of enclosure; and, secondly, enclosure was closely connected with the peasant revolt in the Midlands in 1607, which forms the object of study in Part III. Like Tawney, I shall persist with the term 'enclosure' in order to describe the form of agrarian change associated with the extinction of common rights, depopulation, engrossing and conversion, in spite of the different ways in which others interpret and use the term.[11] This is in agreement with the definition adopted by the Tudor and early Stuart state apparatus in its agrarian policy and by contemporary sixteenth century observers.

Large-scale enclosure was destructive mainly in the areas in which the open-field system predominated. This system was to be found largely in Southern and Midland England and in the North East.[12] Small-scale enclosure by peasants themselves – whether it involved mutual agreements to enclose and consolidate, closes of pasture, or assarts from the waste – while indicating a gradual modification of the open-field system, did not herald its immediate and complete destruction. In the Midlands, the collision of capitalist agriculture and the open-field system took its most extreme form.[13] This region of England was the most densely populated of all open-field areas and land was in chronically short supply. The attenuated commons, pastures and meadowland were increasingly stinted. Moreover, this region contained much heavy clay soil ideally suited to conversion from arable to permanent grass, so that capitalist investment predominantly took the form of large-scale sheep-grazing for wool-growing. Often this investment was undertaken by large lessees, who were particularly prevalent in the Midlands. Wool, which had a high value for its weight, was a very cheap commodity to transport. This made sheep-grazing especially attractive to the many large capitalist farmers who were not able to profit from the extra-regional market in grain, owing to the lack of convenient waterways for transportation. Moreover, sheep-grazing was largely confined to those with capital and/or considerable land, since it required an absolute minimum of 50 acres of pasture and a large outlay on stock, rent and feed for its profitable operation. Sheep-farming was encouraged by the high prices paid for wool during much of the sixteenth century and until the 1620s. In the latter part of the period, cattle-raising and horse-rearing also became important.

However large-scale sheep-grazing on permanent pasture proved to be totally destructive of open-field peasant mixed-farming units, which relied upon an organic interdependence of tillage and pasture. The establishment of such sheep-farms required the engrossing, enclosure and conversion to pasture of large tracts of previously separate and scattered lands, and the extinction of the peasant community's common rights over these lands. Consequently, the most deleterious effects of the development of capitalist agriculture on the Midland peasantry in the Tudor and early Stuart period resulted from enclosure. It is this contradiction between small grain-producing peasant farming units and the large sheep-graziers which forms the basis of the agrarian problem of England in this period.

The enclosure movement in the period 1500–1640 has not yet been adequately integrated into an overall view of enclosure. Discrete periods have been analysed by various authors – the fifteenth century by Beresford, the sixteenth century by Tawney, Gay and Parker, and the seventeenth century by Leonard and Gonner – without any integration of these findings.[14] Overviews of the process of enclosure by such

authors as Gonner, Curtler, Slater and Johnson fail to confront the
retrospective implications of eighteenth-century parliamentary enclosure for the Midlands, which suggest that *over half* the land in these
counties had *already* been enclosed.[15] These works tend to rely upon
Gay's statistics as a summary statement of enclosure in the period 1500—
1640, in which he suggests that less than 3 per cent of the land area was
enclosed. This conclusion has been widely accepted.[16]

Gay's statistics derive from the two most substantial returns of the
special government commissions appointed to investigate enclosures in
the years 1517—19 and 1607. Their enquiries were intended to establish
the extent of possibly illegal enclosure for the periods 1485—1517 and
1578—1607, largely in the Midlands. In support of his argument that
enclosure was widespread and had a great impact, Tawney points out
that the extent of enclosure recorded by these commissions may well
have been underestimated as a result of jury-packing and intimidation
by landlords.[17] Moreover, Tawney argues that Gay's method of
calculation by percentage of total county area underplays the real
impact of enclosure. First, this method ignores the uneven distribution
of these changes within the county – particular villages were hit
very hard, and enclosure was concentrated in certain areas. Secondly,
the significant porportion of enclosure to be calculated is that
which is relative to the *cultivated area* rather than the total county
area.

Rather than rely on Gay, Tawney draws upon the indirect evidence of
contemporary commentators who clearly perceived the seriousness of
enclosure and of the state's sustained attempts to prevent it, in order to
argue that there was considerable enclosure in this period. In Table 8.2, I
have readjusted Gay's figures according to the above comments. In
addition to recalculating the percentages on the basis that the cultivated
area was only 60 per cent of the total county area, I have doubled the
acreage enclosed in order to take account of the missing interval 1518—
77, and doubled the resulting figures in order to take account of both
enclosure of pasture and underestimation of enclosure by the commissions. This is in line with comments made by Gay and Parker on these
figures.[18]

The final column of Table 8.2 gives a more realistic impression of the
impact of enclosure in the Midlands in the period 1485—1607. On
average, 21.1 per cent of the cultivated area was enclosed; approximately
one-fifth of the land was removed from the open-field system of
cultivation. The enclosure movement must have had a fundamental
impact upon the agrarian organisation of the Midlands peasantry in this

TABLE 8.2 Enclosure in the Midlands, 1485–1607

County	County area (acres)	Cultivated area (acres)	Gay's figures: enclosed area (acres)	Gay's figures: % enclosed	Recalculated enclosure (to nearest thousand acres)	% of cultivated area enclosed
Northants	636,000	382,000	41,416	6.15	166,000	43.4
Beds	301,000	181,000	14,141	4.69	57,000	31.3
Bucks	477,000	286,000	16,998	3.56	68,000	23.8
Warwicks	576,000	346,000	15,067	2.61	60,000	17.4
Leics	530,000	318,000	18,070	3.41	40,000	.12.6
Lincs	1,691,000	800,000	20,286	1.20	81,000	10.1
Hunts	233,000	140,000	15,354	6.58	61,000	43.9
Oxon	478,000	287,000	23,662	4.49	95,000	33.0
Berks	459,000	275,000	12,784	2.78	51,000	18.6
Notts	531,000	319,000	8,940	1.66	36,000	11.2
Total	5,912,000	3,334,000	186,718	3.16 (average)	715,000	21.1 (average)

period, especially since it was concentrated within the felden parts of these counties, a matter I shall discuss below.

We are able to relate enclosure in the Midlands both to the extent of depopulation and to the social groups engaged in enclosure activity. Here, depopulation is defined as the loss of peasant mixed-farming household units of production (houses of husbandry decayed). This is consistent with the definition implemented by the state in its agrarian policy; the unit was considered to have at least 20 acres of arable land attached. (Of course, this left unrecorded the loss of many smaller peasant households with less than 20 acres.) Gay's figures on depopulation indicate that the rate of depopulation was maintained throughout the sixteenth century, similar to the rate of enclosure. In the first thirty-two years (1485–1517), 71,634 acres were enclosed and 1404 houses of husbandry were decayed in the thirteen counties for which there are records. In the last twenty-nine years (1578–1607), 69,758 acres were enclosed and 966 houses decayed in six counties.[19] Over the entire period, over 80 per cent of both enclosure and depopulations recorded in England were in the Midlands. Gay argues that this rate of enclosure was maintained in the intervening period, 1518–77, for which there are no generalised figures. In the latter half of the century, it appears that enclosure activity was even more concentrated on the inner Midland group than before, especially in Northamptonshire, Leicestershire and Warwickshire. This distribution is reflected in the returns of the commissions of 1607, and will be further enlarged upon in the context of the revolt of that year.

In Leicestershire in particular, more than one in every three parishes experienced complete or partial enclosure in the period 1485–1607.[20] Such enclosure gave rise to much depopulation as the land was predominantly converted from arable to pasture. More specifically, there was some depopulation in fifty-one of the sixty-seven parishes in which there was enclosure in the period 1578–1607, involving a minimum of 195 houses decayed. The same commissions returned at least 113 houses decayed in Warwickshire, with some depopulation in most of the thirty-four parishes involved in only four hundreds of the county, and returned 358 houses decayed in 118 parishes in Northamptonshire.[21]

We have some indication of the social groups which were chiefly involved in enclosure (see Table 8.3). Semeonov's figures for six Midland counties (including Northamptonshire, Leicestershire and Warwickshire) indicate that lay landlords were predominantly involved in enclosure, closely followed by farmers and lessees.[22] For

TABLE 8.3   Groups involved in enclosure (percentage of total
land enclosed)
(a) *Semeonov's findings, 1485–1517*

	Midlands	Leicestershire only
Lay landlords	42.4	71.2
Ecclesiastical	16.5	19.8
Farmers/lessees	26.4	2.7
Freeholders	9.8	6.3
Copyholders	2.7	–
Total	97.8	100.0

(b) *Parker's findings for Leicestershire*

1485–1550		1551–1607	
Squirearchy	58.4	Squirearchy	72.5
Monastic	17.6	Peasants	19.0
Nobility	12.1	Merchants	6.8
Crown	2.1	Nobility	1.7
Unknown	9.1		
Total	99.3		100.0

Sources: V. F. Semeonov, *Enclosures and Peasant Revolts in England in
the Sixteenth Century* (Moscow and Leningrad, 1949), tables 1, 3, 6, 8,
10 and 11, pp. 161–80; L. A. Parker, 'The Depopulation Returns for
Leicestershire in 1607', *Leicestershire Archaeological Society,
Transactions*, vol. 23 (1947) pp. 83, 149.

Leicestershire, the pattern is similar, while it is likely that lessees and
farmers played a more important part in the latter half of the century
than in the first half, and that the peasantry was possibly more active in
enclosing. This trend is consistent with the increasing prosperity of the
gentry and the yeomen in this period.

In sum, the extent and pace of enclosure in the Midlands was
maintained throughout the sixteenth century and thereby constituted a
considerable and constant problem for the state. Increasing population
and pressure on land may well have exacerbated the problem from the
mid sixteenth century onwards. Enclosure continued to cause depopulation which destroyed or damaged many peasant communities. During
this period, there was a shift from large landlords towards the gentry and

capitalist farmers and lessees as the dominant enclosing group, and some participation by peasants in enclosure.

The early seventeenth century

Prior to the work of Leonard and Gonner, the early seventeenth century was seen as an interregnum between the harsh, landlord-imposed enclosures of the sixteenth century and the beginnings of parliamentary enclosure in the eighteenth century. Leonard and Gonner argue that the pace of enclosure was in fact maintained throughout the seventeenth century, even though the means of enclosure now took the form of enclosure by agreement and eliminated previously prevalent abuses of tenants' interests by landlords. Tenants were included in agreements to enclose and cultivate the land in severalty, and were allotted land accordingly.

This view has been enlarged upon more recently by Beresford.[23] However, enclosure by agreement did not wholly respect tenants' interests. First, it often rested on a basis of *prior* engrossing of holdings and depopulation. By these means, tenants were reduced in numbers and larger freeholders and lessees were able to elicit general if reluctant agreement from the remainder. Even if agreement was not widely obtained, the consent of the freeholders alone was considered sufficient to bring about an enclosure. As a result, enclosure by these means was not necessarily free from depopulation. Both substantial tenants, whose fate was recorded by government commissions, and poor peasants, cottagers and labourers alike were evicted. Parker's six examples of enclosure by agreement in Leicestershire indicate considerable depopulation – an average of ten houses of husbandry were decayed in each parish. Additionally, these agreements involved on average only eleven freeholders and tenants per parish. The association of this form of enclosure with depopulation is reinforced by the fact that the state saw fit to intervene and regulate it in its courts of Chancery and Exchequer. Those participating in agreements had to certify that their actions would cause no depopulations.

Additional indirect evidence that such enclosures transgressed the interests of the peasantry is given by the fact that they elicited fierce hostility from them. Many agreements examined in Chancery had caused enclosure riots. More importantly perhaps, most of the centres of the enclosure riots comprising the Midlands Revolt of 1607 had experienced enclosure by agreement at the cost of considerable depopulation. We can conclude that enclosure by agreement, although it constituted an advance, was often predicated upon considerable prior destruction of peasant landholding, and was itself not immune from a charge of depopulation.

In the three Midland counties primarily involved in the revolt of 1607, enclosure by agreement through Chancery decree was particularly common at that time. In this period (1600–75) twenty-one such decrees have been found for Leicestershire, sixteen for Northamptonshire and thirteen for Warwickshire.[24] In other words, enclosure by agreement was popular precisely where enclosure was causing so many problems and where the peasantry resisted it most strongly. This should warn us against accepting at face value the claims made for this form of enclosure.

However, enclosure which completely ignored the interests of the peasantry and caused considerable depopulation still remained a problem in the Midlands. This is clearly apparent for the period ending in 1607, as Gay's figures and Table 8.2 indicate. Until then, there was no slackening in the movement of illegal enclosure and in the *gross numbers* of depopulations. Of course, as Parker, Beresford and others have suggested, depopulation now took the form of entire desertions of villages only in rare cases. But, as I have argued, the state remained concerned because depopulation diminished the strength of the peasantry.

After the commissions of 1607, we lack the same comprehensive survey of enclosure and records of depopulation.[25] Until the 1630s, the government in the main relied upon individual petitions and reports: after that time sheriffs and JPs of the counties concerned provided rather scattered and unsystematic reports on enclosure, some of which have probably not survived. Depopulations, therefore, were not systematically recorded. Nevertheless, it is apparent that considerable illegal enclosure took place in the early seventeenth century. In Leicestershire, a county for which records are better than elsewhere, some 10,000 acres (more than 3 per cent of the cultivated area) were enclosed in just two years, 1630–1.[26] This rate of enclosure compares well with the rate in the previous century. Records of enclosure in the 1630s exist for other counties, such as Derbyshire, Huntingdonshire, Nottinghamshire, Lincolnshire and Kent. However, I suspect that centrally appointed royal commissions with a clear brief would have upturned much more illegal enclosure and would have left us more comprehensive records.

In the absence of such records, the major evidence (albeit indirect) of the fact that depopulation remained a serious problem is records of fines exacted from depopulators. In the years 1635–8, fines totalling £47,000 were imposed upon 589 offenders, a large number of whom came from Lincolnshire (£18,846).[27] Leicestershire provided 167 offenders (£9425), and Northamptonshire eighty-five (£8678). Other counties involved were (in descending order of importance): Huntingdonshire, Nottinghamshire, Hertfordshire, Rutland, Oxfordshire, Cambridgeshire, Bedfordshire, Buckinghamshire and Gloucestershire. Clearly, Midland and other inland counties remained in the forefront of illegal enclosure.

Having reviewed the question of enclosure and depopulation in the period 1485–1640, we may conclude that it comprised the enduring basis of the agrarian problem throughout the period, especially in the Midlands. This brings us to the issue of the relationship of the absolutist state to enclosure.

THE STRUCTURAL CHARACTER OF ENGLISH ABSOLUTISM

In England, absolutism was only weakly developed and existed for a relatively short period, roughly coincident with the reigns of the Tudors and early Stuarts (Henry VII to Charles I). Aspirations towards a stronger state reached their height in the reign of Henry VIII, especially during Thomas Cromwell's period in power.[28] In the 1530s, these aspirations were manifest in various ways: for instance, in the draft proposal for a standing army in 1536–7; the appointment of the Council of the North in 1537 after the Pilgrimage of Grace, and the creation of the shortlived Council of the West in 1539 – both of which reflected attempts to extend the royal bureaucracy; the proposed Statute of Proclamations of 1539, by which royal authority was intended to usurp parliamentary legislative powers; and the massive dissolution of the monasteries from 1536 onwards. Stone suggests that Cromwell's policy was generally one of the concentration of economic and military power in law and administration, and the attempted replacement of common by civil law. In the previous decade, attempts had been made to reorganise England's army through a system of 'musters' and to extend royal fiscal powers in the subsidy. However, by and large these attempts to create a strengthened absolutism failed; the Tudor state remained severely handicapped by its lack of size and strength, and was forced to rely upon the local administrative structures of the landed class. This character was reflected in its limited fiscal resources, small bureaucracy, and lack of a standing army.

By the fifteenth century, the growing deficiency of the Crown's ordinary revenues from rent, customs and fee-farms, resulted in the increased importance of direct taxation.[29] In spite of attempts in this period to introduce new forms of taxation subject to royal control, the traditional 'Subsidy' and 'tenth and fifteenth' (granted by Parliament) remained the only viable source of revenue. Indeed, it became an accepted principle that the King should rely upon taxation only for rebellion, war, and defence of the realm, at which time he could rightfully claim a subsidy from Parliament.

Parliament increasingly controlled this fundamental condition of existence of absolutism in England, especially in times of war. By the sixteenth century, direct taxation was the only adequate base for royal finance as revenue from land continued to diminish. The King's fiscal problems came to a head in the 1520s, when, under pressure of extensive war expenditure, he attempted to take control of the Subsidy, which had remained unchanged since 1334. However, Parliament refused to grant a subsidy in 1525, after two earlier subsidies and other loans in the previous few years. The monarch's sale of Crown and monastic lands, although delaying the inevitable, set the seal on royal dependence on parliamentary-granted taxation. For a while these land sales enabled the monarch to remain solvent and relatively independent of Parliament in peacetime, but the exhaustion of this land meant that the Stuart state's position became precarious, as a result of the deepening rift between the King and Parliament. Under the Tudors, the nascent capitalist classes represented in Parliament accepted the necessity of absolutist rule as in their interests; by the seventeenth century, absolutism increasingly restricted and retarded the advancement of these classes. Moreover, the state's marginal fiscal base inhibited the formation of a bureaucracy and prohibited the creation of a standing army, both of which might have given it greater autonomy from Parliament.[30]

The early centralisation of the feudal state under the Normans and the Angevins caused the landlord class itself to become highly unified. This unity was expressed in Parliament, a body which acquired extensive negative control over royal legislative power from an early date, in addition to control over taxation. As a result, there was considerable fusion of monarchical and noble judicial and administrative structures at the local level. This fusion blocked the formation either of an extensive royal bureaucracy or of strong baronial control, and evolved into the system of unpaid justices of the peace, recruited from the county gentry. Where differences of interests between central and local administration existed, there were considerable problems in execution of policy, (for instance, agrarian policy). When interests coincided, central government was more likely to exercise a determining influence.[31] None the less, the rise of absolutism led to considerable changes in central administration, even if these were severely constrained by both local administration and limited fiscal resources. As Elton argues, the reign of the Tudors saw the beginnings of a bureaucracy in which financial, legal and administrative functions were clearly demarcated in the Exchequer, Chancery and Privy Council respectively, and were divorced from the maintenance of the monarch's personal household.[32]

During the later medieval period, England's island situation protected her from the impact or threat of invasion, unlike other emergent states in Western Europe. This allowed the early demilitarisation of the landlord class and the conversion of large sectors of it to commercial agriculture. Thus, there was little external reason for a permanent standing army, while the strength of Parliament rendered its formation unlikely. Such an army would have posed a considerable threat to Parliament by strengthening the monarch's hand. As a result, England's military forces remained particularly antiquated in character.[33] Since military service by vassals had long been commuted into money, the state was forced to revert to the militia, which derived from the Anglo-Saxon organisation of military 'levies' from 'shires' mustered when the occasion warranted it. By the late sixteenth century, certain advances were made by the introduction of the 'trained bands', an elite drawn from the militia and trained more regularly. None the less, the state continued to rely upon this outdated mode of military organisation until the Civil War, which saw the introduction of the 'New Model Army'.

State and Peasantry

These constraints on absolutism in England had important consequences for its relationship with the peasantry.[34] The changes wrought by the emergence of capitalism in agriculture forced the state to adopt an anti-capitalist stance for reasons which concern both the maintenance of feudal relations of production in the landholding monopoly, and the state's own survival. In the long run, of course, the latter was integral to the former, since the maintenance of feudalism required the absolutist state form. However, as a result of transformations in the landlord class, the only occasion on which it would rally collectively behind the state was when landed property itself was threatened. When the state's own fiscal and military conditions of existence were threatened this solidarity was notably absent. Political instability, rebellion and revolt directly threatened the maintenance of feudalism and the existence of absolutism as the political manifestation of the continued dominance of the landlord class. This produced a unity between the state and the landlord class. However, although the state's own interests lay in the preservation of its own conditions of existence in fiscal and military strength, when these concerns contradicted the increasingly capitalist interests of members of the landlord class the latter often failed to heed the constraints which absolutism placed on their activities. As a result, English absolutism was often in the contradictory position in the agrarian sphere of having to protect the peasantry while at the same time being very dependent upon the landed class whose interests were often damaged by the state's activities.

Throughout the entire Tudor and early Stuart period, the maintenance of political stability remained the fundamental imperative of state policy with respect to the agrarian problem.[35] In this concern, even justices of the peace, often ardent opponents of much of the state's agrarian policy, were moved to take action: the *political interests of the landlord class as a whole* overrode the *economic interests of its individual members* which were under attack.

The agrarian changes discussed above led to revolts, riots, and other disturbances and posed a considerable threat to political stability throughout the period. Such disturbances stemmed from a multiplicity of effects damaging to the peasantry, such as the expropriation of land by landlords, peasants' exclusion from commons, racking of rents, unfavourable changes in tenure, and enclosure, which itself involved engrossing, conversion of arable land to pasture, and depopulation. The state viewed all these changes as causes of social disorder and sought to control them and thus protect the peasantry.[36] The maintenance of order was made all the more necessary because the state lacked a powerful and ever-ready army to quell any risings which might occur. Indeed, for its army, the state was forced to rely upon the peasantry itself – the very class which was likely to have been provoked into revolt. In particular, where agrarian changes caused depopulation, the state viewed enclosure with consternation, not only because of the potential for disorder, but also because of its impact upon the raising of taxes and an army.

From medieval times, the weight of taxation was disproportionately heavy for the peasantry.[37] The king created a privileged status for villeins on his estates in ancient demesne tenure precisely in order that they would remain sufficiently prosperous to render tallage. As the emphasis in revenue moved from the Crown's own estates to taxation throughout the realm, the King sought to preserve all villein households for the purposes of taxation, from the predation of their lords. In the sixteenth century, taxation remained unequally distributed: absolutism relied heavily upon the peasantry for its financial well-being. Furthermore, the system of assessment resulted in heavier demands on mixed-farming peasant households than on large pastoral farms. This gave an additional impulse to the state's antagonism towards depopulation and enclosure, and forced it to endeavour to protect the peasantry.

Depopulation also threatened the basis of the state itself in its capacity to raise military forces – that is, in its monopoly of violence. The shire levies were largely drawn from the ranks of the better-off husbandmen, yeomen and small gentry, who were sufficiently propertied for the maintenance of arms. Depopulation weakened the peasantry and thereby diminished military strength. The focus on the Isle of Wight in the first anti-depopulation statute of 1488 centred specifically on this issue, and the continual concern to protect the peasantry in the Northern border areas reflected the same problem. More generally, it was commonly believed that the economic and military strength of the country (the 'Commonwealth') required a strong, substantial, and prosperous peasantry. This belief was most forcefully expressed by the so-called 'Commonwealth' men such as More, Latimer, Crowley and Hales.

Agrarian Policy

I have already outlined the determinants of the agrarian policy of the Tudor and early-Stuart state. This fundamental continuity in policy was reflected in legislation throughout the period, and in its enforcement.[38] The lynchpin of all legislation until its replacement in 1597 was the Act of 1489 (4 Hen. VII, c. 19). This Act lay behind all attempts to come to grips with the agrarian problem. It was concerned with the prevention of peasant depopulations – whether of tenants-at-will, copyholders for life, or copyholders of inheritance – by the preservation of agricultural household units with 20 acres of arable land. The status of this Act was confirmed in 1563, after successive attempts to improve it had failed. In 1597 it was repealed technically, but in fact its spirit was retained and further refined by the introduction of a new Depopulation Statute, which remained in force until the Civil War period. Thus, anti-depopulation legislation was at the heart of agrarian policy. It represented an effort to tackle the effects of insecure tenure and amounted to the tacit acknowledgement that much of the peasantry could not be protected in the courts of Equity and were being evicted.

Legislation was made selective from 1515 onwards, in that the sphere of application of statutes was defined by the geographical areas in which peasant mixed-farming and open-field agriculture predominated, where enclosure was most likely to cause depopulation. The Midlands were accorded primary status, whilst a secondary factor of some importance was prevention of depopulation for reasons of defence in the Isle of Wight and areas bordering Scotland. Selectivity was also built in by the practice of appointing royal commissions to obtain information regarding enclosure. The enquiry of 1517–19 included only twenty-two counties, the abortive enquiries of 1548 and 1549 were initially dispatched to the Midlands, and that of 1565–6 also focused on this region. The commissions of 1607, in direct response to the revolt of that year, concentrated upon the Midland counties most involved, while the last enquiries of 1630–6 were largely concerned with central and Midland counties.

The most important means of the selective strengthening of policy lay in the introduction of ancillary statutes which prohibited the conversion of tillage to pasture. These statutes operated over and above the initial implicit preservation of tillage in the Act of 1489. In the Midlands, conversion was largely synonymous with depopulation and was also considered by many at the time to cause grain shortages and high grain prices. To some extent, this was undoubtedly true. Problems of food supply gave rise to serious political instability in this period which was characterised by unemployment, low wages, population expansion, problems in grain distribution, and a marginal balance between food supply and population. These enduring problems were exacerbated in three critical periods involving harvest failures and other difficulties: the mid sixteenth century, the 1590s and the 1630s. At these times, the state strove to combat the problems by placing renewed emphasis on legislation against conversion. The Act of 1515 (6 Hen. VIII, c. 5) formed the basis of later statutes such as those introduced in 1552 and 1563, in the aftermath of the mid-century crisis. In 1533 and 1549, unworkable Acts which indirectly protected tillage were introduced. In the former, it was forbidden to keep more than 2400 sheep or more than one holding, while the latter involved an abortive attempt to tax large flocks of sheep.

Part of the corpus of tillage legislation was repealed in 1593, after a period of good harvests. Paradoxically, harvests then immediately worsened while loosening of the legislation had resulted in an upsurge of conversion. In 1597, two new statutes were enacted, which as separate entities clarified policy on depopulation and conversion. This action arose in the context of serious discontent the previous year. These statutes remained on the books from then on, although the one which concerned tillage was not enforced with any vigour. In conditions of renewed bad harvests in the early 1630s, the state chose to regulate grain-marketing rather than invoke the extant statute.

In sum, the agrarian legislation was motivated primarily by a concern to protect the peasantry from depopulation. This stance was overlaid by more specific attempts by governments of the day to ameliorate conditions when grain supplies were threatened by bad harvests; to this end, conversion to pasture was proscribed. As a result, legislation in this area followed a much more uneven path than did that concerning depopulation, as the government strove to avoid political instability in times of crisis.

Enforcement

Throughout the period, the state faced considerable problems in the implementation of its agrarian policy. The lack of a sizable bureaucracy and consequent reliance upon members of the landed class, against whom this policy was often directed, seriously weakened its impact. In the first half of the sixteenth century, governments relied upon the obsolete relationship between tenant and superior lord for enforcement. The latter was empowered to take half his tenant's (the encloser's) profits.[39] Lords failed to take advantage of this opportunity, largely because they themselves were heavily implicated in enclosure. Through Wolsey's commissions of 1517–18, the Crown sought to remedy this problem in part, since the Crown was thereby empowered to sue its own tenants for half their profits.

The Act of 1536 substantially altered the situation; now the Crown could proceed against and fine any person who had enclosed illegally since 1488. Large numbers of prosecutions followed – since the information provided by the earlier commissions could now be acted upon. In 1552 and 1555 new statutes increased the powers of central government by the creation of permanent bodies of commissioners which could ensure the application of legislation. However, these statutes were soon repealed in 1563. Further commissions were ordered in 1548, 1549 and 1565–6 in renewed attempts to ascertain the extent of enclosure in the Midlands. These met with little success. Throughout the sixteenth century, the state was forced to rely upon the information provided by the much earlier commissions of Wolsey.

A resurgence of problems at the turn of the century gave rise initially to local unofficial enquiries in the Midlands and then to a full-scale set of commissions in this area in the wake of the revolt in 1607. This produced a substantial amount of information and renewed prosecutions. In the early seventeenth century the Privy Council itself increasingly attempted to regulate enclosure by investigation of individual cases. New, more generalised directives were issued to sheriffs and JPs in the 1630s, after bad harvests. The state then made a last desperate effort to effect its policy by the appointment of a Church-derived permanent Enclosure Commission under Archbishop Laud. Through these means, it was hoped that a centralised bureaucracy with some powers could act against enclosing landlords. The temporary success of the Commission only served to increase the antagonism felt towards the state by the landed class and contributed both to Laud's own demise and to the fall of Charles I.

The question arises as to whether agrarian legislation was in fact consistently enforced throughout the entire period. The currently accepted view, represented by Beresford and Thirsk, is that by the seventeenth century honest enforcement had given way to persecution of enclosers in order to extract fines from them.[40] It is more widely acknowledged that in the sixteenth century the state genuinely attempted to enforce the legislation that it had created. Primarily, this was achieved by way of prosecutions on the basis of information yielded by Wolsey's commissions. Such prosecutions virtually spanned the entire century, 1518–99. Although some duplication is likely, Gay and Beresford have traced over 600 cases concerning prosecution of enclosers in Exchequer in this period, whilst Gay additionally cites a further 195 cases in Chancery.[41] Activity was concentrated in two periods: (1) that immediately following the commissions and until 1530, and (2) 1539–1556, the time of the mid-Tudor crisis. In the latter period, new prosecutions were made possible by the Act of 1536, which for the first time allowed prosecution of all offenders. Other legislation in the sixteenth century was either too short-lived or too unwieldy to be enforced. The state continued to rely upon its earlier source of information in the commissions, which were underpinned by the Act of 1489.

The longevity of proceedings indicates both the difficulty but also the determination with which the state attempted to effect its legislation. In some cases suits spanned fifty years or more. Typical problems involved in prosecution were as follows: there were claims that the enclosure had occurred prior to 1485, the retrospective date beyond which prosecutions could not be made; false claims of repopulation (rebuilding of houses) and reconversion to arable – often the court accepted the encloser's plea at face value; claims that the lands were not held of the King (prior to 1536), or that the lands in question had always been under pasture; and disputes over the original information. Furthermore, loopholes in the law were created by proclamations which exempted from the law those who were able to prove that their enclosures were 'more beneficial for the commonwealth of this realm than the pulling down thereof'. Enclosers also bought immunity from prosecution in the form of the King's Pardon by payment of a fine, and promises to rebuild houses and reconvert land.

The onset of serious problems at the end of the sixteenth century and its ultimate expression in the revolt of 1607 forced the government to gather new information on enclosure. A spate of prosecutions followed: at least seventy and probably well over a hundred convictions were secured and fines levied from those presented.[42] After 1608, harvests generally improved and there was less urgency in enforcing the statutes, especially the Tillage Statute.[43] Moreover, no serious disturbances threatened the country. Although the Tillage Statute came under fire at this time, the Depopulation Statute was above criticism. Its execution was considered essential and judges were exhorted to implement it. In 1616 there was a local enquiry in Derbyshire concerning depopulation, and in 1618 a commission was appointed to take fines for enclosure. Throughout this period the Privy Council intervened in individual cases in order to prevent depopulation.

By 1629, bad harvests threatened to create further instability: the 1630s were marked by renewed anti-enclosure activity prompted by the dearth of grain and resulting disorder. In the period 1630–6, the Privy Council sent letters to the sheriffs and JPs of the relevant counties which instructed them to enquire of enclosure and depopulation and send certificates of their findings to the Privy Council. This method of collection of information had its disadvantages, since the local authorities often were themselves participants in illegal enclosure and had shown themselves in the past to be unenthusiastic enforcers of the agrarian legislation. Nevertheless, the commission controlled by Archbishop Laud proved effective in the prosecution of those who did not escape the net. The long list of fines imposed upon offenders in the period 1635–8 is an indication of this.

But these fines did not mean that the state's concern in the prosecution of offenders was confined to pecuniary interest. Throughout the early seventeenth century, the state also sought to ensure the *reformation of offences* in the form of the throwing down of enclosures, the rebuilding of houses of husbandry, and the reconversion of land to arable. In this respect there was continuity with the sixteenth century. Here, I dispute the currently orthodox interpretation articulated by Beresford and Thirsk. Thirsk has suggested that the state's anti-enclosure activity had in the 1630s 'degenerated into a revenue-raising device and little else'.[44] However, we may understand the state's agrarian policy at this time in terms of a continued fundamental opposition to depopulation for the reasons I have discussed, overlaid by the immediate exigencies of the fiscal crisis which became acute at that time. We should not neglect the former aspect, for which considerable evidence exists. As before, the state made continual attempts to ensure reformation of offences. Information gathered from local enquiries was acted upon, and was not just a source of revenue. JPs were ordered to have enclosures in their jurisdictions stopped, or, if already in existence, to have them destroyed. Generally, the Privy Council stated at that time that offenders 'may be admitted to their pardons upon reasonable compositions, and caution to restore the decayes and depopulations in a competent measure'.[45]

I hope now to have demonstrated how agrarian policy was *selected* by the structure of the absolutist state and the necessity for its reproduction within the social formation. It was these imperatives that gave rise to consistent efforts by the state to prevent depopulation and produced ameliorative activity in times of social crisis. But what of the effects of this agrarian policy — was it successful?

The impact of agrarian policy

There is some divergence of opinion on the relative success of the state's agrarian policy. On the one hand, Gay and Gonner suggest that the state had very little impact, while, on the other, Leonard argues that, for the seventeenth century at least, the state's efforts slowed the enclosure movement considerably.[46] However, no one would dispute that the state failed in the long term to halt the advance of capitalist agriculture. Whilst not denying the short-term and minor effects of the state's concentrated efforts in certain periods, we must conclude that the state's objective — to preserve the peasantry — was not realised. But we must not attribute this failure to the inevitable and inexorable progress of the economic forces associated with the rise of capitalism. Failure was determined by the complex relationships between economy, state and class struggle delineated in Chapter 6.

First, agrarian legislation did not get to grips with the essential problem, that of guaranteeing security of tenure together with fixed rents and entry fines. Laws could be applied only when the damage had been done and peasants evicted or their tenure transformed into leasehold. Legislation merely tackled the *effects* rather than the *cause* of insecure peasant landholding. This fatal weakness in the laws reflected the inherent lack of strength of English absolutism relative to the landed class. This was manifest in the increasingly active role played by the House of Commons, which by the seventeenth century was beginning to voice enclosers' interests. Secondly, the weakness of the state was reflected in the lack of a centralised bureaucracy. For enforcement of the statutes, the state was forced to rely upon the landed class – primarily the JPs – against whom legislation was often directed. As Hill states, 'no domestic policy could succeed in the long run without the co-operation of unpaid Justices of the Peace, who controlled local government'.[47] As agrarian capitalism developed and the landed class became increasingly integrated into production for the market, the interests of local administrators and central government diverged more markedly over the solution to the agrarian problem.

We must conclude, along with Tawney, that the state's agrarian policy merely served to mitigate the hardships induced by the enclosure movement, rather than to alter the direction of development permanently. The limits of its intervention were defined by its own structural constraints and its relationship with the landed class. But what of the role of peasant struggles in the determination of development? Was the peasantry able on its own account to protect its position?

PEASANT STRUGGLES IN THE SIXTEENTH AND EARLY SEVENTEENTH CENTURIES

Before assessing any potentially transformative role that peasant struggles may have had in this period, I shall recapitulate briefly on the structural constraints placed upon them. First, struggles were *structurally limited* by the emergence of agrarian capitalism and its relationship with feudalism. The primary form which struggles took was that of a reaction against agrarian transformations such as enclosure and the introduction of leases, raised rents and entry fines. These conditions were themselves a consequence of the *failure* of prior peasant struggles to gain secure forms of landholding, as indicated above. Secondly, the structural character of the state itself and the nature of its agrarian policy *selected* certain forms of peasant struggle: struggles were cast in a 'reformist' and 'legalistic' mould and were directed towards influencing the state on their behalf.

Brenner and Barrington Moore make such conditions of peasant struggles a feature of their analyses of the transition to capitalism in both France and England. Brenner suggests that the form that peasant revolt took in these two countries reflected their divergent political and economic structures.

In England, of course, peasant revolt was directed against the landlords, in a vain last-ditch struggle to defend disintegrating peasant proprietorship against advancing capitalist encroachment. In France the target of peasant revolt was, typically, the crushing taxation of the absolutist state, which ironically had been instrumental in securing and protecting peasant proprietorship (and thus impeding capitalist development).[48]

Barrington Moore gives peasant revolts a leading role in a negative sense, in that, in his terms, the modernisation process 'begins with peasant revolutions that fail'. In the case of England he concludes that 'the enclosures greatly strengthened the larger landlords and broke the back of the English peasantry, eliminating them as a factor from British political life'.[49] In terms of his discussion, English peasant revolts were not likely to play a transformative role. First, the English state, in contrast with the French, was insufficiently developed to be able to extract considerable surplus from the peasantry. Secondly, the commercialisation of the landed class in turn led to the commercialisation of the peasantry, to its increased production for the market, and its extensive internal differentiation. The cohesion of the peasantry was destroyed, and strong links based on common interests were forged between one sector of the peasantry – the yeomanry – and the landed class. Close involvement of landowners with their estates and a corresponding penetration of political authority by JPs ensured that the peasantry remained subordinated to the landed class and that autonomous peasant institutions did not survive. I have commented on these developments in some detail.

These are the broad outlines of the factors that weakened the peasantry and strengthened the landed class in their struggles. However, both Brenner and Barrington Moore fail adequately to consider the question of the efficacy of peasant struggles in England. Even though Brenner's major theme is that of the importance of the 'balance of forces between the contending classes', he analyses the character of peasant revolts in England (and France) only as *effects* of their different economic and political structures. This is not compatible with the perspective adopted here. Moreover, Barrington Moore tends to dismiss any role that English peasant revolts might have had – his discussion of them is limited to one footnote. Below, I shall continue to stress the potentially transformative role of the struggle between peasant and landlord, even though we must recognise the structural limits placed upon such struggles, as discussed above.

In the sixteenth and early seventeenth centuries, tenants continued to attempt to improve their conditions of tenure and to retain unimproved rents. The intervention of the law and the increasingly clear-cut status of various forms of tenure reoriented these struggles towards the establishment at law of favourable terms of tenure. Meanwhile, the increasing pressures upon the peasantry – enclosure, eviction, engrossing, conversion, raised rents and raised entry fines, together with the increased difficulties of small peasant farming in a market context, forced the peasantry to engage in protest on a larger scale. This period saw the poor peasant farmer, the cottager and the labourer in dire straits. The revolts which arose from these conditions were aimed at forcing the state to protect their interests against the onslaught of agrarian capitalism.

Several peasant revolts seriously threatened the social order of England and much energy was expended by the state in its attempts both to prevent and suppress peasant revolts. During the Tudor and early Stuart period, the peasantry was a force to be reckoned with. In the early days of Tudor rule, when the taxation powers of an increasingly ambitious state were a major issue, the commons (including the peasantry) resisted the state's demands for tax: first in Yorkshire in 1489, in Cornwall in 1497, and then in the form of passive resistance to subsidies and tenths and fifteenths in 1513 and 1525.[50] The next rebellion was the Pilgrimage of Grace in 1536, which arose largely as a result of Henry VIII's dissolution of the monasteries and his increasing centralisation of authority. Other aspects of this rebellion more closely associated with the peasantry were the burdens of taxation, gressums (entry fines), enclosure, and the widespread hatred of the Earl of Cumberland, because of his heavy-handed methods of estate-management. (The serious agrarian grievances present in this revolt have not yet been sufficiently analysed.[51])

Not long after this, England experienced conditions which amounted to a sustained economic and political crisis, during which peasant revolts occurred which had the potential permanently to alter England's direction of development. Ket's Rebellion and that in South West England in 1549 occurred at a time when the state was severely weakened politically and overextended militarily and financially, and when the whole of Southern and Midland England was disaffected.

The Mid-Tudor Crisis

Jones has argued trenchantly for a mid-Tudor crisis from 1539–63.[52] The growth of population from the late fifteenth century onwards gave rise to considerable pressure on land by mid-century. In the 1530s and 1540s, the price of wool rose dramatically, thereby encouraging the enclosure and conversion of land to pasture. However, at the same time grain prices increased considerably and grain supply was restricted, because of the bad harvests of the 1550s, and inflation was exacerbated by the practice of debasing the coinage. These economic pressures had their greatest impact upon wage labourers, whose real wages fell drastically and who completely relied on the market in grain; and upon poor and middle peasants, for whom inflation, bad harvests and high grain prices spelt ruin.

To these problems were added those of war and taxation.[53] In the reigns of Henry VIII and Edward VI, England was involved in a huge and expensive war with France, and also with Scotland. War expenditure necessitated heavy taxation in the last years of Henry's reign and during the reign of Edward VI. The commitment of large military forces overseas also weakened the country's ability to preserve internal order, a matter which proved an important precondition in the revolts of 1549. In sum, as Jones suggests,

> The events of 1549 . . . [mark] perhaps the supreme crisis in mid-Tudor government and almost certainly the nadir in relationships between the 'political nation' and the commons of Tudor England. The rebellions of 1549 take on their full meaning . . . in the context of the state of endemic riot which existed in so much of England, and in that of long-run social, economic and religious developments. In short, they marked a crisis of society as well as of government.[54]

In 1548, enclosure riots and other disturbances broke out in many counties – in some before the enclosure commissions that May, in others in reaction to these enquiries.[55] By spring 1549, there were serious disorders in the following Southern and Midland counties: Wiltshire, Sussex, Hampshire, Kent, Gloucestershire, Suffolk, Warwickshire, Essex, Hertfordshire, Leicestershire, Worcestershire and Rutland. In June, the people of Devon and Cornwall rose in rebellion against the introduction of the new English Prayer Book, while there were riots in Oxfordshire, Buckinghamshire, Northamptonshire and Berkshire. In July, disorder again flared up in Kent and Essex, in Midland counties, and in Yorkshire. Ket's Rebellion – which was to involve all Norfolk and parts of Suffolk, Cambridgeshire and Lincolnshire – began at this time in the form of enclosure riots. In this month, the government had two serious revolts on its hands, together with countless minor disturbances in many other areas. In sum, almost all the South and Midlands experienced disturbances of epidemic proportions.

As Stone suggests, the two rebellions of 1549 differed from other discontent and assumed such large proportions partly because the rebels were able to move into a power vacuum, once the local gentry had failed to provide effective resistance.[56] Henry VIII had largely destroyed the power of important regional lords in a move to strengthen the central state. In the South West, the rebellion was primarily caused by the religious changes associated with the Reformation.[57] These causes were compounded by elements of class antagonism towards the gentry and opposition to that year's poll tax on sheep. Enclosure was not a significant problem in this part of England and played no part in the rebellion. Cornwall argues that the strong regionalism of the South West was a crucial factor and that the rebellion represented strong resistance, like the earlier Pilgrimage of Grace, to the Tudor policy of centralisation and unification.

Ket's Rebellion

In Norfolk, the causes of the revolt were overtly social and economic, while it clearly displayed antagonisms based on class differences.[58] Here, the economic grievances of a peasantry under the assault of capitalist agriculture are clearly articulated. The East Anglian peasantry had long participated in an active market in land and was characterised by much freehold (approximately one-third of the population), while manorialisation was tardy and incomplete (see my discussion in Chapter 4). By the sixteenth century, there was much competition for land, holdings were highly fragmented, and as a result of the extensive land market there was much confusion over terms of tenure: freehold and copyhold were intermingled and not easily distinguished. Consequently, the peasantry did not suffer greatly from the problems caused by insecure tenure, as occurred in the Midlands. Rather, their enduring problem arose on account of the land shortage – changed agricultural practices threatened their vital customary rights of common. The introduction of large-scale sheep-farming in East Anglia was particularly facilitated by the regionally specific system of fold-course, which gave landlord graziers the right to pasture their flocks throughout the lands of their manors. These rights derived from medieval manorial rights of fold.[59] In the new context of large-scale and profitable sheep-farming, landlords without any large demesnes of their own were able to exploit this legacy to their advantage and extend their grazing rights to the exclusion of the common rights of peasants. Additionally, landlords could overstock and then enclose the manor's commons, for which only ill-defined rights of common existed.

This situation allowed grazier landlords to circumvent the problems posed by peasant freehold and security of tenure; they could gain access to pasture without having to evict peasants, and the formation of large sheep-farms was allowed without the large-scale depopulating enclosure usually associated with such changes. In Norfolk, the commission of 1517–19 recorded less than 8000 acres enclosed and converted and only seventy houses of husbandry decayed, while Suffolk was outside the scope of the commissions' enquiries altogether.[60] Since East Anglia was the centre of England's cloth industry, sheep-farming was encouraged and became very important. Many Norfolk families enriched themselves through profits from wool-growing in the first half of the sixteenth century.

None the less, the peasantry still vented its anger on the many enclosures that did exist as tangible symbols of exclusion from their rightful commons. Levelling of enclosures was endemic in the period before 1549. The enclosure riots prevalent in the area of Wymondham (which catalysed the larger revolt) formed part of a long tradition of such protest.

However, in 1549 other factors ensured that these riots assumed the proportions of a revolt. First, in 1546 Henry VIII had imprisoned the Duke of Norfolk. This caused a breakdown in the traditional power structure of the region. Ecclesiastical authority was also weak, as a result of the unpopularity of the Bishop of Norwich. Secondly, the government's military resources were taxed to the limits by the simultaneous risings in Oxfordshire, Buckinghamshire and the South West. Somerset was unable to release the Earl of Warwick to deal with the rebels at Norwich until Lord Russell had suppressed these other risings. These two factors allowed the Norfolk rebels time to assemble, organise, recruit, and spread the sphere of influence of the revolt. After the initial enclosure riots, nearly a month passed before the Earl of Northampton's disastrous attempts to repress the revolt, and a further month slipped by before Warwick defeated the rebels at Dussindale.

In spite of the time available, the rebels failed to establish contact with other risings, even though all of Southern England was in some measure disaffected. Moreover, the rebels in Norfolk focused their attentions on Norwich, the regional capital, rather than moving towards London, as the rebels of the South West had been about to do before they became fatally lodged in the siege of Exeter. In this situation, Somerset was given time to deal with risings elsewhere before concentrating upon Ket's Rebellion. If communication and co-ordination between risings had been established, the state would have found itself over-extended militarily and the political future of England would have hung in the balance.

The reasons why the rebellion was confined to Norfolk and surrounding areas are clarified by an examination of the demands made by the rebels. The underlying thrust of these demands was an appeal to the King and his councillors for aid against the corrupt, dilatory and oppressive local authorities. As the symbolic representative of the absolutist polity, the King was petitioned for the implementation of laws which, the rebels argued, had not been applied diligently in Norfolk, and for the redress of wrongs experienced by the peasantry. Unlike the Pilgrimage of Grace and the rebellion in the South West in 1549, the dominant theme was not that of a split between regions and centre, but of a demand that central authority be used to protect the peasantry. Like the smaller risings in the South and Midlands, Ket's Rebellion was based upon the class divisions of peasant and landlord.

The specific demands made in Ket's Rebellion make this clear.[61] Of the twenty-nine demands, seventeen were concerned with land, the problem of rights of common, rents, prices, and laws governing property and tenure. Although enclosure was specifically mentioned in only one demand, in a wider sense the appropriation of land by the landed class at the expense of the peasantry underlay many of the demands, which were concerned with the overstocking of commons, restrictions to be placed on the size of herds, prohibition of the conversion of freehold to copyhold, protest against landlords passing on expenses to tenants, rising rents, high land prices, and so on. All these issues related to the emergence of capitalist agriculture.

However, Ket's Rebellion did not constitute a turning-point in the political relationship between the peasantry, the state and the landed class, even though it re-emphasised the fragility of political stability and the dependence of absolutism upon the continued support of the peasantry. At the time, the state's priority was to restore order rather than to consider the rebels' demands. The Norfolk rising was suppressed. There was no question of the state implementing in full the rebels' demands, even though its general agrarian policy was in sympathy with them. After the crisis of 1549, the state introduced draconian 'anti-combination' laws in 1550, in an attempt to prevent further assemblies of peasants, outbreaks of enclosure rioting, and resistance to the payment of rents by the peasantry. Renewed attempts to improve the anti-enclosure legislation were made in the 1550s and 1560s. The state's activities, both in its repression and anti-enclosure legislation, together with improved harvest conditions and a slackening of the enclosure movement in conditions of lower wool prices, resulted in the relative quiescence of the peasantry. However, by the mid-1590s bad harvests had returned, and enclosure increased at a time when some of the tillage legislation had been repealed. Again, peasant revolt was close at hand: in the Midlands, there was an attempted rising in the Vale of Oxford in late 1596, which was foiled when the authorities were alerted by an informant. This rising was caused by the combination of extensive recent enclosure in a group of four parishes near Oxford and the extremly high grain prices experienced during the famine years of 1596–7.[62]

Not long after this, in 1607, the peasantry of the Midlands rose in what was to be the last peasant revolt in England. Using the Midlands Revolt of 1607 as a case-study, I shall both illustrate the impact of agrarian capitalism upon the peasantry, and assess the impact of peasant revolts in halting, diverting or deflecting the course of agrarian capitalism in the long term.

PART III

Case Study: the Midlands Revolt of 1607

9 The Midlands Revolt of 1607

The Midlands Revolt was, like Ket's Rebellion in 1549, essentially a movement of protest against the advance of agrarian capitalism,[1] but with the difference that protest was most explicitly directed against enclosures. For this reason the revolt is central to an understanding of the relationship of agrarian transformation to peasant revolt in the transitional period in England. It was also the last concerted effort by the peasantry to halt these changes. Never again was there such a resurgence of strength by the peasantry itself.

The revolt took the form of a wave of enclosure riots spreading outwards from north-west Northamptonshire to Warwickshire, Leicestershire and beyond. At the point at which it might have developed into a more organised form, an armed Northamptonshire gentry force confronted, fought and dispersed a large assembly of rebels at Newton, and managed to suppress the revolt by exemplary executions in Northamptonshire and neighbouring counties.

PRECIPITATING FACTORS

The causes of the revolt are relatively straightforward: a time of protracted economic difficulties in the Midlands, including chronic bad harvests in the wake of the crisis period of 1596–7, coincided with a quickening of the enclosure movement, and culminated in a threatened dearth of grain in early 1607. (The general economic difficulties experienced by the Midland region are examined in Chapter 10.)

After the terrible years of 1596–7, in *national* terms, harvests recovered and were average to good until 1607.[2] (See Figure 9.1.) However, from the 1590s until the 1620s the Midlands experienced a chronic scarcity of grain irrespective of harvest quality. While grain prices were stable in Southern England in the period 1601–5, prices at

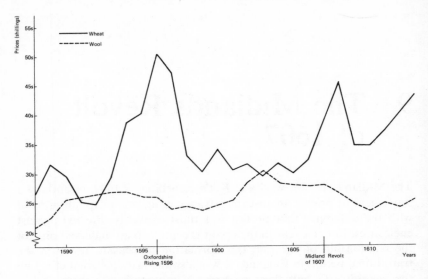

FIGURE 9.1   Movement of wheat and wool prices, 1590–1610

Source: Bowden, 'Agricultural Prices, Farm Profits, and Rents', in J. Thirsk (ed.), *The Agrarian History of England and Wales*, vol. IV (Cambridge: Cambridge University Press, 1967).

Wormleighton in the Warwickshire felden rose by nearly 20 per cent. Furthermore, the annual pattern of fluctuations in Wormleighton prices displayed characteristics indicating deep-seated poverty. Instead of peaking in summer before the harvest, prices abated slightly – indicating a decline in demand which more than offset the growing scarcity, because the poor had already used up their cash reserves and had switched to inferior cereals such as oats. The Midlands' grain supplies became even more inadequate when harvest difficulties were experienced further south. By 1604, the export of grain from East Anglian ports was forcing up prices in Warwickshire, and in the following year grain prices in Southern England shot up 40 per cent; in Exeter in the South West they rose by more than 50 per cent over the two years 1605–7. These problems reverberated to even greater effect in the Midlands. On top of all this, the winter of 1606–7 was extremely severe and gave rise to a bad harvest in 1607.[3] Referring to Figure 9.1, we can see these problems reflected in the national figures for wheat prices as a sudden upswing in prices from 1605 to 1608. However, it should be noted that the price of oats increased from as early as 1602.[4] (Oats rather than wheat was commonly consumed by poorer people, especially in times of shortage.)

By April 1607 – just before the onset of serious enclosure riots – the peasantry would have been aware that even harder times were on the way, owing to the meagre condition of the coming harvest. The rebels' concern for the grain supply is revealed by their petitions to the King. The 'Diggers of Warwickshire from Hampton Field' feared a famine on the scale of that of the early fourteenth century, and suggested that it were 'better . . . wee manfully dye, than hereafter to be pined to death for want of yt which these devouring encroachers do serve theyr fatt hogges and sheep withall'.[5] Other Warwickshire rebels suggested that the conversion of land to pasture made 'the porest sorte reddy to pyne for wante'.[6]

Commentators of the time confirm that the interrelated problems of grain supply and conversion to pasture were the major immediate concern of the revolt. Robert Wilkinson, reflecting on the revolt in a sermon given at Northampton on 21 June 1607, constantly stressed its origins in the lack of grain. He suggested that the law should be used to promote the cause and take up the complaints of the 'expelled halfe pined, and distressed poore, that they should rebell no more'.[7] Five years later, Standish, in his introduction to the *Commons Complaint*, referred to enclosure and conversion as causes of the dearth of grain which led to the revolt: 'by means thereof . . . Corne . . . doth continue at too deare a rate for the poor Artificer and labouring man; by which dearth, too oft ariseth discontentments, and mutinies among the common sort, as appeared of late by a grievance lately onely for the dearth of Corne in Warwickshire, Northamptonshire, and other places'.[8] Furthermore, Shakespeare's play *Coriolanus*, written at Stratford-on-Avon in Warwickshire in 1608, exhibits these concerns. In this play, the dearth of grain is a constant theme and is ascribed to social factors, while contemporary Stuart class distinctions appear within the Roman context.[9]

In conclusion, there can be little doubt that a central precipitating cause of the revolt was the rise in grain prices in the early years of the seventeenth century, underpinned by chronic problems of grain supply, and combined with bad harvests in 1607–8 that were felt with full force in the Midlands.

The causes of grain shortages in the Midlands, as the rebels correctly perceived, lay partly in the withdrawal of a considerable amount of land from tillage. As Figure 9.1 indicates, at the turn of the century wool prices rose considerably in relation to grain prices. Moreover, the government had in 1593 repealed much of its legislation protecting tillage. In consequence, there was a considerable increase in enclosure and conversion of arable to pasture. Indeed, the pace of enclosure reached a peak in the five years preceding the revolt. In the six Midland counties for which the commissions of 1607 recorded enclosure, of the total area enclosed during the period 1578–1607 some 61 per cent was enclosed *after*1593, two-thirds in the years 1598–1607.[10]

The salience, for the disaffected peasants in 1607, of enclosure causing conversion is highlighted by the fact that all but one of the centres of enclosure riots in the revolt had been completely enclosed, depopulated and converted to pasture only a few years before the revolt. In the case constituting the sole exception to this, the peasant community was fighting desperately against the same fate. (See Chapter 10 for further discussion of this point.)

These two factors – increasing problems of grain supply and rising prices, coupled with an onslaught by enclosers – produced a crisis situation which reached breaking-point in the early summer of 1607.

THE PATTERN OF DEVELOPMENT

The chronological pattern of development of the revolt may be analysed in five phases reflecting the expansion and coalescence of riots into a revolt and its suppression.

(1) Discontent

During the previous year and in the months prior to May 1607, there was an unusually high number of cases of enclosure riots, reflecting increased peasant discontent. These riots gave rise to at least seven cases heard in the Court of Star Chamber from the Midland counties of Northamptonshire, Warwickshire, Leicestershire, Gloucestershire and Huntingdonshire.[11] Pressure was mounting, both because of the acceleration of enclosure and the onset of deteriorating harvests.

(2) The month of May

On May Eve (30 April), the first enclosure riots directly associated with the revolt occurred in Northamptonshire. At the same time, disturbances were reported in Derbyshire.[12] It is more than likely that the festivities associated with May Day served to broaden and intensify the

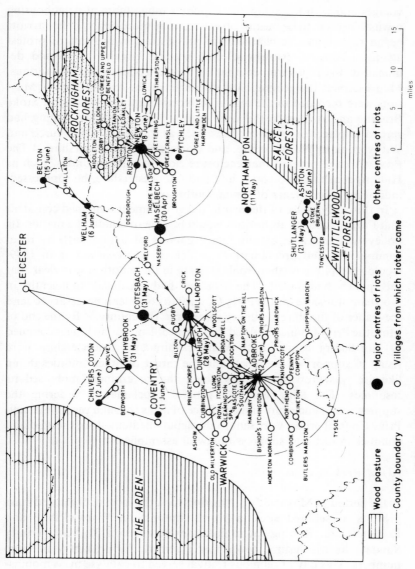

MAP 1 The Midlands Revolt of 1607: the extent of enclosure riots

riots, just as the feast of St Thomas did in Wymondham, Norfolk, in 1549. Throughout May, wider contacts were established between villages and with the sympathetic poorer inhabitants of neighbouring towns. Through these means, objectives were more clearly defined; riots began to assume the character of an abstract movement of protest against enclosure. Rioters selected specific targets that would demonstrate to the government that the problem of enclosure was serious. Map 1 depicts the geographical character of the revolt. In early May, riots were recorded in the region of Northampton town and at Stoke Bruerne and Ashton in the same county.[13] By late May, rioting had spread to places in other counties, such as Ladbroke, Dunchurch and Withybrook in Warwickshire, and Cotesbach in Leicestershire.[14] The Privy Council ordered that enclosure riots in other counties, such as Huntingdonshire, Worcèstershire and Gloucestershire, be suppressed, indicating official fears of similar outbreaks.

In this early phase of the revolt, the government remained confident that the civil county authorities would be able to handle the matter. Its policy was to avoid extraordinary courses of action such as royal commissions and proclamations, which, it was believed as in 1549, would precipitate further troubles. Late in the month it was clear that this policy had failed. The troubles had escalated sufficiently in Northamptonshire for the Privy Council to consider it necessary to send the leader of the shire's military forces into the county.[15] By the end of May, the Privy Council realised that the problem was no longer confined to Northamptonshire: both Warwickshire and Leicestershire were rising in support of the rebels and the threat of other counties doing likewise was growing. At this point, the government mobilised its resources. The King issued a general proclamation ordering the suppression of enclosure riots by force of arms through the militia, and Privy Council orders were sent to the deputy lieutenants of the Midland counties in order to suppress unlawful assemblies.[16]

(3) A week of crisis

In the period 31 May to 8 June, the riots took the form of organised mass protests at selected sites in Northamptonshire, Warwickshire and Leicestershire. Rioting intensified considerably on 31 May, Trinity Sunday, at which time townspeople joined the peasantry in large numbers. This day of religious festival served to catalyse mass mobilisation of both peasants and their allies. In Northamptonshire, there were documented riots at Haselbech, Newton, Pytchley and Rushton; in

Warwickshire, at Ladbroke, Hillmorton, Withybrook, Coventry and Chilvers Coton; and, in Leicestershire, at Cotesbach and Welham.[17] Rioters were drawn not only from felden areas (in which enclosure was such a problem), but also from adjacent wooded – pastoral regions and principal towns, such as Northampton, Coventry, Warwick and Leicester.

The crisis-point was reached on 8 June, at which time an armed gentry force confronted the rebels at Newton in Northamptonshire.[18] The leading gentry of the area, having failed to muster the trained bands, had armed and mounted their retainers and had assembled makeshift bands of foot soldiers from their household servants. This force confronted a thousand rebels at Newton, who had been encamped there for several days in order to destroy the enclosures. After twice reading the King's proclamation to the rebels in an attempt to disperse them, the gentry charged into their ranks. After an initial unsuccessful charge, the gentry routed the peasants' poorly armed forces, and in the process killed some forty or fifty of them and captured others, some of whom were hung, drawn and quartered, and their remains displayed in local market towns. The gentry's defeat of the rebels at Newton signalled the failure of the rising. From this time on, there were no further large-scale demonstrations by the peasantry.

(4) Shock-waves

By mid-June, the rising had spread belatedly to other counties in the region, but gave rise only to isolated and small-scale riots in places such as Belton in Leicestershire; in Bedfordshire; and in later months at Peachley in the parish of Hallowes, Worcestershire, at Cogges in Oxfordshire, Nassington in Northamptonshire, and at Chapel-en-le-Frith in Derbyshire.[19] The three major counties involved themselves remained in a disturbed condition until the end of June. However, the government had now marshalled its forces, and had tightened security throughout the Midlands. There was little chance of another major outbreak. By mid-July, the government felt confident enough to organise royal commissions to inquire into offending enclosures.[20] Throughout August and September the depopulation commissions for the counties concerned sat in the appropriate county towns and heard information regarding illegal enclosure. At the same time, commissions of Oyer and Terminer were sent to the counties, and the local authorities recorded rebels who had submitted themselves to the King's Pardon, ordered by proclamation.[21]

(5) Aftermath

During the remainder of this year and in 1608, the extent of rioting against enclosure was higher than usual. In this period there were
ten Star Chamber cases concerning such riots in Midland
counties, including Northamptonshire, Warwickshire, Leicestershire,
Oxfordshire, Gloucestershire and Berkshire.[22] Clearly, the same areas
remained disaffected. The bad harvest in 1608 and the state's inability
rapidly to reform enclosures maintained this discontent. Indeed,
throughout the next decade consciousness of the revolt in 1607 was
engraved on the minds of peasants and authorities alike. It was
frequently referred to either as an exemplar for further action or as a
warning of the potential ramifications of riots.[23] Moreover, the passage
into common usage of the terms 'Levellers' and 'Diggers' – first used
during the 1607 revolt to describe the destruction of enclosures –
indicates the long-term impact of the Midlands Revolt.

Narrative of Involvement: Country and Town

At this point, I shall describe in some detail events in Ladbroke, a
Warwickshire felden village, and in Leicester, a local county town. Both
were heavily involved in the revolt. In the former, the rioters' actions,
and, in the latter, the authorities' attempts to suppress the revolt are well
documented. In this way I hope to give greater insight into the precise
character of the larger revolt.

Ladbroke had been entirely enclosed in 1598 in the wake of the years
of dearth at the end of the sixteenth century. This enclosure had been
instigated by Sir Robert Dudley, lord of the manor, and William
Burton, an enterprising rich yeoman or small gentleman. Although
Ladbroke had been enclosed by agreement, considerable depopulation
and conversion to pasture resulted (see Chapter 10). For some time
before the revolt, Dudley was absent from the country, and this meant
that Burton's enclosures (which comprised some 200 acres) were the
focus of attention. Early in the 1600s, inhabitants of nearby unenclosed
peasant communities (comprising both 'open' and 'freehold' communities), presented Burton at the local assizes for blocking highways
through Ladbroke with his hedges. This background made Ladbroke a
clear target for the rioters in 1607: its lands had recently been illegally
enclosed to ill effect and adjacent peasant communities had already
mobilised against the enclosures.

During May, when the revolt was gathering force in Northamptonshire, there were assemblies of discontented peasants at Ladbroke. Matters came to a head on 2 and 3 June when inhabitants of villages in the area 'to the number of four hundred' gathered at Ladbroke:

> all of them being armed, arraied and weaponed with long bowes, arrowes, long piked staves, bills, mattocks, spades, shovels, axes, hatchets and suche other weapons, engins and tooles fitt to exercise and putt in theire said lawless, lewd and wicked purposes.[24]

They proceeded to Burton's enclosures, ignoring other smaller enclosures, and levelled the hedges and ditches:

> Thomas Harris beinge armed and weaponed . . . and mounted on horsebacke . . . and Wyncles havinge a tabor and pipe did . . . as captaines and leaders goe before, sett on and encourage the said lewde and ill disposed persons . . . playinge, pypinge and vauntinge themselves.

Another leader was Francis Harrolde, yeoman or small gentleman of Ladbroke, who was mounted on a gelding and armed with a sword and dagger.

The rioters then made various speeches and threatened Burton, saying that 'they would bringe him quicke in the ditches'. Burton, fearing for himself, 'did then refoote to his dwelling house . . . and shutt the doors – for his better saffegard against their saide fury and malice'. At which point, Robert Russell, 'beinge a notorious offendor and one of the cheefest leaders', entered the house and was forcibly detained by Burton. Meanwhile, outside the assembled peasants threatened to pull the house down and to 'cut him [Burton] in peeces and bury him quick in the saide ditches'. Burton, terrified by these threats, let Russell free.

The riots were actively supported by one John Cook, gentleman of Harbury, and his wife Christian, and by John Meacocke, the Constable of Harbury. This parish was adjacent to Ladbroke and acted as an organisational and resource centre for the rioters. There, many rioters were fed, boarded, and gathered together over the several days that the work of levelling the enclosures took. The above-mentioned people also transported rioters to Ladbroke in carts and brought food and drink to refresh them during their labours. Contact was established with Cotesbach in Leicestershire, another major centre of riots, and support was promised from there for Ladbroke.

There is an odd sequel to these events which highlights existing divisions within the village. Burton evidently bore great resentment towards the freeholders of Ladbroke, whose own enclosures had not been touched. (They had not been party to the original enclosure, which they had been forced to accept on conditions of a reduction in land held and the transformation of tenure into freehold.) In a futile attempt to incite local people, Burton and his son published a libellous poem in various fairs, markets and churches, which attacked Ladbroke's free-holders for their enclosures. This activity landed them both in the court of Star Chamber (and, incidentally, resulted in the recording of prior events cited above).

Events in Leicester town illuminate both the role of the involvement of towns in the revolt, and details of the attempts by the authorities to suppress the revolt.[25] Some seventy-one townspeople are recorded as having joined with the rebels; undoubtedly many more were in fact involved.

By the end of May, the county JPs were aware that the rising had spread to Leicestershire and that town-dwellers could well join them. On 30 May, they ordered the town's authorities to prevent anyone leaving Leicester. In spite of this, many inhabitants slipped out of the town the following morning, Trinity Sunday, under pretence of 'ordinarie shoe of recreacion' and journeyed to centres such as Cotesbach in Leicestershire and Withybrook in Warwickshire, a good fifteen miles distant. The next day, the Mayor of Leicester was peremptorily ordered by the county authorities to take action, so he sent his aldermen and others to retrieve errant inhabitants. At Lutterworth, they met the returning rioters, who had completed the levelling of enclosures at Cotesbach and other places.

In the light of such developments, the Lord Lieutenant of the county, the Earl of Huntingdon, ordered that the town muster and put in arms a force of forty men. This force was held in reserve during the week of crisis 1–8 June rather than ordered into the field, because Sir Thomas Cave, one of the county's deputy lieutenants, had been able to muster the militia. (This indicates that Leicestershire had, perhaps, not become as deeply involved as Northamptonshire in the revolt.) However, it is unlikely that the Leicester motley band would have been an effective military force: a significant proportion of their number had joined the riots earlier that week!

Huntingdon arrived from London on the morning of Friday 5 June, having been ordered by the King to take control of a deterio-rating situation. He arrived well aware of the seriousness of the revolt, since he had just traversed the hostile and disturbed county of

Northamptonshire and had stayed the previous night in Northampton. Huntingdon immediately set about organising the more effective suppression of the rising. He ordered that a gibbet be set up in the town's market-place and that the town have ready considerable supplies of gunpowder and ammunition, which were to be kept under guard in the town hall. He also ordered a strong watch of more than a hundred men to be placed over the various exits and gates to the town in order to prevent another mass exodus. He sent co-ordinating letters to those in charge of suppression in the other counties, organised Leicestershire's own forces under the deputy lieutenants, JPs and the Mayor of Leicester, and sent a letter to the Privy Council informing it of his actions. He then dispatched his cousin Henry Hastings to escort the captured John Reynolds, the supposed 'Captain Pouch' and leader of the rebels, to London to be examined by the Privy Council.

That same day, Saturday 6 June, Huntingdon and his forces marched to Welham to suppress enclosure riots there. On arrival, he found that the rioters had been forewarned and had scattered before making much impression on the enclosures. Huntingdon was able to round up only a few people involved, 'very poor creatures', who were threatened with hanging from a nearby windmill (there being no trees handy). On their submission to the King's mercy, Huntingdon spared their lives and returned with them to Leicester as hostages to be put to death 'if the least stir had again risen'.

On Monday 8 June, it being 'a raynye morning and . . . little companye stirringe', the gibbet was pulled down by the Beadle, the town gaoler, his underkeeper, a prisoner, 'dyvers boyes', and others. The Mayor was unable to have the gibbet re-erected, owing to a general refusal to do so, so the dismantled structure was taken to an alderman's yard for safekeeping, 'fearinge the same shoulde be stoulne or cut in peeces'. This instance of the Mayor's lack of authority and enthusiasm for his job proved to be the last straw for Huntingdon, who relieved him of his duties and placed him under house arrest for dereliction of duty. (The sympathy shown by Leicester's authorities for the rioters is discussed in the following chapter.)

Huntingdon finally left the town on the evening of Saturday 13 June, having successfully surmounted the crisis and organised the county's forces. On his arrival at Ashby-de-la-Zouch in the north of the county, he confidently assured the Privy Council that Leicestershire was now quiet. From this point on, matters were chiefly concerned with the legal process in the aftermath of the revolt. Commissions of Oyer and Terminer were held in the town on 26 and 27 June and records were made (for future reference) of those who submitted to the King's Pardon. Some three months later, the Depopulation Commission sat at Leicester and heard information regarding illegal enclosure.

PROBLEMS OF REPRESSION

During May (phase two), central government left the problem of control in the hands of the local authorities. This was later acknowledged to have been an error. JPs took effective action only when there loomed a direct threat to their own enclosed properties. They were taken to task by the Privy Council for their unwillingness to take quick and decisive action. In many instances, it appears that even the normal course of the law was pursued only half-heartedly. The Mayor of Northampton town and the Sheriff and JPs of the county were prosecuted in Star Chamber for not raising the militia and trained bands in order to suppress the revolt. The authorities of Leicester town were almost in open sympathy with the rebels and the county gentry were slow to act. In Warwickshire, the Sheriff and JPs compromised themselves by parleying with the rebels and implicitly accepting their demands.

There are several reasons for this inactivity and distinct lack of enthusiasm. First, there would be some among the local authorities – a definite minority – who might covertly sympathise with the reformist goals of the rebels if not their means. This was certainly the case with the authorities of Leicester town and probably also of Puritan Northampton and Coventry. There were also specific reasons for those controlling *towns* to have this attitude, which relate to their location within the Midlands economy. (This is discussed in the following chapter.) Secondly, one could argue that riots, and, more specifically, enclosure riots, were a ritualised form of protest which were to some extent accepted by local authorities as a legitimate means of political expression.[26] This might explain inactivity in phase one and the early part of phase two, but it cannot explain why JPs remained ineffective when rioting became more widespread and co-ordinated, and posed a definite threat to social order. Moreover, at this time authorities were given explicit and unequivocal instructions by Council to suppress the disturbances.

In order to explain this seeming immobility, we must understand that the local authorities were largely *unable to impose order* because they were isolated from the grass-roots of the administrative structure in the richer peasantry – the village constabulary. The interests of JP and constable diverged strongly over the issue of enclosure, the cause of the rebellion. On the one hand, many JPs in these counties had themselves enclosed and depopulated their lands. In Northamptonshire thirteen of the twenty-six resident JPs were heavily implicated in enclosure, while in Leicestershire ten of the twenty-two, and in Warwickshire eight of the twenty-five resident JPs were thus involved.[27] On the other hand, the constabulary were largely aligned with, or at least in strong sympathy with the rebels. They were themselves often involved in the enclosure riots.[28]

As the rising gathered force, it became impossible to muster the militia and trained bands, usually drawn from the local peasantry. Perhaps, if strong action had been taken before the end of May, at a time when the whole countryside was not yet committed to the revolt, the militia could have been brought out. By June, this was no longer possible – many members of the militia themselves became involved in the rising, either actively or by voting with their feet and failing to attend the muster.[29] Thus, there was a cleavage in the military – between gentry and peasantry – analogous to that in the structure of local civil authority. This created great difficulties in repressing the revolt. In this sense, the key to the further expansion of the rising beyond localised riots lay in the *allegiance of the richer peasantry*. If they had remained integrated within the authority structure of the landlord class, suppression would have proved an easy matter. As it was, the rising threatened to get out of hand and become a fully fledged revolt.

The only reason why widespread revolt did not develop further was that the threatened Northamptonshire gentry formed a 'vigilante' group and dispersed the rebels. This emergency action was prompted by attacks on their own enclosures. The destroyed enclosures at Newton belonged to Thomas Tresham, JP. Previously, other JPs' enclosures had been levelled at Haselbech (William Saunders) and Pytchley (Euseby Isham), in this part of the county, a prime area of enclosure and sheep-pastures. Other JPs resident in the area, such as Robert Osborne (Kelmarsh), James Pickering (Titchmarsh), Walter Montagu (Hanging Houghton), William Belcher (Guilsborough) and John Isham (Lamport) would have felt similarly threatened, since their recently enclosed lands would have been prime targets. In addition to the threat posed to their enclosures, the fact that the Northamptonshire gentry formed a close network which was itself based on mutual enclosing served to weld them into a group with strong interests in common. The revolt itself was most intense and enduring in this part of the county, and this made emergency action all the more necessary.

In Warwickshire and Leicestershire, enclosure was rather more widely distributed. None the less, rioting was intense, especially where the two counties met with Northamptonshire, and the co-ordination established between centres was high, as Map 1 suggests. The centres of riots in both counties were predominantly owned by landlords who were relatively defenceless and unable to act against the rebels, rather than by members of the judiciary, as in Northamptonshire. This meant that it was fortunate for the government that the revolt did not take a stronger hold than it did in Warwickshire and Leicestershire. There was little effective suppression of the revolt in these counties. Hillmorton was owned by the widow of a Norfolk gentleman, and Ladbroke by an absentee landlord, while Cotesbach was owned by a citizen and draper of London, and Welham by a person of recently risen yeoman status. Two of the lesser centres – Chilvers Coton and Withybrook – were held by JPs but neither man was able to suppress the riots effectively.

It should be noted that, if the force of Northamptonshire gentry had itself been defeated, a temporary power vacuum would have been created because of the failure to muster the county militia. The peasant forces could then have linked up with other disaffected areas, in Lincolnshire, Oxfordshire and Derbyshire, organised their troops, and cemented their alliance with the townspeople. Victory would have given them confidence, radicalised their goals, and given them access to the county stores of arms and ammunition.[30] Indeed, at this point the Midland rising would have taken on the character of a fully fledged revolt. However, by defeating the rebels in Northamptonshire (at the heart of the revolt), the gentry sealed its defeat. By this time, the rising was already subsiding in both Warwickshire and Leicestershire.

FORM OF PROTEST

It must be stressed that this revolt constituted a consciously organised movement of protest against enclosure in the areas affected. As Map 1 indicates, the detailed linkages evident in Warwickshire establish the more general pattern of the revolt in the other two counties involved. The revolt consisted of a series of non-violent enclosure riots extending outwards from western Northamptonshire in the region of Haselbech and Northampton town. These riots were based on the convergence of peasants (and townspeople) from a 10 to 15 mile radius on a chosen site of protest; for example, Ladbroke and Newton. These linkages were supplemented by co-ordinating links between centres of riots (for instance, Ladbroke and Cotesbach, and Withybrook and Chilvers Coton), through which support and encouragement was given to the rebels. This protest movement extended throughout western Northamptonshire, southern Leicestershire and eastern Warwickshire and, along with the peasant communities of the felden, drew in all the towns of the region, together with many inhabitants of the wooded—pastoral regions.

The motivating force unifying the rioters drawn from many peasant communities was their shared perception of the extent of enclosure which required legal redress by the government. Hence, they chose to throw down enclosures in already largely depopulated parishes rather than attack less significant enclosures within their own parishes. In every major centre of riots apart from Hillmorton, the indigenous peasant community had already been largely destroyed. The rioters came from other villages in order to demonstrate their point. In rioting, peasants felt that they were putting the King's laws into execution. Such laws had long been neglected by the local JPs, who were doubly ill-thought-of, because they were often the very offenders against the enclosure statutes. These aspects were clearly established in the statements made by rioters who assembled at Chilvers Coton to destroy enclosures belonging to Sir John Newdigate, JP. They suggested that Newdigate pursued his own 'private benefitt' in spite of the 'public hurt' caused thereby, and that he 'should not doe men justice but would wronge them in suche matters as they would bringe before him'.[31] This 'legalistic' attitude was reflected in the fact that rioters claimed to have held warrants from the King endorsing their actions.

The limited and 'reformist' goals of the revolt were evident in the fact that the rebels actually promised to cease their activities if the King would take action to reform enclosures within six days:

> they answered . . . that the cause of theyr rysing was oute of no undutifull mynde to his Majesty but only for reformation of thos late inclosures which made them of the porest sorte reddy to pyne for wante, and that they myght heare answere from his Majesty within six dayes and that his Highness wolde promis to reforme thos abuses, they wolde then all departe home, and rely uppon his Majesty's promis and performance therof.[32]

The riots were remarkably free from violence against persons; all feelings were directed against the offending hedges, fences and ditches. However, late in the movement (when the major riots had subsided) more radical utterances were recorded (if a bill of complaint in Star Chamber is to be believed). After the riots at Chilvers Coton, a leader at an assembly of still discontented peasants reportedly said 'that all that had bene done by the said Captayne Powch and other his adherents would doe little good unto the comonaltie concerning inclosures but that he hoaped to have a daye of the gentlemen'.[33] This statement shows some awareness that the previous demonstrations, which drew attention only to the lack of execution of the laws, would inevitably fail to halt the enclosure movement. More far-reaching action involving the elimination of the enclosing class was required to this end. At Northampton, Robert Wilkinson, who delivered a sermon to the Earl of Exeter (Lord Lieutenant) and others concerned with repression of the revolt, observed,

> First they professe nothing, but to throwe downe enclosures, though that were indeed no part of the common powre; but afterward they will reckon for other matters, They will accompt with Clergiemen, and counsell is given to kill up Gentlemen, and they will levell all states as they levelled bankes and ditches.[34]

Even though the riots were largely non-violent, considerable forces were mobilised by the peasantry and their allies, the poorer townspeople. Stowe's Chronicle gives some 5000 men, women and children at Cotesbach and a further 3000 at Hillmorton, while the gentry force confronted a thousand at Newton field, and it was estimated that some 5000 were involved in Northamptonshire as a whole.[35] Although these figures may not be accurate, at least they give us some indication of the numbers involved. Perhaps more precise are the numbers cited in the bills of complaint of cases in Star Chamber following the riots – 400 at Ladbroke, 200 at Chilvers Coton, 200 at Stoke Bruerne and Ashton, and 100 assembled outside Coventry's walls. These large numbers of assembled participants were fed, boarded, supplied with tools and transported to the sites of protest by peasant communities adjacent to the enclosed parishes. Riots often extended over a period of several days, as considerable time and energy was required to throw down thousands of acres of enclosures. The exact method usually employed was as follows: the quickset hedges were cut down and piled into the adjoining ditch (the hedges usually grew on a mound created by the excavation of a ditch), where they were burnt and then buried by the levelling of the mound into the ditch. In this way, the landscape was returned to its previous state and could again be used in common.

The enclosure riots comprising the revolt built on a long tradition of protest through these means. Riot, it is increasingly being appreciated, was an important mode of political expression for a population otherwise excluded from the political process. Enclosure riots had strong ritual and symbolic components to them. They were often catalysed by holidays and religious festivals, times when hierarchies and modes of social control could be symbolically and ritually over-turned and temporarily inverted, without fear of reprisal. From the point of view of the authorities such festivities could get out of hand as the symbolic overturning became transformed into questions of actual power and control. Rioting against enclosure often arose as a con-sequence of the traditional annual processional confirmation of com-munity boundaries during Rogation Week, and the ceremonial opening of common pastures at Lammas. At both these times, the detrimental impact of enclosure on communities would have been forcefully brought home. As we have seen, the Midlands Revolt itself was closely associated with the May Day festivities and with Trinity Sunday.

Enclosure riots often produced leaders who were given the name of 'Captain' and who claimed supernatural powers and direction by God. 'Captain Pouch', the purported leader of the Midlands Revolt, was so-named because of his large magical pouch which contained 'sufficient matter to defend them against all commers'. He also claimed 'Authoritie from his majestie to throwe downe enclosures, and that he was sent of God to satisfie all degrees whatsoever, and that in this present worke, hee was directed by the lord of Heaven.'[36] When captured, John Reynolds, the supposed Captain Pouch, had his pouch examined, but only a piece of green cheese was found in it. (Apparently, those who captured him were sufficiently worried about his legendary powers to feel the need to check!)

Either Captain Pouch was in fact a mythical symbol of unity, or in the shape of Reynolds he covered a lot of ground in the three counties concerned. It may well have been the former. Reports concerning Pouch in the ensuing Star Chamber cases give no name but refer to him in abstract as granting authority to throw down enclosures and as the guarantor of the rebels' safety. Rebels captured at Chilvers Coton said that Pouch authorised them to go to Coventry and Bedworth for support, and, further, that he gave them authority to throw down enclosures between the towns of Northampton and York. When a JP announced that Pouch had been captured (in an attempt to disperse assembled rioters), they refused to believe him and continued in their work. Captain Pouch was reported to have been at Withybrook in

Warwickshire on 2 June, though he was, in the form of Reynolds, captured in Leicestershire only a day or so later. In all probability, the eponym of Captain Pouch had its origins in the initial Northamptonshire riots. Whatever the case, Pouch acted as an effective unifying and legitimating force and became a symbol for the activities of the Midlands rebels; he was to be recalled as such in later years.

The riots themselves were organised and consciously led. They often took the form of a procession, at the head of which was the leader (a local constable or other significant figure within neighbouring villages), who was perhaps mounted on a horse; those following him were armed both with tools for the work in hand and with more offensive weapons, and the whole was accompanied by the playing of music and beating of drums. In many cases, church bells would be tolled as a signal for assembly, while the occasion was generally seen as one of celebration. Men, women, young people and children alike would participate; indeed, entire communities became involved.

Women played a significant role in enclosure riots throughout the period.[37] This was probably for several reasons. First, there is no reason to assume a strong sexual division in such activity; both sexes were very much involved in the peasant economy organised around the household. Secondly, at that time it was commonly thought (perhaps mistakenly) that women had a certain immunity from prosecution under the law, and this would have encouraged their participation. Thirdly, the often generalised ritual inversion of traditional hierarchies (frequently expressed in a reversal of sex roles), further encouraged women's active participation in riots. Finally, there are some cases of participants in riots, both men and women, wearing the other sex's clothes. Whether this is part and parcel of the role reversal or a more elementary need for disguise is hard to tell. It is worth noting that the restricted wardrobe of impoverished peasants may well have left them with no alternative for disguise other than their spouse's clothing.

In spite of the ritualistic components, it is important to remember the fact that many enclosure riots in general and the Midlands Revolt in particular represented a real threat to social order and were perceived as such by the authorities. We should not over-emphasise the integrative and functional role of enclosure riot as a form of political protest. Although the government in one sense admitted the legitimacy of the rebels' claims, it had no hesitation in suppressing the revolt forcefully. The Act concerning rebellious assemblies – created in the wake of the crisis of 1549 and concerned primarily with enclosure riots – was to be continued until the next Parliament after the revolt, precisely in order to ensure the existence of legislative means to suppress further incipient trouble at its roots.[38]

Here, Wilkinson's comments on the revolt are pertinent and reflect the mutual but opposed dilemma of state and peasantry. He used biblical imagery to argue that the rebels should not turn stones (break down walls enclosing pasture) into bread (arable land), even though enclosers had turned bread into stones, and by so doing had 'turned men into beasts, and made them wild and rebellious'. For Wilkinson, the two illegal forms of activity were incommensurate:

> I think the sin of these men [the rebels] by many degrees to exceed the other [enclosers], for pasture-men indeed do horrible mischiefe, but they do it by degrees . . . but that which growes by mutinies being sodaine and violent is lesse resistible. Pasture-men indeed destroy a few townes, but mutiners by civill commotion depopulate whole Kingdoms.[39]

These comments reflect the thinking of the government of the day. As I have suggested previously, the role of the state was to repress peasant revolt and thereby protect landed property, before peasant demands could in any sense be admitted as legitimate. This was the situation in which James I and his Council found themselves during May and June 1607.

10 Town, Forest and Felden in the Revolt

In this final chapter, I shall seek both to draw out the involvement of the peasantry and its allies in the revolt in terms of the specific economic structure of the Midland region, and to focus upon the Warwickshire felden peasant communities whose path has been traced, thus far, till the fifteenth century. We must take our analysis beyond the broad preconditions and precipitants for the revolt in order to understand the detailed reasons why peasant communities and townspeople participated in the rising. This requires an analysis of the precise location of types of peasant community and Midland towns within the regional economy. For the former, this entails distinguishing between the forest (or wooded–pastoral) community and the felden community. Within the felden itself, we may distinguish between the two types of peasant community already noted: 'open' and 'freehold' communities. In this way, the involvement of the peasantry in the revolt of 1607 can be linked back into and explained by the transformations which were experienced from the medieval period onwards.

CENTRES OF THE REVOLT

Before examining the structural location of peasant communities and towns in the Midlands, it is necessary to specify the character of the enclosed parishes in the felden which served as centres of enclosure riots in May and June 1607. Only then may we understand the involvement of peasants and townspeople. As we shall see, centres of riots had almost invariably been totally enclosed and depopulated, and converted to pastureland, within the decade prior to the revolt.

Northamptonshire

There is documentation of riots at four centres in this county: Haselbech, Rushton, Newton and Pytchley. It is more than likely that Great Houghton, adjacent to Northampton town, also experienced serious riots. These parishes lay in a part of Northamptonshire which had suffered greatly from enclosure, depopulation and conversion, and had become noted for its sheep-farming. Rushton, Newton and Pytchley formed a group adjacent to the wooded—pastoral area known as Rockingham Forest, while Haselbech lay in the very centre of the area of intense enclosure and Great Houghton was only a mile or so from the county town. In other words, the geographical location of these centres reflected the involvement of felden, forest and town in the revolt.

The western part of the county, in which these parishes lie, consists of clay vales (eminently suited to conversion to pasture), upon which nucleated peasant communities practised open-field mixed farming.[1] This area was similar in character to much of southern and eastern Leicestershire and the south-eastern Warwickshire felden, to which the revolt spread from its centre in Northamptonshire in 1607. In these areas, the peasant economy was entirely destroyed by enclosure where it occurred. In this part of Northamptonshire, enclosure was a problem of considerable magnitude and it remained so through into the seventeenth century. Activity by enclosers was particularly intense in the area around Haselbech itself and in the south-western corner of the county.[2] Surveys of sheep held on enclosed pasture, undertaken in 1547 and 1564, indicate definite concentrations in these areas. Further enclosure then occurred, as a survey in 1595 of enclosure since 1564 suggests. The abortive Oxfordshire Rising of 1596 prompted local inquiries, focusing on parishes near Haselbech, into the relationship of sheep-farming with enclosure and depopulation. The findings of the commission of 1607, concerning enclosure in the period 1578—1607, reinforce our conclusions that the area around this parish was a centre of enclosure and sheep-farming. The government convicted numerous enclosers from this area after 1607. Enclosing for sheep-pasture received considerable impetus from the remarkable increase in wool prices relative to grain prices at the beginning of the seventeenth century. This situation is reflected in the increase in the Isham flock at Lamport in Northamptonshire from a low point of 731 sheep in 1596 to a peak of 1498 in 1606.[3] Landowners in Northamptonshire by and large expanded or at least maintained their flocks until the decline in wool prices in the 1620s.

In sum, in this county the impetus of the enclosure movement was maintained in the second half of the sixteenth century and even intensified, especially in the last decade of the sixteenth and the early years of the seventeenth century. This increased activity by enclosers was felt to the fullest effect in the area surrounding Haselbech, where the first serious riots which precipitated the revolt occurred.

The high incidence of enclosure was facilitated by an extensive and close-knit network among the gentry of the area, based on marriage, kinship and land.[4] This network was distinctive in that it was overwhelmingly based upon horizontal and homogeneous links between members of the gentry with interests in common. The landowning structure of the county was dominated by newly risen gentry with recently acquired titles. This may be explained by the extensive market in land after the dissolution of the monasteries, combined with the fact that there were very few traditional large estate-owners of medieval origin. What was perhaps unusual was that the network was grounded in land, in a complex and interlocking pattern of ownership and tenancy in various parishes. This feature probably derived from the fragmented and dispersed nature of the monastic estates on which aspiring landowners based their move into the county and their rise into the ranks of the gentry.

This network assisted greatly in the business of enclosing. Enclosers could rely upon the co-operation of members of their own class who were similarly interested in enclosure and who were often prominent freeholders and lessees in the parish concerned. Landowners with unconsolidated and fragmented lands in separate parishes could exchange lands for their consolidation and enclosure. Similarly, landowners in adjacent parishes were able to extinguish their mutual common rights and enclose their lands. In this way, the barriers posed by fragmented landownership were surmounted and enclosure greatly facilitated.

In Figure 10.1 I have illustrated part of this network among the enclosing gentry, centred upon Thomas Tresham of Rushton. I shall examine his activities in some detail. Not only was he closely integrated into the network, but in addition his 'improvements' manifested the worst excesses of the enclosure movement. (The 'improvement' of land was a contemporary euphemism for enclosure and its associated effects, such as conversion, raising of rents, and often depopulation.) Until a few years before 1607, he had been the owner of Haselbech and was chiefly responsible for the demise of its peasant community. He was also the lord and encloser of Rushton, another centre of revolt. But Tresham's

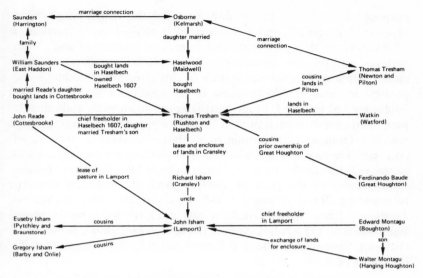

FIGURE 10.1 The gentry network in the area of Haselbech

improvements went beyond the depopulation of these two parishes and made him notorious throughout the county.

Tresham was an unusual member of the Northamptonshire gentry class in that he inherited an early-established and consolidated estate which could not easily be improved without considerable disturbance to the peasantry.[5] Tresham's improvements paradoxically coincided with the decline of the family, which was hastened by the massive recusant fines levied upon him as a prominent Catholic. Mounting debts forced him to resort to drastic measures in order to extract the maximum amount of revenue from his estate in the short term, through pasturing sheep, leasing pasture, raising entry fines and rents, mortgages, and finally through selling land. These actions antagonised the peasantry in both felden and forest, as well as the townspeople in the area.

In Orton-in-Rowell, Tresham introduced massive and contentious entry fines on tenants' leases. In Great Houghton, he raised entry fines, attempted to buy out freeholders and tenants, and planned an enclosure of the parish which, he calculated, would certainly cause depopulation. However, he was forced to abandon these plans for fear of a popular uproar. But this did not prevent him from selling the manors in Great Houghton in 1601 and 1604 to Ferdinando Baude for the precise purpose of enclosure. Baude duly enclosed the entire parish by a supposed 'agreement', and was convicted in 1607 of the conversion of 1320 acres, the decay of thirty-one houses of husbandry and eleven cottages, and the eviction of some 240 people.[6] Tresham himself was clearly implicated in the elimination of this peasant community – the grossest instance of depopulation in the county at that time. (The inhabitants of nearby Puritan Northampton town were undoubtedly motivated to destroy enclosures in Great Houghton by their antagonism towards Tresham as a prominent Catholic recusant as well as an encloser.) Tresham was also involved in the pasturing of many sheep and cattle in the Little Park at Brigstock in Rockingham Forest. Improvement of the park in 1603 sparked off enclosure riots by surrounding forest villages; these were largely directed against Tresham.[7] Even though Tresham was dead by 1607, his symbolic significance for the rebels remained. His actions exemplified those of the enclosing gentry as a whole, as is demonstrated by the changes wrought in centres of revolt.

Haselbech

Haselbech had been owned by Thomas Tresham of Rushton. Before 1579, tenants had enjoyed copies for life or lives, rents at customary levels, and did not have to pay entry fines. After that time, rents were raised fivefold and tenants came under massive pressure, which culminated in the forced abandonment of holdings, virtually equivalent to outright eviction. This depopulation came in early 1596, just before the famine of that year really began to bite, and was well remembered by the peasantry, for that reason. The stark facts of the complete enclosure by 'agreement' of Haselbech are displayed in an exceptionally well preserved map of the parish in 1599.[8] At that time there were only two landowners of any standing – Thomas Tresham of Rushton (and lord of the manor), and another prominent county sheep-farmer, John Reade of Cottesbrooke. (See Figure 10.1.) They were charged in 1607 with the enclosure and conversion of 1600 acres, the decay of fourteen houses of husbandry, and the eviction of at least seventy-two people. Haselbech's importance to the rioters and its status as a centre of protest early in the revolt arose from these factors. The parish lay right in the centre of an area where the excesses of the enclosure movement were displayed for all to see, and it was Tresham who enclosed the parish in brutal fashion.

Rushton

In Rushton, Tresham's home manor, the process of enclosure was more attenuated than in Haselbech, but gave rise to the same effects – depopulation and conversion to pasture.[9] As early as 1540 common rights were under assault, causing enclosure riots. By the 1550s, well over 3000 sheep were pastured in Rushton and adjacent Glendon and Barford. By the end of the century pressure on tenants had reached a peak. In 1600, a tenant of Rushton accused Tresham in the Queen's Bench of converting a thousand acres of arable land during the period 1558–97. In order to facilitate such enclosing, Tresham had attempted to buy up freeholds, and, when that failed, had resorted to the appropriation of land and denial of freehold tenure. By 1601, the 'improvement' of the parish by enclosure was virtually complete. In 1607, Tresham was convicted (posthumously) of the enclosure of 670 acres (388 acres of which was converted), the decay of twelve houses of husbandry, and the eviction of seventy-three people. Ensuing court cases clearly indicate that, in fact, the entire parish was enclosed.

Newton

Newton was owned by another Thomas Tresham, cousin of Tresham of Rushton, and he was engaged in activities similar to those of his namesake.[10] As early as 1564, some 650 sheep were grazed in the parish. Tresham of Newton was investigated by those enquiring into depopulation and sheep-farming in 1597–8, and in 1607 he was convicted of the enclosure and conversion of 400 acres and the decay of nine houses of husbandry in Newton. Yet this did not represent the true magnitude of his enclosure. In fact, the whole parish was under grass and had been leased out. It would appear that Newton was enclosed in the mid-1590s, only a few years before the revolt. Like his cousin, Tresham of Newton was widely known for his oppressive enclosures. He was also responsible for the enclosure of Pilton on the eastern edge of Rockingham Forest.

Pytchley

This manor was owned by Euseby Isham, another grazier gentleman with considerable family connections in the county.[11] Indeed, the Isham family, centred at Lamport, was among the foremost sheep-farming families in the county. Euseby Isham and his cousin John enclosed the manor by 'agreement' in 1604 at the cost of considerable depopulation. In 1607, Euseby Isham was convicted of the conversion of 400 acres, the decay of nine houses of husbandry, and the eviction of forty-five people. The Isham cousins, together with Tresham of Newton, were the chief organisers of the gentry forces which attacked and dispersed the rebels assembled at nearby Newton.

Leicestershire

Previously, it was thought that Leicestershire's involvement in the revolt was confined to the huge demonstrations at Cotesbach, on the border with Warwickshire.[12] However, the strength of these riots, combined with the considerable involvement of Leicester town in the revolt, argues otherwise. Indeed, further evidence of the serious situation in Leicestershire is the fact that the King himself ordered the county's Lord Lieutenant there post-haste. Also, it was necessary to muster the militia, and then afterwards considerable energy was expended in the prosecution of rebels. In addition to the major riots at Cotesbach, there were riots at Welham and at Gracedieu in the parish of Belton, in the area of most intense enclosure activity in the south-east of the county. We should also remember that the revolt took place in the context of endemic enclosure rioting in the county.[13]

Cotesbach

Like the centres in Northamptonshire, this parish was rapidly and completely enclosed not long before the revolt.[14] In the sixteenth century, certain changes prepared the way for this final enclosure. Prior to the 1517–19 commissions, some 220 acres had been enclosed from the leased demesnes, causing the depopulation of five households. This resulted in the loss of one-fifth of the open fields and the addition of a sheep-grazier to the community. By the late sixteenth century, customary tenure had been replaced by leasehold, but the precise means by which this was achieved remain unclear. None the less, the community remained largely intact.

Two sales of the manor of Cotesbach in the 1590s resulted in ownership by John Quarles, citizen and draper of London. Having paid a hefty sum for the manor, he was determined to recoup some of his expenditure either by the renewal of leases at an increased rate, or by enclosure. Upon expiry of the leases in 1602, Quarles demanded exorbitant rents from tenants; these demands were rejected. He then made plans for the complete enclosure of the parish, which involved the purchase and control of only the two freeholds – the tenants could be safely ignored. Quarles enclosed the manor by royal licence on the basis of a supposed 'agreement' with tenants and freeholders. Some tenants were evicted outright, others saw no reason to remain, since they had to pay such high rents on their enclosed allotments. As a result, the five remaining sheep-graziers (including Quarles) were able to consolidate the lands of the parish into blocks of pasture so that, only three years after the enclosure, the peasant community was utterly destroyed. Quarles and the two freeholders were charged in Star Chamber with the enclosure and conversion of 520 acres and the decay of eighteen houses of husbandry. These figures accurately represented the entirety of the open fields and the peasant community of Cotesbach.

Welham

Welham was owned by William Halford at the time of the revolt.[15] He had risen from yeoman status in the sixteenth century, and by 1614 was styled 'Esquire'. The Halfords had bought the manor in 1551, at which time over half its lands were already in pasture and meadowland, and they consolidated this possession by the purchase of four other properties in Welham, including some lands previously belonging to Launde Priory. The Depopulation Returns of 1607 declared that Halford had converted 131 acres to pasture and decayed one house of husbandry, but this failed to indicate the full extent of enclosure. In reality, the whole parish was enclosed at some time between 1601 and 1606.

Belton

At Gracedieu – the site of a dissolved monastery in Belton – there were enclosure riots on 15 June 1607, some time after the major disturbances had subsided.[16] These lands, including many closes of pasture, were first purchased by the Earl of Huntingdon and then by the Beaumonts, well-known Leicestershire enclosers, who were the owners at the time of the revolt. It is not clear whether the closes of pasture under attack at the time had been recently enclosed. None the less, Belton's peasant community claimed that their rights of common had been taken away.

Warwickshire

There were a considerable number of centres of enclosure riots in Warwickshire. Although the seriousness of rioting (apart from at Hillmorton) did not approach the level recorded in Northamptonshire, the extent of co-ordination established between centres ensured that the overall effect created by these protests was great.

Hillmorton

By the seventeenth century, the peasant community in Hillmorton was fighting for its survival.[17] Mary Astley, 'lord' of the manor, took up residence in Hillmorton in the late sixteenth century, after her husband died. Immediately, she began to instigate 'improvements' in the manor. The community promptly responded with lawsuits and riots. Indeed, both sides became enmeshed in large numbers of lawsuits in the period 1600–6. The conflict gave rise to some eight to ten suits in Chancery and Star Chamber, and a reported twenty in Common Law! The peasants engaged lawyers and established funds for the struggle at law.

The disputes fell into two phases: (1) earlier disputes relating to Astley's enclosure of 350 acres from the common pastures, and (2) more serious conflict concerning her attempts to enclose a further 400 acres of demesne lying in the community's open fields. The multiformity of the detailed disputes derived from the fact that Astley was essentially attempting to transform the parish's traditional agricultural practices. Her various tactics – such as withdrawal of land from common, disruption of the system of rotation, growing of wheat on pasture-ground, pasturing of cattle in the hay meadows and sheep in the beef-pasture, enclosure of pathways leading to the river, and rabbit-breeding near the arable fields – created all sorts of disruptions for the peasants and led to fierce and sustained resistance. There were many riots involving large numbers of participants in the period 1600–7. The lengthy conflict drew in many others from villages within a radius of some 12 miles of Hillmorton (see Map 1).

By 1606 the situation of the peasant community was precarious indeed. After considerable manoeuvering, Astley had arranged for a local (encloser) JP to put into effect an equivocal 'enclosure agreement' which, contrary to the understanding of the peasants of the village, allowed her to enclose all her lands and cause considerable depopulation. (She was convicted in 1607 of the enclosure and conversion of 300 acres and the decay of fifteen houses of husbandry in the period 1602–7.)

In these circumstances, the community considered the supposed 'agreement' to have been rescinded. This was the situation reached in the year prior to the revolt; the community was under threat of total destruction and all legal means had failed. Thus, Hillmorton became a focal point for the protest movement of 1607.

Chilvers Coton

As mentioned in Chapter 9, the reasons for the occurrence of enclosure riots in Chilvers Coton are more complex than for other centres. Indeed, the extent of illegal enclosure recorded by the 1607 commission was relatively minor: Sir John Newdigate, JP and lord of the manor, and William Whitehall converted 80 acres of land to pasture and decayed two houses of husbandry.[18] None the less, Newdigate in particular had aroused much ill feeling in the area because of his alleged neglect of his public duties and pursuance of his own private gain. His enclosures exemplified this improbity. Chilvers Coton had a history of discontent against enclosure which became fused with the grievances of the out-of-work coal-miners of both Griff, in the parish of Chilvers Coton, and nearby Bedworth. Both mines were closed at this time. The miners would have suffered greatly from the lack of work, and like all other labourers in those years were at the mercy of high grain prices and inadequate supply. In addition, it was Newdigate and Whitehall who owned, operated (and closed) the mine in Griff, while the neighbouring Bedworth mine was operated by Sir Thomas Beaumont, JP and encloser. This conjunction of private profit-seeking, manifest in enclosure and mining, with the neglect of public obligations made these two gentlemen particularly disliked.

Coventry

The riots outside Coventry's walls provide an interesting case because they indicate that the disaffection present in the countryside thoroughly penetrated the Midland towns and caused townspeople to initiate their own protests against enclosure of the towns' commons.[19] Such actions were by no means unusual. Indeed, we have considerable documentation of the sustained conflict over Coventry's own commons from the late fourteenth century until the end of the seventeenth century. This conflict became entangled with the broader forms of conflict inherent in the town: between the rich merchant oligarchy; the body of craftsmen; and the journeymen, labourers and the poor. An alliance between the latter two groups was relatively easy to effect over the issue of enclosure because the merchants largely exercised control over the common lands. The riots in 1607 were an integral part of this protracted struggle by the craftsmen, labourers and the poor to retain their commons.

Ladbroke

In considering Ladbroke, we rejoin the account (contained in Chapter 5) of the Warwickshire felden peasant communities, such as the 'open' communities of Harbury, Napton, Fenny Compton and Tysoe, and the 'freehold' communities of Prior's Hardwick, Prior's Marston, Southam, Bishop's Itchington, Cubbington, Burton Dassett and Hillmorton. All these communities (apart from Hillmorton, which was struggling for its own existence) were involved in the riots which took place at Ladbroke in 1607.

Ladbroke was situated right in the middle of the most developed and concentrated sheep-pastures in the Midlands.[20] It was from Hodnell, Radbourne and Wormleighton (all deserted villages adjoining Ladbroke) that the renowned graziers, the Spencers, originated. The Spencers pastured their huge flocks of sheep on massive tracts of pasture in these deserted villages and other, adjacent sheep-walks, such as Chapel Ascote, Wills Pastures, Watergall and Stoneton. They also owned lands in Fenny Compton and in Ladbroke itself. It is hardly surprising, then, that we find evidence of considerable transformation of manorial structure and the early emergence of sheep-farming in Ladbroke. By the late fourteenth century, the Catesbys (owners until 1597) had purchased and consolidated sufficient lands in the parish for them to be considered lords of the manor.[21] At that time, they worked the large arable demesnes entirely by wage labour, and grain sales accounted for much of their income. Traditional feudal dues were of lesser importance. Additionally, the Catesbys grazed more than 400 sheep in Ladbroke and another flock of equivalent size in adjacent Radbourne.

Ladbroke probably appears in John Rous's list of depopulations, made in the late fifteenth century, but the depopulation was only partial. It is likely that such enclosed lands were grazed by the sheep of Thomas Lucy (of Charlecote) in the early sixteenth century and were then purchased by Sir John Spencer, who also leased a small manor in Ladbroke at that time. Thus, the effect of sheep-grazing on the parish was strong long before Ladbroke's final enclosure at the end of the sixteenth century. None the less, after the initial depopulations the community remained relatively stable at about thirty five to forty households until the end of the sixteenth century.[22]

The crucial event in Ladbroke's continued development proved to be Robert Catesby's sale of the manor to Sir Robert Dudley in the period 1596–8, because of his mounting recusant fines. After a series of speculative transactions, Dudley consolidated his holdings in the parish by purchase of further lands, some of which belonged to the Spencers. He thereby gained unity of ownership in Ladbroke and proceeded to make further purchases of small parcels of land from peasants and attempted to buy out the Rector. The underlying purpose behind these moves is obvious; Dudley was preparing the way for the comprehensive enclosure of Ladbroke. This was greatly facilitated by the fact that tenants had held their lands entirely at the will of the lord under Catesby and Spencer. By the time of the enclosure, all such 'tenures' had disappeared; only freehold remained. It is clear that some larger tenancies were reduced in size and transformed into freehold, while other tenancies were absorbed into Dudley's estate. It would seem that larger tenants negotiated with Dudley and smaller tenants were simply evicted from their holdings. These changes are summarised in two features involved in the complicated land transactions: the disappearance of tenure-at-will, and the accumulation of several small properties into a unified single manor with huge demesnes.

William Burton – the rich yeoman against whom anger was directed in May and June 1607 – moved into Ladbroke on purchase of an unimproved 200 acres in 1597. The following year, he set about enclosing his lands and building himself an expensive mansion on the site of the two peasant houses decayed by him, in a bid for elevated status. Dudley enclosed his lands in conjunction with Burton under an 'agreement', which caused the conversion to pasture of 1280 acres and the decay of sixteen houses of husbandry. Note that these enclosures occurred in the wake of the famines of 1596–7.

In sum, Ladbroke was situated in the part of the Warwickshire felden where the injurious effects of enclosure were most evident (compare Haselbech in Northamptonshire), and was itself enclosed precipitately and with considerable depopulation within the ten years prior to the revolt.

THE TOWNS

The reasons for the participation of all the principal towns in the disaffected areas are not immediately apparent. The difficulty in accepting their involvement arises from the assumption that such towns were sufficiently divorced from the surrounding countryside that their interests were divergent from those of the peasantry. The Privy Council itself, in commenting on the revolt at the time, made such an assumption.

> We hold such Townsmen, whether they be Artificers or others, as did put themselves into this Rebellion among the countrey people to have more heynouslie offended than some others, in respect *they had lesse pretence of greevance, having little or nothing to do with Enclosures*; and yet ministering most healp by numbers of men, weapons, and other means of assistance.[23] [Emphasis added]

I shall argue that Midland towns were very much involved with and dependent upon their rural hinterlands, and that this provided good cause for their involvement in the revolt of 1607.

Dependence of Midland Towns upon the Countryside

In the first half of the sixteenth century, most English towns experienced considerable economic difficulties caused by the diversion of investment from town to countryside (both to farming and to rural industry), problems in foreign trade, bad harvests, high prices and high taxation.[24] Later in the century, the position of many towns had superficially improved, as a result of the considerable expansion of internal trade. However, the underlying weakness of urban economies remained (except perhaps in the case of London) and became increasingly obvious. This was especially apparent in medium-sized centres such as Midland provincial towns. Their fundamental instability was accentuated by the continued attraction of capital into the countryside, large increases in the town poor (largely as a result of the influx of rural poor), rising urban unemployment, and the tremendous expansion of relief necessary to cope with the swollen poorer sector of the population. These factors had a massive impact on town economies from the 1590s onwards, and 'accentuated the close economic dependence of provincial towns on the countryside. Even established towns offered little or no resistance to the vagaries of the rural economy. Serious harvest failure had immediate repercussions for the whole economic structure of a town.'[25]

Midland towns were very much dependent upon the surrounding felden countryside for their food supplies. The region was not supported by any complementary specialised arable areas nearby, but was fringed by a wooded–pastoral economy which itself was reliant upon grain from outside. This vulnerability was amplified by the land-locked nature of the region, which made grain-importation difficult. The consequent problems of grain supply, although felt with considerable force in the countryside, had their greatest impact in the towns, where the largest concentrations of consumers were to be found.

The position of Midland towns was made worse by the extreme fragility of the rural economy, which was under attack by enclosers. Enclosure and conversion to pasture of large areas had seriously eroded the character of the region as an area of peasant grain-production. These agrarian changes caused overpopulation in the countryside and pressure on resources in unenclosed communities. Cottagers, the poor without common rights, and evicted peasants were forced to seek a living in the towns, thereby swelling the urban poor and increasing the demand for grain. Enclosure and conversion to sheep-pasture had another detrimental if more indirect effect on local towns. Many town labourers depended upon nearby arable farms for seasonal employment. The introduction of extensive sheep-walks with low labour requirements drastically reduced employment opportunities. General downturns in the agrarian economy created difficulties for Midland towns not only on account of dependence on grain supplies but also because they had developed specialised rural-related industries and trades such as leather, tanning, shoemaking and butchery. These had emerged in response to the increasing extent of land under sheep- and cattle-pasture.[26] In this way, the dependence of towns on the countryside was accentuated even further.

These problems became increasingly severe as the sixteenth century developed, during which time there was a concentration of wealth at the top and a broadening of the base of the social pyramid, as a result of population increase and a flood of rural migrants. Perhaps two-thirds or more of Midland towns' populations lived at or below the poverty line at this time, constituting an 'ever-present menace to the community in years of high food-prices or bad trade'.[27] Thus, it is understandable why townspeople, especially the poor, should perceive enclosure as a threat to their existence.

Those towns chiefly involved in the Midlands Revolt exemplify these characteristics. Leicester's integration into its rural hinterland was pronounced.[28] Capitalist farmers were the largest employers of labour and provided the most important source of industrial capital in the town. They also came to dominate other sectors of the community –

such as craftsmen and shopkeepers – by their wealth and influence. Most of Leicester's labouring population relied upon employment in agriculture, and husbandry remained the most common by-occupation of the townspeople. The tanning and butchering trades experienced rapid growth and became very important – all leather crafts taken together constituted the largest industrial grouping in Leicester. Kerridge concludes that 'Leicester existed to serve the needs of the countryside and was itself part of the countryside . . . the town had a profoundly rural aspect'. Leicester was more an overgrown village than an autonomous urban centre. This was reflected in the fact that the town retained its own common fields until the eighteenth century.

Northampton was a town of similar size and structure to Leicester. It became noted for shoemaking and other leathercrafts, and its common fields were not enclosed until 1778.[29] Coventry was considerably larger and sustained two specialist industries – textiles and metals – not directly related to agriculture. Although this gave Coventry some autonomy from the countryside, the town was still very much dependent upon the local felden economy for grain and it retained its common fields.

Town populations were frequently involved in riots against enclosures.[30] These disturbances were usually related to the enclosure or intended enclosure of the town's own common fields. The usual pattern was a polarisation between the rich town oligarchy (who wished to enclose the commons for their own gain) and the poorer craftsmen and labouring population (whose interests lay in maintaining access for all to the town lands). In the Midland towns involved in the revolt of 1607, there was a strong tradition of protest against enclosure. The outstanding example of sustained resistance to enclosure is provided by Coventry.[31] There, conflict over the town's common fields was prolonged over three centuries until the eighteenth century and caused considerable unrest. This conflict became entwined with the broader cleavages within the town – between the rich merchant oligarchy and the body of craftsmen. When the latter group held civic power the offending enclosures were often ordered to be laid down. Such antagonism towards enclosure by Midland town authorities was not unusual. For example, in the first half of the seventeenth century Leicester town petitioned Parliament and took legal action against enclosures, while also refusing to ratify the nomination of a local encloser for Parliament.[32] This antagonism and the covert sympathy displayed by towns for the rebels of 1607 arose as a consequence of the location of Midland towns in the regional economy. Town authorities might well fear the consequences of enclosure, especially considering the weight of the poor and the paramount importance of the maintenance of order.

Involvement in the Revolt of 1607

By the beginning of the seventeenth century, Midland towns were experiencing great difficulties. The bad harvests of the 1590s and consequent food shortages and high grain prices coincided with a huge influx of migrants from nearby rural areas. This was immediately followed by outbreaks of plague among town populations weakened by malnutrition. At the same time, an acceleration of the enclosure movement threatened to diminish grain supplies and employment even further, and to create fresh waves of migration to the towns.

In these conditions, the town corporations of Leicester and Coventry in 1597 were forced to import grain from Danzig in order to relieve the poor.[33] Earlier, in 1586 (another year of bad harvests) there was agitation against Northampton town's maltsters, and fears that the poor might rise on account of the grain shortages. The pressure created by the chronic scarcity of grain, combined with a decrease in employment and an increase in migration to towns, was maintained throughout the first two decades of the seventeenth century, and constituted a protracted crisis. These conditions weakened the physical resistance of the population, causing regular outbreaks of the plague.[34]

Given these circumstances, it is hardly surprising that ongoing enclosure and conversion of land to pasture might be blamed for the problems besetting the towns. After several years of comparative relief from bad harvests, the up turn in grain prices in early 1607 threatened renewed hard times. When the moment arrived, townspeople eagerly joined with those of the countryside in the protest against enclosure.

The records made by Leicester's authorities of those from the town who joined the riots in 1607 clearly indicate that all occupational groups from the poorer sectors of the town's occupational structure were present.[35] (See Tables 10.1 and 10.2.) Nearly 40 per cent of the rioters were labourers, apprentices and journeymen. The leading occupations of the town, especially in leather and clothing, were well represented, while nearly half the rioters (48 per cent) came from other than the leading occupations analysed in Table 10.1, indicating a wide spread of involvement in the riots. Other occupations recorded were (among others) smiths, coopers, whittawers, slaters, painters, woolwinders, joiners, saddlers and costermongers. The single most prominent occupation was shoemaking, a trade well known for radical dissent. In

TABLE 10.1   Leading occupations of Leicester rioters

| Occupation | Excluding apprentices and journeymen | | Including apprentices and journeymen | |
	No.	% of total (74)	No.	% of total (74)
Labourers	14	19	14	19
Shoemakers	10	14	15	20
Tailors	5	7	6	8
Carpenters	3	4	5	7
Weavers	3	4	3	4
Tanners	3	4	3	4
Total	38	52	46	62

TABLE 10.2   Occupational structure of rioters and of Leicester town

| Occupational group | Rioters | | Occupational Structure of Leicester* | |
	% excluding apprentices and journeymen	% including apprentices and journeymen	% (Hoskins)	% (Kerridge)
Labourers	19	19	–	–
Apprentices and journeymen	(19)	–	–	–
Leather	23	32	19	25.0
Clothing	14	20	15	12.5 (textile)
Building	15	19	4	3.4
Food and distributive	7	7	21 (food)	13.6
Agriculture	3	3	–	15.9 (husbandmen)
Total	100	100	59	70.4

* *Sources*: W. G. Hoskins, 'English Provincial Towns in the Early-sixteenth Century', *Tr RHS*, 5th ser., vol. 6 (1956) table, p. 14; E. Kerridge, 'The Social and Economic History of Leicester, 1509–1660', in *VCH Leics*, vol. IV (1958) table, p. 78.

Leicester, many poor shoemakers, especially the journeymen, had broken away from guild control and operated outside the town's walls in the 'suburbs'. It is worth noting, however, that the agricultural sector was significantly under-represented. Indeed, the two recorded agricultural occupations were distributive (cornman) and marginal (herdsman), rather than those central to agriculture. This emphasises the point that towns became involved in the revolt of 1607 on the basis of strictly *urban* criteria deriving from a generalised antagonism towards enclosure, rather than because the interests of townspeople engaged in agriculture were directly under attack.

We have no detailed information on the people from Northampton who participated in riots, but that which we have regarding Coventry tends to support our conclusions concerning Leicester.[36] Of seven rioters whose occupations were recorded, four were shoemakers, two were silkweavers and one a cutler. The latter two occupations reflect Coventry's status as a textile and metal working centre.

FOREST VILLAGES

In explaining the involvement of forest or wooded–pastoral peasant communities in the revolt of 1607 in the felden, we face questions similar to those concerning the participation of townspeople. In neither case were rioters directly threatened by enclosure. The widespread disorder of the forest areas has often been noted, both by contemporary observers and by modern historians. But this leaves open the question why this disorder came to be channelled into violence against hedges in the felden.[37]

Dependence of Wooded–Pastoral Areas on the Felden

Scattered throughout England in the sixteenth and seventeenth centuries were regions with a distinct social and economic structure – here designated 'wooded–pastoral' regions.[38] These areas had been by-passed in the process of the establishment and consolidation of feudalism in the medieval period because they consisted of expanses of forest in which it was difficult to extend the manorial economy. These circumstances were reflected in a low incidence of labour services and villein tenure, and a lack of nucleated settlements centred upon intensive open-field arable cultivation. Generally, the absence of 'feudal' impartible inheritance customs allowed extensive fragmentation of land. From the sixteenth century onwards, these areas were characterised by scattered hamlets and farms, fragmented and extensive landownership, considerable areas of woodland and wastes with associated resources, the dominance of pastoral over arable farming, and an absence of strong manorial and religious control. From that time, such areas experienced much immigration from neighbouring mixed-farming areas, because of the shortage of land and agrarian changes occurring in the latter. The wooded–pastoral environment held the attraction of a plenitude of resources for a cottage economy, and there was open access for settlement. As a result, wooded–pastoral areas became increasingly heavily populated, mainly by poverty-stricken cottagers and landless labourers. These groups often relied upon craft and industrial by-employments in winter, and agricultural work in summer in nearby mixed-farming areas.[39] Most importantly, the wooded–pastoral regions, as a result of their pastoral and industrial-dominated economy, necessarily became dependent upon nearby mixed-farming areas for grain.

Wooded–pastoral regions were to be found in many parts of England, such as East Anglia, Somerset, the Weald of Kent, Wiltshire, Yorkshire, Lincolnshire and Sussex, as well as in the Midlands. The wooded–pastoral part of Norfolk, for example, was densely populated and consisted of small hamlets and farms largely free from manorial control. Partible inheritance led to the fragmentation of holdings, while the many poor were reliant on the cloth industry for employment. From the sixteenth century onwards, the area was heavily dependent upon the supply of grain from the light mixed-farming parts of the county.[40] However, the latter areas themselves had suffered from enclosure and the overstocking of commons with sheep, and from the extensive differentiation of their peasant communities. Relatively few arable farmers now serviced all in both felden and woodland with grain. This relationship in Norfolk was strikingly similar to that of wooded–pastoral villages in the Arden in Warwickshire and Rockingham Forest in Northamptonshire. However, in the Midlands the problem was made even worse because enclosure was much more closely connected with the conversion of land to pasture than in Norfolk. Conversion directly threatened the essential grain supplied to wooded–pastoral areas.

The Arden

I have already briefly described the character of this part of Warwickshire in the medieval period, and its strong contrasts with the felden, in Chapter 5. In the medieval period, the Arden experienced rapid colonisation and expansion of village populations, and increasing pressure on its limited arable resources. By the late thirteenth century, the density of peasant households per unit of arable was four times that of the felden, which indicates that even at this time a pastoral economy predominated. This situation was reflected in the movement of grain surpluses from the felden to the Arden.[41]

From then on, as a result of differentiation, immigration from the land-hungry felden and population increase, the Arden's social structure was transformed from a relatively egalitarian freeholder society to one of great inequality which was numerically dominated by the poor.[42] By the mid seventeenth century, labourers, craftsmen, smallholders and lesser husbandmen constituted nearly 80 per cent of the entire population. Between one-quarter and one-half of village populations were forced through poverty to rely on craft and industrial by-employments. The Arden became increasingly dependent upon the importation of grain by purchase in the markets of Warwick, Stratford-on-Avon, Alcester and Bidford-on-Avon in felden Warwickshire.[43]

During this long-term population expansion, there was one particularly significant period from the 1590s to the 1620s. At that time, there was extensive migration into the Arden from those Warwickshire felden areas which rose in revolt in 1607, as a result of the chronic crisis conditions experienced in the felden (see Chapter 9). Such migration, in turn, tipped the balance of resources and population in the Arden and caused the same situation of constant dearth of grain which culminated in a period of crisis from 1613 until 1619. This situation, however, had its roots further back in the sixteenth century. As early as 1587, JPs met in emergency session in Warwick and bound over local felden grain-producers to market grain to supply those in the Arden. From this point on (and until the situation was remedied by a compensating shift in the ratio of arable to pasture in the mid seventeenth century) the grain scarcity was perennial – as is indicated by the local price index, which was some 13 per cent above the national figure.

Rockingham Forest

We do not have data for Rockingham Forest comparable to that for the Arden before the sixteenth century. From that time, however, a similar pattern is apparent.[44] By the early sixteenth century, forest villages were densely populated (they had twice as many households on average as felden villages), and were dominated by the landless or near landless poor (over three-quarters of the population were labourers, cottagers and other poor). Throughout the sixteenth century there was, as in the Arden, considerable migration into the forest from the felden. Those villages not subject to strong landlord control experienced dramatic increases in numbers. By the latter half of the seventeenth century, the poor totally dominated the profile of social stratification in forest villages: nearly half their populations were exempt from the hearth tax of 1670.

Although industrial by-employments developed later in the century, in the early seventeenth century such opportunities for employment were lacking. This forced many members of Rockingham communities to rely upon seasonal agricultural work in the felden. At the same time, populous forest villages increasingly were forced to rely upon the arable open-field felden areas of Northamptonshire for grain. These characteristics of Arden and Rockingham Forest villages placed them in structurally similar relationships with the adjacent felden, and caused them to experience increasing difficulties, culminating in a crisis situation by the end of the sixteenth century.

Involvement in the Revolt of 1607

A common view of contemporary commentators such as John Norden was that forest areas were particularly disorderly. According to him '[they] will breed and bring forth more and more idleness, beggary and atheism and consequently all disobedience of God and King'.[45] Such a propensity for disorder is explicable in terms of the chronic under-employment in these areas, the dominance of a marginal squatting economy, and the lack of manorial and religious control. The very fact that there were large concentrations of the marginal and poor in these areas was sufficient to raise fears of the 'many-headed monster' – in Hill's graphic phrase – in the minds of many.[46] The lack of secular or religious authority allowed greater mobility and greater freedom of expression of tensions, protest and dissent than was possible in the more hierarchical and closely controlled felden communities. It also contributed indirectly to the instability of forest areas because of the absence of any barriers to large-scale immigration.

A readiness for disorder was increased by the existence of strong communication links with mixed-farming areas. Not only were forest areas internally fluid and mobile, but they also maintained an openness and constant contact with wider events. These connections were based on the three structural linkages discussed above: the perennial transportation of grain into the forest; the seasonal movement of labour between forest and felden; and the settlement of migrants in forest villages. These links resulted in broadened horizons of experience and close contact with other areas. Broggers and badgers (middlemen dealers in grain and other goods), cornmen, shepherds, drovers and itinerant pedlars and tinkers brought news of events elsewhere. Labourers in spring and summer journeyed to the felden in search of work and returned in autumn. The constant flow of impoverished and dispossessed peasants and cottagers into forest villages increased awareness of agrarian changes in the felden.

These three axes of structural location in relation to the felden provided Midland forest areas such as the Arden and Rockingham Forest with good cause for rioting against felden enclosures. Enclosure diminished both grain supplies and employment opportunities for those in the forest, in addition to precipitating new waves of migration which threatened to swamp already overburdened communities. Given that an upsurge of enclosure and conversion in the felden coincided with a situation of crisis in Midland wooded–pastoral areas, it is hardly surprising that Rockingham Forest villages (see Map 1) and probably Arden villages became involved in the rising of 1607.

Detailed examination of those Rockingham villages which were involved in the revolt – Weldon, Corby, Benefield, Middleton, Little Oakley and Stanion – bears out this analysis. Of the rioters recorded by Sir Edward Montagu at Boughton House near Newton, more than half came from these villages.[47] (Weldon and Corby individually contributed the greatest number of rioters of all villages named in the document.) Such forest inhabitants travelled to enclosed parishes on the fringe of the forest – such as Newton, Pytchley and Rushton – and joined with felden peasants to throw down the hedges. In at least four of these six villages the problems pinpointed above were oppressive.[48] Weldon, Corby, Benefield and Middleton (from which virtually all recorded forest rioters came) had experienced massive population expansion from the early sixteenth century, so that by this time they were densely populated and overburdened with poor. Before the mid seventeenth century, few industrial by-employments had developed in the forest. Brigstock, a populous but decayed market town adjacent to Stanion, had no such employment, and neither did King's Cliffe, a similar centre in the north-east of the forest.

Rockingham Forest villages were also drawn into the revolt for more direct reasons. At the time, plans concerning the disafforestation and enclosure of the forest were mooted. Local inhabitants were given a taste of things to come in 1602–3, when Sir Robert Cecil, in association with Sir Thomas Tresham of Rushton, began to 'improve' Brigstock Parks.[49] The parks were enclosed and leased out as pasture. These moves immediately caused riots by the peasants of Brigstock and Stanion in attempts to restore their rights of common. The fact that Tresham was involved in this conflict related the struggles of forest villagers to retain their own commons directly to the problems they faced as a result of enclosure in the felden. Tresham's activities undoubtedly strengthened the solidarity of forest and felden communities during the revolt.

We may infer that Arden villages were involved in attacking enclosures at nearby enclosed or partly enclosed felden parishes such as Chilvers Coton and Withybrook, as well as at Coventry, even though we have no direct evidence for this. The decay of coal-mining operations in Chilvers Coton and Bedworth may well have destroyed an important source of industrial employment for Arden communities in the area. (It is also possible that inhabitants of villages in Salcey and Whittlewood forests in Northamptonshire joined the riots at Shutlanger and Ashton nearby; see Map 1.)

Entire forest communities were involved in the 1607 revolt.[50] Tables 10.3 and 10.4 indicate that the rioters represented a cross-section of both occupations and wealth within occupations, with the exception of wealthier yeomen. We should note that, as one might expect, less than 10 per cent of those recorded were primarily involved in cultivation of the land, and over half depended on their own labour, while more than one-third of rioters were engaged in crafts.[51] (This distribution of occupations contrasts strongly with that of felden rioters in Table 10.8 below.) We may conclude that support for the revolt was not confined to any one particularly hard-pressed group within forest communities. Their

TABLE 10.3   Occupations of forest rioters

	Landholding	Labouring	Crafts
No.	7 husbandmen	39 labourers 3 shepherds 42	28
% of total	9	55	36

TABLE 10.4   Wealth and occupation of forest rioters

	Husbandmen	Labourers	Crafts	
			Landless	Landed
Rich	1	2	1	1
Middle	2	2	2	1
Poor	—	1	3	—

involvement must be explained in terms of the structural links which bound entire communities into precarious dependence upon the felden and drew them into the protest movement against enclosure.

FELDEN

Our analysis of town and forest suggests reasons why such communities became allies of the felden peasantry in the revolt. Now we should consider the involvement of felden peasant communities themselves. To a considerable extent, the general parameters of the involvement of the felden have been set out in the previous chapter – a period of sustained problems of grain supply was combined with a marked increase in enclosure in the Midlands. In order to provide a more detailed and precise explanation, we must focus on the specific types of community characteristic of the felden. This we may do by recourse to the two structurally distinct types of felden peasant community – 'open' and 'freehold' communities – introduced earlier.

Open and Freehold Communities

In Chapter 5, the preconditions for the formation of both open and freehold communities in felden Warwickshire were analysed. These two types of peasant community emerged with clarity in the sixteenth century (see Figure 5.1). The first was characterised by its poverty, fragmented freehold landownership, and density of population; the second by its strong and wealthy freeholders among whom land was equally distributed. Both types of community remained, in large part, free from extensive enclosure. Already enclosed parishes were mingled with these communities.[52] The Warwickshire felden was characterised by 'large tracts of surviving open fields . . . interspersed with townships which had been enclosed at an earlier period'.[53] (See Map 2.) The pattern of involvement of the peasantry in the Warwickshire felden in the revolt of 1607 was of the convergence of both open and freehold communities upon enclosed parishes which lay nearby. Such was the case with Ladbroke. (See Map 1.)

Enclosure

It might appear odd that freehold communities emerged from those peasant communities which were the most thoroughly manorialised in

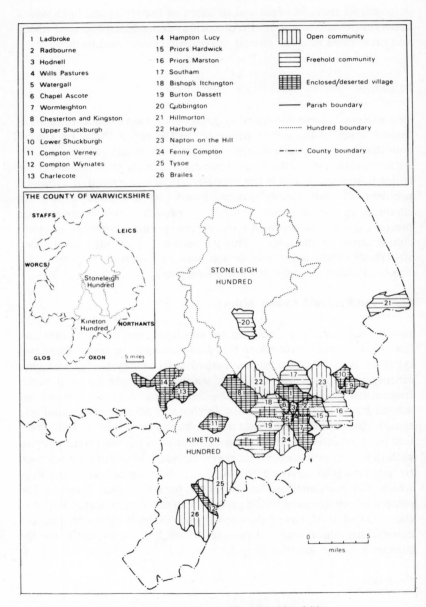

1 Ladbroke	14 Hampton Lucy	▥ Open community
2 Radbourne	15 Priors Hardwick	
3 Hodnell	16 Priors Marston	▤ Freehold community
4 Wills Pastures	17 Southam	
5 Watergall	18 Bishop's Itchington	▦ Enclosed/deserted village
6 Chapel Ascote	19 Burton Dassett	
7 Wormleighton	20 Cubbington	—— Parish boundary
8 Chesterton and Kingston	21 Hillmorton	
9 Upper Shuckburgh	22 Harbury	·········· Hundred boundary
10 Lower Shuckburgh	23 Napton on the Hill	
11 Compton Verney	24 Fenny Compton	—·—·— County boundary
12 Compton Wyniates	25 Tysoe	
13 Charlecote	26 Braıles	

THE COUNTY OF WARWICKSHIRE

STAFFS

LEICS

WORCS

Stoneleigh Hundred

Kineton Hundred   NORTHANTS

GLOS   OXON   5 miles

STONELEIGH HUNDRED

KINETON HUNDRED

0   5
miles

MAP 2 Parishes in the Warwickshire felden

the medieval period. One might assume that factors such as the heavy demands for rent, the lack of freedom, and domination by a powerful landlord such as Coventry Priory would have given rise to peasant communities characterised by very insecure tenure and land only marginal for subsistence. In order to understand the transformation of such highly villeinised communities into freehold communities, we must examine the critical period of the fifteenth and early sixteenth centuries. We have seen in Chapter 5 how tenants in manors belonging to a Warwickshire religious house, the Bishop of Coventry, managed to have rents commuted and tenure improved. As I have discussed at the end of Chapter 7, in the early fifteenth century in Coventry Priory manors, specifically peasant communities began to control manorial demesnes.The balance of power was shifting in favour of peasant communities. But peasants had not yet transformed tenure of land into freehold. Such communites were thus extremely vulnerable to depopulation. Indeed, parts of Prior's Hardwick, Prior's Marston, Bishop's Itchington, Burton Dassett and Hillmorton were enclosed in the fifteenth century, but their communities largely remained intact.[54] Fortunately, Coventry Priory – which held Prior's Hardwick and Marston, Southam and Bishop's Itchington – maintained possession until its dissolution in the 1530s, and, furthermore, did not engage in large-scale sheep-farming, unlike the neighbouring Warwickshire Cistercian abbeys of Stoneleigh, Merevale, Bordesley and Combe.[55] Probably the introduction of sheep-farming became impossible once the Priory had lost control of its demesnes in these manors. The continuity of possession by the Priory largely protected its peasant populations from depopulation in the fifteenth century, so that the freehold communities were able to consolidate their position and transform their tenure into freehold. It is likely that this remarkable transformation ultimately derived from successful struggles waged at the end of the fourteenth century.

By the time of the dissolution of the Priory, the peasant communities were sufficiently strong and freehold was well-enough established for them to resist any large-scale enclosure and depopulation, in spite of considerable speculation in their lands by well-known gentry enclosers, and the fact that their single manors gave such landlords a unity of ownership.[56]

Priors' Hardwick and Marston and Southam were first bought by the Knightleys, upon dissolution of Coventry Priory. Before long, the Spencers held lands in the first two parishes, and by the seventeenth century they owned both manors. The Throckmortons purchased Southam from the Knightleys in the late sixteenth century and proceeded to enclose part of the manor. Approximately one half of Bishop's Itchington (Nether Itchington) was depopulated by Thomas Fisher in the sixteenth century, but the other half of the parish remained open. The non-Coventry freehold parishes also survived relatively unscathed in spite of speculation. Cubbington was purchased by the Master of the Great Wardrobe and a skinner from London, upon the dissolution of Stoneleigh Abbey, while Peter Temple first leased and then bought Burton Dassett's pastures, for which Edward Belknapp had been charged with depopulation by the 1517 commission.

However, less well-developed freehold communities such as Hillmorton and Southam came under increasing pressure from enclosers. Both were weakened by their intermediate position between the freehold and open types. On the one hand, unlike open communities they were not resistant to enclosure on the grounds of the fragmentation and dispersal of land amongst many small freeholders, while, on the other, their freeholders were not very prosperous. The Astley family had been in sole control of Hillmorton, supplying the resident squire, from the twelfth century onwards. Much later, the family moved elsewhere. In spite of the lack of a resident lord, population growth and immigration remained low, so that Hillmorton resembled more the freehold communities of the fertile Avon valley, even though it was located in the poor clay lands, where many open communities were to be found. Additionally, the community managed to survive the enclosure of some 1200 acres in the late fifteenth century. But, on the death of her husband, Mary Astley moved back to Hillmorton in the late sixteenth century. She immediately began to enclose much of the manor and threatened to destroy the peasant community. By contrast, Southam developed towards the open type and away from the freehold type of community in the sixteenth century. Immigration of poor people into the parish was assisted by the increasing fragmentation of its manors and the absence of a resident lord. As a market town, it attracted many migrants in search of employment. As a result, its population expanded rapidly: there was an increase of 127 per cent in the period from 1525 to the 1660s. By the seventeenth century, the Throckmortons had consolidated their lands so that they owned half of the reconstituted manor. In 1620, Clement Throckmorton enclosed one-quarter of the parish lands, a matter which gave rise to proceedings in Chancery and Star Chamber.[57]

Both Hillmorton and Southam became deeply involved in the revolt of 1607. Their only marginal freehold position induced landlords to attempt to enclose the parish lands. However, in both cases the communities ultimately were able to resist complete enclosure. Astley's enclosures in Hillmorton were never again restored after their destruction in 1607; like Southam, the parish remained substantially open until enclosed by Parliament in the following century.[58]

The many manors contained within the open parishes were similarly sold and resold for profit in the sixteenth century, and often ended up in the hands of enclosers.[59] The lands of Kenilworth Priory in Harbury were bought by the Fishers, while those of Combe Abbey were leased by William Catesby, associated with Ladbroke. Other small manors in the parish followed similar paths. In Napton, the Shuckburghs (depopulators of Upper Shuckburgh) were the major landowners, and the Spencers also owned a manor and leased lands there. William Cope (the depopulator of Wormleighton) held a manor in Fenny Compton in the late fifteenth century. By the early sixteenth century, the Spencers owned two manors in this parish. The depopulator of Compton Wynyates, William Compton, held the major manor in Tysoe. (See Chapter 7 for these depopulated parishes.)

In spite of such close attention from enclosers, open parishes largely remained open: they were difficult to enclose. The extensive, entrenched and fragmented freehold, combined with the characteristic fragmented manorial structure of these parishes prevented any unity of ownership. Moreover, such parishes were unattractive to enclosers because they were often situated in the poor heavy clay uplands of the border with Northamptonshire. As a result the position of those open and freehold communities which managed to weather the storm of the fifteenth century was increasingly strong by the sixteenth century. Enclosers turned to easier targets.

Involvement in the Revolt

In the sixteenth and seventeenth centuries, open communities felt the general expansion in population most severely: they became increasingly populous and poverty-stricken. Migration into such communities was widespread, because of the absence of strong landlord control and the possibility of a marginal squatting existence based on the extensive wastes of such parishes. Elsewhere in the felden, land was not freely available. Open communities often comprised large villages which were or had been market towns and thus easily accessible to migrants. In the period from 1525 to the 1660s, Napton's population increased by 244 per cent and Harbury's by 123 per cent; and, in the period from 1563 to the 1660s, Fenny Compton's population increased by 176 per cent and Tysoe's by 133 per cent (see Tables 10.5, 10.6, and 10.7).

TABLE 10.5   Open and freehold parishes in the Subsidy of 1525

	No. assessed/(%)			Average		Total
	At 4d.	4d.–2s.	More than 2s.	s.	d.	
Freehold parish						
Southam	21 (50)	8 (19)	13 (31)	1	8	42
Bishop's Itchington	2 (6)	16 (50)	14 (44)	2	2	32
Cubbington	0 (0)	12 (80)	3 (20)	1	9	15
Hillmorton	32 (62)	10 (19)	10 (19)	1	8	52
Open parish						
Harbury	22 (56)	16 (41)	1 (3)	1	2	39
Napton	3 (10)	17 (55)	11 (35)	1	10	31

Such marked expansion in population made open communities increasingly defenceless against downturns in the agrarian economy. The sustained problems of food supply in the Midlands at the end of the sixteenth century created a situation of crisis in these villages, since the bulk of their populations was forced to buy in grain, usually from freehold parishes. At that time, Warwickshire JPs sent directives to the owners of valuable pasturelands in parishes such as Burton Dassett, Kingston, Radbourne, Hodnell, Watergall and Chapel Ascote, which were adjacent to the open parishes of Harbury, Napton, Fenny Compton and Brailes. These directives instructed the graziers to support financially the poor in these open communities. (Such pastures were themselves the end-product of considerable depopulation; see Chapter 7.) Such a letter of 1599 to John Temple, sheep-farmer of Burton Dassett, described the pitiful condition of Brailes (at a time when harvests had returned to normal outside the Midlands): 'The greater part of the town's ninety laborers, for want of work, must beg, steal, or starve. Everybody in the parish who is able to pay does so weekly.'[60] Considering that the number cited represented well over half the households of Brailes, the magnitude of the problem is clear.

The causes of this distress lay not only in the dearth of grain but also in the lack of available employment, as the above description of Brailes clearly states. The labouring populations of open communities were forced to move outside their parish for employment. As in later centuries, open communities comprised a large pool of underemployed labour which could be utilised by wealthy capitalist arable farmers in adjacent enclosed, sparsely populated parishes. Unfortunately, such

TABLE 10.6 Population growth in open and freehold parishes: 1525–1660s
(households)

	1525	1563	1660s	% increase 1525–1563	% increase 1563–1660s	Overall % increase
Freehold Parish						
Southam	56	62	127	11	105	127
Bishop's Itchington	42	30	55	−30	83	28
Cubbington	20	32	66	60	106	230
Burton Dassett	–	42	75	–	79	–
Hillmorton	69	71	108	3	52	57
Open Parish						
Harbury	52	58	116	12	100	123
Napton	41	80	141	95	76	244
Fenny Compton	–	34	94	–	176	–
Tysoe	–	66	154	–	133	–

TABLE 10.7   Open and freehold parishes in the hearth tax of the 1660s

	Not liable	No. assessed/(%) At one hearth	No. assessed/(%) More than one hearth	Average no. of hearths/ household	Total hearths	Total households
Freehold parish						
Prior's Hardwick	10 (29)	7 (20)	18 (51)	1.9	70	35
Prior's Marston	12 (16)	31 (42)	31 (42)	1.5	114	74
Southam	35 (32)	26 (24)	48 (44)	1.9	210	109
Bishop's Itchington	18 (33)	39 (71)	? ?*	1.6	91	55
Cubbington	15 (27)	22 (40)	18 (33)	1.4	99	55
Burton Dassett	37 (46)	11 (14)	33 (41)	2.1	152	81
Hillmorton	35 (35)	48 (48)	18 (18)	1.4	143	101
Open parish						
Harbury	24 (24)	57 (56)	20 (20)	1.4	147	101
Napton	16 (13)	83 (65)	28 (22)	1.3	175	127
Fenny Compton	41 (48)	28 (35)	16 (19)	1.4	126	85
Tysoe	31 (23)	26 (20)	76 (57)	1.6	222	133

* J. M. Martin's figures for Bishop's Itchington fail to add up correctly.

capitalist *arable* farming had not developed by the early seventeenth century. Some employment was to be found on the larger arable holdings of wealthier yeomen and freeholders (often in freehold parishes), but this would have been insufficient at the best of times and was drastically curtailed in periods of harvest difficulties.

The large open communities in the felden were thus located in the economy in a manner analogous to forest villages. They were dependent upon other felden communities (often freehold ones) both for grain supplies and for employment, while they were hard hit by migration, caused in part by enclosure. In certain respects the position of felden open communities was even more precarious than that of forest villages, because of the lack of industrial crafts and extensive common rights. Crafts remained subsidiary and strongly attached to agriculture. Craftsmen serviced the peasant community and usually were also involved in farming themselves.[61]

These problems were conjoined with a great expansion in population in open communities in the decades prior to 1610 and an upsurge in enclosure and conversion. Such conditions culminated in a period of intense pressure upon resources, and the involvement of open communities such as Harbury, Napton, Fenny Compton and Tysoe in the revolt of 1607. These peasant communities had good cause to blame enclosure for the chronic problems they experienced. Like forest villages, open communities displayed a propensity for disorder. They were often free from the close control of a resident landlord and incorporated mobile persons who did not fit into a stable and hierarchical social structure. The constant flow of immigrants in and labourers out in search of work ensured communication with other communities and awareness of their problems and grievances. Links would have been forged between open and freehold communities on the basis of the seasonal agricultural work available in the latter.

In freehold communities, the retention of manorial control and the strength of the yeoman community enabled the preservation of holdings, the strict stinting and control of commons, and the prevention of encroachment on the wastes and overcrowding by the poor and landless. The freeholders often consolidated their lands and extended them by purchase or lease of the manorial demesnes. Often such communities chose not to enclose their lands: the parishes remained open until enclosed by parliamentary means. There was sufficient flexibility in the open-field system for the introduction of improved methods of peasant farming without resort to enclosure.[62]

Freehold communities resolutely opposed enclosure when accompanied by depopulation. This threat constantly hung over them. As I have described, the peasant community of Hillmorton was fighting for its very existence, while that of Southam was also in considerable danger. Other freehold communities often existed alongside a well-known encloser and sheep-grazier in the same parish. As I have noted, the Spencers were the dominant landholders in both Prior's Hardwick and Prior's Marston; much of Bishop's Itchington was already enclosed; and half the land in Burton Dassett was grazed by the Temple's sheep.

There were other good reasons for the antagonism of freehold communities towards enclosure. Along with enclosed parishes largely in pasture, wealthy freehold communities were made liable to support increasingly impoverished open parishes. The wealthy yeomen baulked at having to pay for what they viewed as the end-product of depopulating enclosure.[63] More specifically, the yeomen and husbandmen of the freehold parishes of Priors' Hardwick and Marston became involved in the Ladbroke riots because their rights of thoroughfare through Ladbroke to Warwick were denied as a result of the enclosures. These peasants spearheaded the protests against the blocked highway in Ladbroke. Problems of passage invariably arose when entire parishes were enclosed, and thus neighbouring peasant communities were impelled to protest against the offending enclosures.

It is clear that entire felden peasant communities were involved in the revolt of 1607.[64] Tables 10.8 and 10.9 suggest that the rioters represented a cross-section of occupations, and wealth within occupations. At one extreme, we may instance William Chambers, labourer of Harbury, who left in the inventory attached to his will of 1629 only £1 7s. 8d., comprising his goods in his rented room – three bedsteads, two

TABLE 10.8   Occupations of felden rioters

	Landholding	Labouring	Crafts	Trades
No.	2 gentlemen 9 yeomen 31 husbandmen 1 grazier 4 cottagers $\overline{47}$	26 labourers 2 shepherds $\overline{28}$	27	9
% of total	43	25	24	8
% in felden at large	40	30	30	

TABLE 10.9   Wealth and occupation of felden rioters

	Yeomen	Husbandmen	Labourers	Crafts	Trades
Rich	2	4	1	2	1
Middle	4	4	–	3	1
Poor	1	9	1	2	1

coffers, and one press (for storing clothes), implements in the house, a hen-pen and two hens; while Ellis Burbury, husbandman of Harbury, was so poverty-stricken that he died in gaol in 1610 having been committed for unpaid debts.

At the other extreme were two very wealthy yeomen. Nicholas Bodington, freeholder of Cubbington, held 2 yardlands there, together with lands in Great Harborough, Pailton and Stretton Baskerville. On the death of his father in 1610, he was left the bulk of the estate of £550, while his two brothers received a total of £280. Nicholas himself died in 1636 leaving property worth £306. In all the available rioters' inventories, there is only óne person who exceeded Bodington in wealth: Henry Mister, husbandman of Napton, who left property worth £369 on his death in 1634. In terms of his wealth, Mister was undoubtedly of wealthy yeoman status.

But what of the many poor husbandmen present in Table 10.9? This is perhaps the only over-represented group among the rioters. Upon examination of their distribution by parish, it is striking that they belonged, with one exception, to the open communities of Napton (six) and Harbury (two). By contrast, five of the seven yeomen came from the freehold communities of Knightcote (in Burton Dassett), Prior's Hardwick, Cubbington and Stockton. These divergent origins of rioters reflect the distinct structurés of these two types of peasant community.

CONCLUDING REMARKS

This brings us full circle in understanding the changing relationship between peasant and landlord in England. The Midlands Revolt of 1607 represented the final stage in peasants' struggle with their landlords over land. This sustained struggle reached back across the centuries into the medieval period. It began in the twelfth and thirteenth centuries, when landlords sought to impose servility on their tenants and to control peasant land and property; by the late fourteenth century, peasants had broken down much of this power over them. In the fifteenth century landlords denied peasants secure tenure in land, while in the sixteenth and seventeenth centuries the peasantry felt the effects of insecure tenure to the full, and fought to preserve their existence against the encroachment of capitalist agriculture.

At all times, these struggles played an important part in determining English agrarian development. Throughout this book, such struggles have been illustrated in detailed fashion by reference to Warwickshire and have been related to their structural constraints at large. In order to explain the forms that struggles took and to understand English agrarian development, it has been necessary to go back and to revise considerably existing Marxist theory concerning feudalism, the transition to capitalism, and the absolutist state. I have provided a reformulation of feudal economic and political structure and of the place of commodity relations so that the trajectory of feudal development and the place of class struggle between peasant and landlord might be understood. This reformulation aids us considerably when considering the transition towards capitalism and the role of the absolutist state in that process, and allows us to analyse the configuration of agrarian capitalism, feudalism, the state, and the struggle between peasant and landlord in the period up to the mid seventeenth century. This configuration was encapsulated and writ large in the Midlands Revolt of 1607.

The open and freehold communities involved in this revolt were in one sense exceptions that prove the rule. Due to the specific conditions which I have traced, they were able to establish control over land and survived long enough to play a leading role in the protest of 1607 against the destruction of less fortunate peasant communities. None the less, the more usual route led to the extinction of communities, both by a process of internal erosion and by attack from outside. The peasantry had been caught between the pincers of internal differentiation and external appropriation. Its solidarity, which had long been based upon common economic interests, was rapidly vanishing, and, as a result, so was its capacity as a political force to be reckoned with. Although it was not apparent at the time, with the benefit of hindsight it is clear that the Midlands Revolt represented the final outburst by a peasantry already largely undermined by prior developments. But this is not to deny the revolt of 1607 any efficacy: it surely succeeded admirably in its goal, which was to provoke ameliorative action by the government. However, the state could only grapple with the *effects* of the underlying problem in insecure tenure, and even this it could do only ineffectively, because of the resistance of the landed class.

By the mid seventeenth century, the relationship of the peasantry, the landed class and the state was significantly altered. The peasantry was no longer the decisive economic and political force that it had been. The ultimate failure of both the mid-sixteenth-century risings and that of 1607 confirmed this development. The state still attempted to protect the peasantry but its agrarian policy became increasingly ineffective and entangled with its financial problems and served only to exacerbate the split between capitalist agrarian interests and the state. The political and economic interests of the landed class had advanced beyond those that could be secured by the absolutist state. Since peasant revolt had receded as a significant threat, absolutism now constituted only an obstacle to the further development of agrarian capitalism. The lines of conflict were now set. The landed class and its representatives in Parliament, especially the House of Commons, saw agricultural improvement by enclosure and the establishment of individual property rights as the unequivocal means of advancement of their interests. Their point of view ultimately prevailed; by this time it could hardly have been otherwise. Enclosure rarely caused large-scale depopulation, thanks to the simple fact that there were relatively few peasants in the way. All, or all who mattered (those with recognised property in land), could agree to enclose and cultivate their land in severalty for their mutual benefit and profit. It was the era of enclosure by agreement, clearing the way for the parliamentary enclosures of the eighteenth century.

Politically, the question of continued capitalist agrarian development was resolved by the English Civil War and the consequent destruction of the absolutist state apparatus. From then on, the state endorsed and approved enclosure, and the great agrarian transformation culminating in the disappearance of the peasantry received its political ratification. The fate of the English peasantry was now sealed.

Marxists have often underplayed the contingent nature of agrarian transformation in England in providing an essential precondition for the emergence of industrial capitalism. The contribution made by the expropriation of the land from the peasantry is usually accepted as a *fait accompli*, from which one can then build an explanation of the origins of English capitalism. But this transformation was by no means an inevitable process. The disappearance of the peasantry was itself dependent upon the determination of the struggle over the land. Taking this into account, I hope that I have illuminated the process of agrarian transformation, which culminated in the defeat of the peasantry and the release of the land for the further advance of capitalism.

Notes

NOTES TO CHAPTER 1: FEUDAL STRUCTURE

1. K. Marx, *Capital*, vol. III, (Moscow: Progress Publishers, 1971) pp. 790–1. See M. Dobb, *Studies in the Development of Capitalism* (London: Routledge and Kegan Paul, 1963) pp. 35–6.
2. Marx, *Capital*, vol. III, pp. 790–1.
3. R. H. Hilton (ed.), *The Transition from Feudalism to Capitalism* (London: New Left Books, 1976) p. 14.
4. L. Althusser and E. Balibar, *Reading 'Capital'*, trs. B. Brewster (London: New Left Books, 1970) pp. 218–24; N. Poulantzas, *Political Power and Social Classes*, trs. T. O'Hagan (London: New Left Books, 1973) pp. 25–33.
5. P. Anderson, *Lineages of the Absolutist State* (London: New Left Books, 1974) pp. 403–4. Anderson's detailed discussion of feudalism is contained in *Passages from Antiquity to Feudalism* (London: New Left Books, 1974) pp. 147–53.
6. Anderson, *Lineages of the Absolutist State*, p. 404.
7. Godelier's work in anthropology is founded on a basis similar to that of Anderson.

8. This is made clear in E. Hobsbawm (ed.), *Karl Marx: Pre-capitalist Economic Formations*, trs. J. Cohen (London: Lawrence and Wishart, 1964), esp. pp. 20, 41–5, 87–9, 99. Hobsbawm cites numerous examples from *Capital*.

9. V. Lenin, *Collected Works*, vol. III: *The Development of Capitalism in Russia* (Moscow: Progress Publishers, 1972) pp. 192–3.

10. Dobb, *Studies in the Development of Capitalism*, pp. 50–65.

11. Marx, *Capital*, vol. III, p. 790.

12. Similar confusion occurs in analysis of the Asiatic mode of production by Balibar and Poulantzas, both of whom rely upon the same passage in Marx. See Hobsbawm (ed.), *Pre-capitalist Economic Formations*, p. 69; Althusser and Balibar, *Reading 'Capital'*, p. 219; Poulantzas, *Political Power and Social Classes*, p. 31.

13. P. Sweezy, 'A Critique' and 'A Rejoinder', in Hilton (ed.), *Transition from Feudalism to Capitalism*.

14. M. Dobb, 'A Reply', ibid.

15. J. Banaji, 'The Peasantry in the Feudal Mode of Production: Towards an Economic Model', *JPS*, vol. 3, no. 3 (1976). My critique is based on J. E. Martin, 'A Reply to Banaji on the Feudal Mode of Production', *JPS*, vol. 4, no. 4 (1977).

16. B. Hindess and P. Hirst, *Pre-capitalist Modes of Production* (London: Routledge and Kegan Paul, 1975).

17. Ibid., p. 232. (From *Capital*, vol. III, p. 791.)

18. For criticism of Hindess and Hirst's general discussion of productive forces, see J. Taylor, 'Review of *Pre-capitalist Modes of Production*', *Critique of Anthropology*, vols 4–5, 6 (1975–6); T. Asad and H. Wolpe, 'Concepts of Modes of Production', *Economy and Society*, vol. 5, no. 4 (1976).

19. Hindess and Hirst, *Pre-capitalist Modes of Production*, p. 246.

20. Hindess and Hirst mention these aspects of the feudal economy but fail to consider their implications for economic structure and political conditions of existence.

21. M. Bloch, *Feudal Society*, 2 vols, trs. L. Manyon, foreword M. Postan (London: Routledge and Kegan Paul, 1965) vol. I, pp. 251–2; G. Duby, *Rural Economy and Country Life in the Medieval West*, trs. C. Postan (London: Edward Arnold, 1968) pp. 224–31, 239–52.

22. This assumption has been made for the sake of analysis. In reality, medieval economies almost invariably involved exchange. relationships. See M. Bloch, 'Natural Economy or Money Economy: a Pseudo-dilemma', in *Land and Work in Medieval Europe* (London: Routledge and Kegan Paul, 1967).

23. For discussion of the middle peasant, see Lenin, *Development of Capitalism in Russia*, pp. 181, 191, 207; E. Kosminsky, *Studies in the Agrarian History of England*, trs. R. Kisch, intro. R. Hilton (Oxford: Blackwell, 1956) pp. 230–7, 355; W. Kula, *An Economic Theory of the Feudal System: Towards a Model of the Polish Economy, 1500–1800* (London: New Left Books, 1976) pp. 44ff; R. H. Tawney, *The Agrarian Problem of the Sixteenth Century* (London: Longmans, 1912) p. 92.

24. See the discussion of the 'farm' system in P. Vinogradoff, *Villeinage in England* (Oxford: Clarendon, 1892) pp. 301–5.

218 *Notes*

25. M. M. Postan, *The Medieval Economy and Society: An Economic History of Britain in the Middle Ages* (London: Weidenfeld and Nicolson, 1972) pp. 124–5.
26. R. H. Hilton, *Bond Men Made Free: Medieval Peasant Movements and the English Rising of 1381* (London: Methuen, University Paperback, 1977) pp. 32–3.
27. Marx, *Capital*, vol. ɪ, pp. 146–9, 150; vol. ɪɪɪ, p. 328.
28. Banaji, in *JPS*, vol. 3, no. 3, p. 306. See Kula, *Economic Theory of the Feudal System*, pp. 28–75. I have extended Kula's analysis – intended to apply only to Eastern Europe – to commodity forms of enterprise in general.
29. Thus, landlords' expansion of consumption is not a *necessary* effect of the feudal economic structure, as Banaji suggests, but of course as an index of profitability it tends to give rise to increasing consumption.
30. Money rent is the end-product of a process of abstraction from concrete labour in the form of labour services, whereby labour time is given an exchange value. This process is analogous to the development of exchange (Marx, *Capital*, vol. ɪ, part 1). Produce rent occupies the same intermediate position as 'barter': in both cases exchange is still tied to the particular use values of the products, their equivalence with one another, and to the concrete labour time involved in their production (Kosminsky, *Studies in the Agrarian History of England*, pp. 152ff).
31. Commodities from the demesne – whether produced by means of wage labour or labour services – are subject to the same form of calculation.
32. See, for example, the institution of *propinacja* in Poland (Kula, *Economic Theory of the Feudal System*).
33. Kosminsky, *Studies in the Agrarian History of England*, pp. 354–5; Lenin, *Development of Capitalism in Russia*, p. 181; Hilton, *Bond Men Made Free*, p. 94.
34. I. Wallerstein, *The Modern World-system: Capitalist Agriculture and the Origins of the European World Economy in the Sixteenth Century* (London: Academic Press, 1974).

NOTES TO CHAPTER 2: FEUDAL ENGLAND

1. For this section, see M. Bloch, 'The Advent and Triumph of the Watermill', in *Land and Work in Medieval Europe*; R. Bennett and J. Elton, *The History of Corn Milling*, 4 vols (London: Simpkin, Marshall, 1898–1904); L. White, *Medieval Technology and Social Change* (Oxford: Clarendon Press, 1962).
2. Bloch, in *Land and Work in Medieval Europe*, p. 154.
3. Another monopoly particularly important in the medieval economy was that of the manorial sheep-fold. The lord was able to fold his tenants' sheep on his own land and thus derive the benefits of their dung. (The primary restriction upon productivity of land was lack of manure.) See S. B. H. Van Bath, *The Agrarian History of Western Europe, A.D. 500–1850*, trs. O. Ordish (London: Edward Arnold, 1963) ch. 2.
4. Hindess and Hirst, *Pre-capitalist Modes of Production*, p. 244.
5. For this section, see White, *Medieval Technology and Social Change*, and Vinogradoff, *Villeinage in England*, pp. 238–9.

6. White and Vinogradoff explain the origins of the open-field system in terms of the large plough-team. The latter also suggests that the fragmented and scattered composition of peasant holdings in the open fields resulted from the community's desire to maintain equality of land distribution in quality and quantity (see Vinogradoff, *Villeinage in England*, pp. 234–6).

7. Ibid., p. 253.

8. Kosminsky, *Studies in the Agrarian History of England*, pp. 73–4. He suggests that only 45 per cent of communities coincided with manors.

9. Postan, *The Medieval Economy and Society*, p. 117.

10. Kosminsky, *Studies in the Agrarian History of England*, p. 273; also see pp. 279–80.

11. Ibid. (the following sections are based on this work).

12. Kosminsky (ibid., p. 96) defines manorial size as follows:

> large manors – over 1000 acres of arable;
> medium manors – 500–1000 acres of arable;
> small manors – under 500 acres of arable.

13. Ibid., p. 284. However, in the late thirteenth century, less than half of villein land was attached to labour services. This implies that, on large manors, less than half of their demesnes could be cultivated by services. The point I am making is that the ratio of demesne to villein land was suitable for a labour-service worked demesne, if landlords chose to introduce such a system.

14. This conclusion is reinforced by Kosminsky's analysis of small manors elsewhere (ibid., pp. 264, 271). However, the significance of wage labour should not be overstressed. Both Kosminsky and Hilton (in his earlier work) in following Lenin's example overemphasise this development. As a result they see 'portents' of incipient capitalism on small manors. See Hilton's recent comments in 'Reasons for Inequality among Medieval Peasants', *JPS*, vol. 5, no. 3 (1978).

15. Here Kosminsky (ibid., p. 214) uses a different definition of manorial size:

> large manors – more than 360 acres of villein land;
> medium manors – 240–360 acres of villein land;
> small manors – 120–240 acres of villein land;
> very small manors – less than 120 acres of villein land.

16. Ibid., p. 217.

17. Ibid., pp. 242–3.

18. For this section, see ibid., pp. 143, 168, 187–95. In the Eastern counties are included Essex, Suffolk, Norfolk, Cambridgeshire, Hertfordshire, Huntingdonshire, Northamptonshire, Middlesex and Lincolnshire.

19. Of course, many of the 8 per cent of rich free tenants would fall outside the bounds of the feudal economy. Their exclusion would make the contrast between free and villein tenants even more marked.

20. Kosminsky, *Studies in the Agrarian History of England*, p. 233.

21. Ibid., pp. 168–9.

22. M. M. Postan, *The Medieval Economy and Society*, pp. 144–5, and *Essays on Medieval Agriculture and General Problems of the Medieval Economy*

(Cambridge University Press, 1973) pp. 107ff. His view strongly contrasts with that of Vinogradoff, who emphasises legal incapacity (*Villeinage in England*, p. 134).

23. F. Pollock and F. W. Maitland, *The History of English Law before the Time of Edward I*, 2 vols, 2nd edn (Cambridge University Press, 1968) vol. I, p. 417.

24. E. A. Kosminsky, 'Services and Money Rents in the 13th Century', *Ec HR*, vol. 5, no. 2 (1935) p. 41; Kosminsky, *Studies in the Agrarian History of England*, pp. 331–8.

25. We should not view 'custom of the manor' as a preordained and timeless set of practices apart from the classes whence it originated. Custom resulted from a specific resolution of struggle between landlords and tenants (see R. H. Hilton, 'Peasant Movements in England before 1381', *Ec HR*, 2nd ser., vol. 2, no. 2 (1949) p. 122). We should also not assume that custom necessarily protected the position of peasants. This misunderstanding is based upon an illegitimate extrapolation back in time from the fifteenth and sixteenth centuries, a period in which peasants attempted to protect themselves by an appeal to customary rights.

26. Bloch, *Feudal Society*, vol. I, pp. 272–7. He suggests that the strength of English manorial structure prohibited the creation of the autonomous communal political structures that occurred on the Continent.

27. W. O. Ault, *Open-field Farming in Medieval England: A Study of Village By-laws* (London: Allen and Unwin, 1972) pp. 18–19, 58, 62–3.

28. For this section, see G. Homans, *English Villagers of the Thirteenth Century* (New York: Russell and Russell, 1960); Pollock and Maitland, *History of English Law*, vol. I, pp. 568–82; G. G. Coulton, *The Medieval Village* (Cambridge University Press, 1925); H. S. Bennett, *Life on the English Manor: A Study of Peasant Conditions, 1150–1400* (Cambridge University Press, 1937).

29. Homans, *English Villagers of the Thirteenth Century*, p. 320; Kosminsky, *Studies in the Agrarian History of England*, p. 331.

30. Bloch, *Feudal Society*, vol. I, p. 271. For this section, see Homans, *English Villagers of the Thirteenth Century*, pp. 322–4; Pollock and Maitland, *History of English Law*, vol. I, pp. 568–82; D. M. Stenton, *English Society in the Early Middle Ages, 1066–1307* (Harmondsworth: Penguin, 1965) pp. 149–50. Frankpledge originally was a local system of policing the countryside by reliance upon collective responsibility within communities. It was found in those parts of England where feudalism was most highly developed.

31. Pollock and Maitland, *History of English Law*, vol. I, p. 581; A. N. May, 'An Index of Thirteenth Century Impoverishment? Manor Court Fines', *Ec HR*, 2nd ser., vol. 26, no. 3 (1973).

32. Vinogradoff, *Villeinage in England*, pp. 151–66.

33. For this section, see Pollock and Maitland, *History of English Law*, vol. I, pp. 356–83, 412–32; Vinogradoff, *Villeinage in England*, chs 1, 2, 4 and 5; Postan, *The Medieval Economy and Society*, pp. 144–5, and *Essays on Medieval Agriculture*, pp. 113ff.

34. For this section, see Homans: *English Villagers of the Thirteenth Century*, pp. 109–32; 'The Rural Sociology of Medieval England', *P&P*, no. 4

(1953); and 'The Explanation of English Regional Differences', ibid., no. 42 (1969). Also see J. Thirsk, 'The Common Fields', ibid., no. 29 (1964); J. Z. Titow, 'Medieval England and the Open-field System', ibid., no. 32 (1965); C. Howell, 'Peasant Inheritance Customs in the Midlands, 1280–1700', in J. Goody, J. Thirsk and E. P. Thompson (eds), *Family and Inheritance: Rural Society in Western Europe, 1200–1800* (Cambridge University Press, 1976); R. Faith, 'Peasant Families and Inheritance Customs in Medieval England', *Ag HR*, vol. 14 (1966).

35. Vinogradoff, *Villeinage in England*, p. 246; R. H. Hilton, 'Freedom and Villeinage in England', *P&P*, no. 31 (1965) p. 10n.

36. Postan, *Essays on Medieval Agriculture*, pp. 107ff. Landlords could afford to be indulgent about villein purchase of land but not villein sale of land, which threatened removal of that land from control by the landlord.

37. For this section, see P. Hyams, 'Origins of the Peasant Land Market in England', *Ec HR*, 2nd ser., vol. 23, no. 1 (1970); Vinogradoff, *Villeinage in England*, p. 158. Also see R. H. Hilton: in *Ec HR*, 2nd. ser., vol. 2, no. 2, pp. 121, 132; in *P&P*, no. 31, p. 16; and *The Decline of Serfdom in Medieval England* (London: Macmillan, 1969) p. 44.

38. For this section, see Pollock and Maitland, *History of English Law*, vol. I, pp. 356–83, 597; Bloch, *Feudal Society*, vol. I, pp. 251–2; Bennett, *Life on the English Manor*, pp. 127–38; Coulton, *The Medieval Village*, pp. 55–64; Vinogradoff, *Villeinage in England*, pp. 67, 163–4.

39. For tallage, see Pollock and Maitland, *History of English Law*, vol. I, pp. 574ff.; Postan, *The Medieval Economy and Society*, pp. 124–5. Also see Hilton: *The Decline of Serfdom*, pp. 15–17; *Ec HR*, 2nd ser., vol. 2, no. 2, p. 120; *The English Peasantry in the Later Middle Ages* (Oxford: Clarendon Press, 1975), esp. the chapter 'Rent and Capital Formation in Feudal Society', pp. 125, 199.

For the exaction of the heriot and entry fines, see Hilton, 'Rent and Capital Formation' and 'Lord and Peasant in Staffordshire', ibid., esp. pp. 197–9, 234–5. The severity of the heriot is emphasised by the fact that both middle and rich peasants usually had no more than one draught animal.

For merchet, see Hilton: in *Ec HR*, 2nd ser., vol. 2, no. 2, p. 121; *The Decline of Serfdom*, pp. 15, 18; and *P&P*, no. 31, p. 9. Also see Vinogradoff, *Villeinage in England*, p. 153; Postan, *The Medieval Economy and Society*, pp. 124–5; E. Searle, 'Freedom and Marriage in Medieval England: an Alternative Hypothesis', *Ec HR*, 2nd ser., vol. 29, no. 3 (1976), and 'Merchet in Medieval England', *P&P*, no. 82 (1979). J. Scammell suggests a different analysis which I find unconvincing – J. Scammell, 'Freedom and Marriage in Medieval England', *Ec HR*, 2nd ser., vol. 27, no. 4 (1974), and 'Wife-rents and Merchet', ibid., vol. 29, no. 3 (1976).

40. Hilton, 'Lord and Peasant in Staffordshire', *The English Peasantry*.

41. For this section, see N. S. B. Gras, *The Evolution of the English Corn Market: From the Twelfth to the Eighteenth Century* (Cambridge, Mass.: Harvard University Press, 1915) pp. 18–19, 27n.; Vinogradoff, *Villeinage in England*, p. 156. Also see Hilton: in *Ec HR*, 2nd ser., vol. 2, no. 2, p. 121; in *P&P*, no. 31, pp. 9–10; and *The Decline of Serfdom*, p. 15.

42. For this section, see Pollock and Maitland, *History of English Law*, vol. I, Vinogradoff, *Villeinage in England*. For chevage, see ibid., p. 157; Hilton, in *Ec HR*, 2nd ser., vol. 2, no. 2, pp. 120–1.
43. For this section, see Pollock and Maitland, *History of English Law*, vol. I, p. 423; Vinogradoff, *Villeinage in England*, pp. 59–64, 153.
44. For this section, see B. Putnam, *The Enforcement of the Statute of Labourers (During the First Decade After the Black Death, 1349–1359)* (New York: Columbia University, 1908) pp. 153–60, 220–3.

NOTES TO CHAPTER 3: CLASS STRUGGLE AND
HISTORICAL DEVELOPMENT

1. This term was first used by Hindess and Hirst in their criticisms of Balibar's work (*Pre-capitalist Modes of Production*, pt VI: 'The Transition from Feudalism to Capitalism'). Here, I have extended it to a more general analysis of historical change.
2. Dobb, *Studies in the Development of Capitalism*, pp. 42–70.
3. Anderson, *Passages from Antiquity to Feudalism*, pt II, ch 5, esp. pp. 197–204.
4. Merrington develops further such an analysis of the role of towns in terms of their simultaneous internality and externality: J. Merrington, 'Town and Country in the Transition to Capitalism', in Hilton (ed.), *Transition from Feudalism to Capitalism*. However, this approach merely combines aspects of internal and external dissolution theories explicitly, rather than resolving the antinomy between them as Anderson suggests (*Lineages of the Absolutist State*, p. 21n.).
5. Anderson, *Passages from Antiquity to Feudalism*, p. 198n.
6. E. A. Kosminsky, 'The Evolution of Feudal Rent in England from the Eleventh to the Fifteenth Centuries', *P&P*, no. 7 (1955) pp. 22–6.
7. Kosminsky, *Studies in the Agrarian History of England*, ch. 7: 'The Struggle for Rent in Thirteenth Century England'.
8. Hilton, *Bond Men Made Free*, p. 13. For example, see Duby, *Rural Economy and Country Life*, bk IV, ch. 3: 'The Peasants'.
9. Hilton (ed.), *Transition from Feudalism to Capitalism*, p. 115.
10. Dobb, *Studies in the Development of Capitalism*, pp. 19–20, 181; Dobb and Sweezy, in Hilton (ed.), *Transition from Feudalism to Capitalism*, pp. 46–9, 61–3.
11. Anderson, *Lineages of the Absolutist State*, esp. pt I, ch. 1.
12. Sweezy, in Hilton (ed.), *Transition from Feudalism to Capitalism*, pp. 42–3.
13. Poulantzas, *Political Power and Social Classes*, p. 15. Also see pt II, ch. 3, esp. p. 157.
14. Althusser and Balibar, *Reading 'Capital'*, ch. 5: 'Marxism is not an Historicism'; and Brewster's Glossary, ibid., pp. 321–2.
15. Both Balibar and Poulantzas shelve the problem, commenting that little work has yet been done on the articulation of modes of production: ibid., pp. 207n., 300n.; and Poulantzas, *Fascism and Dictatorship* (London: New Left Books, 1974) p. 118n. This point is clearly established by A. Foster-Carter, 'The Mode of Production Controversy', *NLR*, no. 107 (1978).

16. Both authors' analyses of transition are influenced by Bettelheim's work. For example, see C. Bettelheim, *The Transition to Socialist Economy*, trs. B. Pearce (Hassocks, Sussex: Harvester, 1975), esp. ch. 1; Althusser and Balibar, *Reading 'Capital'*, pt iii, ch. 4: 'Elements for a Theory of Transition'; Poulantzas, *Political Power and Social Classes*, pt ii, ch. 3: 'The Absolutist State, the Transitional State'.
17. Hindess and Hirst, *Pre-capitalist Modes of Production*, pp. 274–5.
18. Ibid., pp. 274–87.
19. Ibid., p. 280. Their analysis involving the severance of class struggle from its means of conceptualisation is carried through to its logical conclusions in B. Hindess and P. Hirst, *Mode of Production and Social Formation: An Autocritique of Pre-capitalist Modes of Production* (London: Macmillan, 1977).
20. Asad and Wolpe, in *Economy and Society*, vol. 5, no. 4, pp. 497–501. Also see I. Gerstein, 'A Theory of Modes of Production', *Insurgent Sociologist*, vol. 7, no. 4 (1977) pp. 70–1.
21. Hindess and Hirst, *Pre-capitalist Modes of Production*, p. 279.
22. Poulantzas, *Political Power and Social Classes*, p. 95.
23. E. O. Wright, *Class, Crisis and the State* (London: New Left Books, 1978) ch. 1.

NOTES TO CHAPTER 4: FEUDALISM AND CLASS STRUGGLE

1. P. Vinogradoff, *The Growth of the Manor*, 2nd edn (London: Allen and Unwin, 1911), and *Villeinage in England*. These points are made in less analytic terms by both Kosminsky and Hilton: E. Kosminsky, in *P&P*, no. 7, pp. 12–13, and 'The Hundred Rolls of 1279–80 as a Source for English Agrarian History', *Ec HR*, vol. 3, no. 1 (1931) pp. 16–20; R. H. Hilton, *The Decline of Serfdom*, pp. 18, 30, and 'Kibworth Harcourt: a Merton College Manor in the Thirteenth and Fourteenth Centuries', in W. G. Hoskins (ed.), *Studies in Leicestershire Agrarian History* (Leicester: Leicestershire Archaeological Society, 1949) pp. 18–19.
2. Postan, *The Medieval Economy and Society* and *Essays on Medieval Agriculture*.
3. J. Z. Titow, 'Some Evidence of the Thirteenth Century Population Increase', *Ec HR*, 2nd ser., vol. 14, no. 2 (1961), and *English Rural Society, 1200–1350* (London: Allen and Unwin, 1969); I. Kershaw, 'The Great Famine and Agrarian Crisis in England, 1315–1322', *P&P*, no. 54 (1973); E. Miller, 'The English Economy in the Thirteenth Century: Implications of Recent Research', *P&P*, no. 28 (1964); J. Hatcher, *Plague, Population and the English Economy, 1348–1530* (London: Macmillan, 1977).
4. Kosminsky, in *P&P*, no. 7, esp. p. 77, and *Studies in the Agrarian History of England*, pp. 176–8. Also see Vinogradoff, *Villeinage in England*, pp. 311, 342; Hilton, *Bond Men Made Free*, pp. 86–7.
5. Ibid., ch. 2.
6. See Kosminsky, in *Ec HR*, vol. 3, no. 1, p. 24.
7. Kosminsky, in *P&P*, no. 7, p. 18.

8. M. Bloch, *French Rural History*, trs. J. Sondheimer (London: Routledge and Kegan Paul, 1966) pp. 91–106.
9. Hilton: in *Ec HR*, 2nd ser., vol. 2, no. 2; in *P&P*, no. 31; and *Bond Men Made Free*, pp. 87–8.
10. R. H. Hilton, 'Peasant Society, Peasant Movements and Feudalism in Medieval Europe', in H. A. Landsberger (ed.), *Rural Protest: Peasant Movements and Social Change* (London: Macmillan, 1974) p. 74.
11. Hilton in *Ec HR*, 2nd ser., vol. 2, no. 2, p. 122. For example, the court rolls of the manor of Halesowen, Worcestershire, indicate no sign of the continual conflict from 1234–1387 recorded centrally.
12. Vinogradoff, *Villeinage in England*, ch. 3; B. P. Wolffe, *The Royal Demesne in English History* (London: Allen and Unwin, 1971).
13. For this section, see Kosminsky, *Studies in the Agrarian History of England*, esp. pp. 341–8; Vinogradoff, *Villeinage in England*, ch. 3 and p. 204.
14. J. E. Martin, 'Peasant and Landlord in the Development of Feudalism and Transition to Capitalism in England' (University of Lancaster, PhD thesis, 1979). Therein, references are given for detailed examples cited below.
15. Hilton, in Landsberger (ed.), *Rural Protest*, p. 80. Also see Hilton in *P&P*, no. 31, p. 18.
16. Here, I rely upon Kosminsky, *Studies in the Agrarian History of England*.
17. Hyams, in *Ec HR*, 2nd ser., vol. 23, no. 1; Homans, in *P&P*, no. 4.
18. For the Midlands, see, in addition to Kosminsky, R. H. Hilton, 'Medieval Agrarian History' in *VCH Leics*, vol. II (1954), and *The Economic Development of Some Leicestershire Estates in the Fourteenth and Fifteenth Centuries* (London: Oxford University Press, 1947).
19. E. Power, 'The Effects of the Black Death on Rural Agricultural Organisation in England', *History*, new ser., vol. 3 (1918). For the above comments, see Kosminsky, *Studies in the Agrarian History of England*, pp. 172–8.
20. Kosminsky, ibid., pp. 174–7. Dobb makes the same observation in response to Sweezy, in Hilton (ed.), *Transition From Feudalism to Capitalism*, p. 61.
21. Kershaw, in *P&P*, no. 54.
22. G. A. Holmes, *The Estates of the Higher Nobility in Fourteenth Century England* (Cambridge University Press, 1957) pp. 114–15. Hatcher supports the thesis of the resilience of the economy of the large estates (*Plague, Population and the English Economy*, p. 40).
23. For these criticisms, see J. Bean, 'Plague, Population and Economic Decline in the Later Middle Ages', *Ec HR*, 2nd ser., vol. 15, no. 3 (1963); B. F. Harvey, 'The Population Trend in England Between 1300 and 1348', *Tr RHS*, 5th ser., vol. 16 (1966); Kosminsky, in *P&P*, no. 7, p. 18.
24. Ibid., p. 22. Also see R. Brenner, 'Agrarian Class Structure and Economic Development in Pre-industrial Europe', ibid., no. 70 (1976).
25. Hilton, *Bond Men Made Free*, pp. 145, 166–7.
26. Martin, 'Peasant and Landlord', appendix I.
27. See J. Tillotson, 'Peasant Unrest in the England of Richard II', *Historical Studies*, vol. 16 (1974).
28. Postan, *The Medieval Economy and Society*, p. 153; Power, in *History*, new ser., vol. 3, pp. 112–16; E. Lipson, *An Introduction to the Economic History of England*, vol. I: *The Middle Ages*, 3rd edn (London: Black, 1923) pp. 128–9;

C. Oman, *The Great Revolt of 1381*, 2nd edn (Oxford: Clarendon Press, 1969) pp. 152–4; R. B. Dobson (ed.), *The Peasants' Revolt of 1381* (London: Macmillan, 1970) p. 27; M. McKisack, *The Fourteenth Century, 1307–1399* (Oxford: Clarendon Press, 1959) pp. 338–9.

29. Hilton adopts this approach (*Bond Men Made Free*, p. 150).
30. The following section is based on R. H. Hilton: ibid.; 'A Crisis of Feudalism', *P&P*, no. 80 (1978); *The English Peasantry*, p. 61; and in *Ec HR*, 2nd ser., vol. 2, no. 2.
31. Tillotson, in *Historical Studies*, vol. 16, p. 16.
32. Throughout this chapter I have refrained from analysing peasant struggles in all their aspects. Rather, building on Chapter 3, I have argued for their importance in the determination of feudal development.
33. Hilton, *Bond Men Made Free*, p. 184.
34. Martin, 'Peasant and Landlord', appendix I.

NOTES TO CHAPTER 5: DEVELOPMENT IN WARWICKSHIRE

1. This chapter is largely based upon J. B. Harley, 'Population and Land Utilisation in the Warwickshire Hundreds of Stoneleigh and Kineton, 1086–1300' (Birmingham University, PhD thesis, 1960), and his 'Population Trends and Agricultural Developments from the Warwickshire Hundred Rolls of 1279', *Ec HR*, 2nd ser., vol. 11, no. 1 (1968); Hilton, 'Social Structure of Rural Warwickshire in the Middle Ages', *The English Peasantry*; Kosminsky, *Studies in the Agrarian History of England*, pp. 97–9, 162, 223, 285–91.
2. Another Warwickshire religious lord – the Bishop of Coventry – had similar powers in nearby Staffordshire, where he owned seven main manors, held a view of frankpledge in three, and hundredal jurisdiction in all its manors. He also held extensive rights of free warren and the profits of six markets and fairs in the county. Manors were largely organised around large labour-service worked demesnes. See Hilton, 'Lord and Peasant in Staffordshire', *The English Peasantry*.
3. The higher *overall* percentage of demesne land on small rather than large manors masks the emergence of two types of manor: (1) those without demesnes, such as many of the Templars' Warwickshire manors (the Templars for their own financial reasons preferred money rents and no demesnes – B. A. Lees (ed.), *Records of the Templars in England in the Twelfth Century: The Inquest of 1185* (London: Oxford University Press, 1935) p. xxvii; and (2) manors containing large demesnes but few or no tenants – not true manors at all but precursors of capitalist farms.
4. Hilton notes that in a full quarter of all parishes in Kineton hundred, the 1332 Subsidy indicates the absence of a resident lord – R. H. Hilton, *A Medieval Society: The West Midlands at the End of the Thirteenth Century* (London: Weidenfeld and Nicolson, 1966) p. 90.
5. Ibid., pp. 172–3, 176; Kosminsky, *Studies in the Agrarian History of England*, pp. 216–24.
6. It is important to stress manorial control as a factor in the balance of

population and land. Land availability was determined by the political control established over land by lords.

7. Hilton, *The English Peasantry*, table, pp. 126–7. Note his error: the correct percentage for Kineton hundred villeins is 57 per cent not 47. I have taken his figures, which include Leam parishes such as Bishop's Itchington in the Kineton hundred.

8. The sources for this section, especially its tables, are discussed in Martin, 'Peasant and Landlord', appendix VIII. Briefly, here I have relied upon (a) the Domesday survey of 1086 analysed in Harley, 'Population and Land Utilisation', and transcribed in *VCH Warwicks*, vol. I (1904); (b) the Hundred Rolls of 1279 – Harley, ibid., and in *Ec HR*, 2nd ser., vol. 11, no. 1; (c) the Lay Subsidy of 1332 – W. F. Carter (ed.), *The Lay Subsidy Roll for Warwickshire of Edward III, 1332* (London: Dugdale Society, 1926). Other material was gleaned from the appropriate volumes of *VCH Warwicks*.

9. For this section, see Homans, *English Villagers of the Thirteenth Century*, pp. 276–84; E. Fryde (ed.), 'The Tenants of the Bishops of Coventry and Lichfield and of Worcester after the Plague of 1348–9', in R. F. Hunnisett and J. B. Post (eds), *Medieval Legal Records: Edited in Memory of C. A. F. Meekings* (London: HMSO, 1978). Also see Hilton: in *Ec HR*, 2nd ser., vol. 2, no. 2, pp. 128–9; *A Medieval Society*, pp. 155–61; and *The English Peasantry*, pp. 61–2.

10. E. G. Kimball (ed.), *Rolls of the Warwickshire and Coventry Sessions of the Peace, 1377–1397* (London: Dugdale Society, 1939) p. lxxviii. The term 'villein' was not recorded once in these rolls. However, we should note that the revolt reached Worcester manors; see above.

NOTES TO CHAPTER 6: TRANSITION TO CAPITALISM

1. Dobb, *Studies in the Development of Capitalism*, pp. 20–1, ch. 3.
2. Sweezy, in Hilton (ed.), *The Transition From Feudalism to Capitalism*, pp. 41ff.
3. Merrington, ibid. See above, ch.3, n. 4.
4. Anderson, *Passages from Antiquity to Feudalism*, p. 22n.
5. Anderson, *Lineages of the Absolutist State*, p. 40.
6. P. P. Rey, *Sur l'articulation des modes de productions*, vols 13 and 14 of *Cahiers de Planification*, ed. C. Bettelheim (Paris: Centre d'Études de Planification Socialiste, École Pratique des Hautes Études, 1968). For a summary and criticism of Rey's work, see A. Cutler and J. Taylor, 'Theoretical Remarks on the Transition from Feudalism to Capitalism', *Theoretical Practice*, no. 6 (1972).
7. E. Laclau, 'Feudalism and Capitalism in Latin America', *NLR*, no. 67 (1971); S. Amin, *Unequal Development: An Essay on the Social Formations of Peripheral Capitalism*, trs. B. Pearce (Hassocks, Sussex: Harvester, 1976); J. G. Taylor, *From Modernisation to Modes of Production: A Critique of the Sociologies of Development and Underdevelopment* (London: Macmillan, 1979); H. Wolpe, 'Capitalism and Cheap Labour-power in South Africa', *Economy and Society*, vol. 1, no. 4 (1972); C. Bettelheim, 'Theoretical Comments', appendix I, in A. Emmanuel, *Unequal Exchange: A Study of the*

Imperialism of Trade, trs. B. Pearce (London: New Left Books, 1972), and *The Transition to Socialist Economy*, trs. B. Pearce (Hassocks, Sussex: Harvester, 1975). This type of theory is cogently discussed by A. Foster-Carter in *NLR*, no. 107 (1978).

8. H. Alavi, 'India and the Colonial Mode of Production', *Socialist Register*, 1975; J. Mandle, 'The Plantation Economy: an Essay in Definition', *Science and Society*, vol. 36 (1972); B. Davey, 'Modes of Production, Socio-economic Formations: Combined and Uneven Development', *South Asia Marxist Review*, vol. 1, no. 2 (1972); J. Banaji, 'For a Theory of Colonial Modes of Production', *Economic and Political Weekly*, vol. 7, no. 52 (1972).

9. K. Tribe voices such a criticism of Marxists who look at English development – 'Capitalism and Industrialisation', *Intervention*, vol. 5 (1975).

10. This feature is emphasised by P. Anderson in 'The Origins of the Present Crisis', *NLR*, no. 23 (1964).

11. In respect of the observations made below, Marx's own writings have largely not been superseded in their broad outlines – Marx, *Capital*, vol. i, pt viii, esp. chs 27–30.

12. C Hill in 'State and Revolution in Tudor and Stuart England', *Communist Review*, July 1948, summarises the debate among English Marxists, in which it was concluded that absolutism was a feudal state. See also K. Takahashi, 'A Contribution to the Discussion', in Hilton (ed.), *Transition From Feudalism to Capitalism*, p. 87; B. Porchnev, 'Popular Uprisings before the Fronde, 1623–1648', in P. J. Coveney (ed.), *France in Crisis, 1620–1675* (Totowa, NJ: Rowman and Littlefield, 1977) p. 100; G. Therborn, *What Does the Ruling Class Do When It Rules?* (London: New Left Books, 1978).

13. Anderson, *Lineages of the Absolutist State*, pt i, chs 1 and 2.

14. Here, see the now-classic debate between Miliband and Poulantzas, contained in brief in R. Blackburn (ed.), *Ideology in Social Science: Readings in Critical Social Theory* (London: Fontana, 1972).

15. See P. Hirst's lucid critique of Anderson for this point – 'The Uniqueness of the West', *Economy and Society*, vol. 4, no. 4 (1975).

16. Poulantzas, *Political Power and Social Classes*, pt 2, ch. 3: 'The Absolutist State, the Transitional State'.

17. E. K. Trimberger, 'State Power and Modes of Production: Implications of the Japanese Transition to Capitalism', *Insurgent Sociologist*, vol. 7, no. 2 (1977).

18. This section is based upon Anderson, *Lineages of the Absolutist State*; and Kula, *Economic Theory of the Feudal System*.

19. M. Kimmel, 'Absolutism in Crisis: the English Civil War and the Fronde', in W. L. Goldfrank (ed.), *The World System of Capitalism: Past and Present*, vol. ii: *Political Economy of the World-system Annuals* (London: Sage, 1979).

20. T. Skocpol, *States and Social Revolutions: A Comparative Analysis of France, Russia, and China* (Cambridge University Press, 1979) pp. 24–33.

21. H. Draper, *Karl Marx's Theory of Revolution*, vol. i: *State and Bureaucracy* (New York: Monthly Review, 1977) pp. 475–83.

22. A. D. Lublinskaya, 'The Contemporary Bourgeois Conception of Absolute Monarchy', *Economy and Society*, vol. 1, no. 1 (1972).

23. This form of analysis is adapted from Wright, *Class, Crisis and the State*. I retain certain reservations about his approach, which often betrays eclectic and formalistic tendencies. In this instance I feel justified in using such a model since each mode of determination is elaborated upon in the following chapter.

NOTES TO CHAPTER 7: 15TH CENTURY: LANDHOLDING AND STRUGGLES

1. Brenner, in *P&P*, no. 70. Also see Bloch, *French Rural History*, pp. 127–9.
2. Postan, *The Medieval Economy and Society*, p. 140, and *Essays on Medieval Agriculture*, pp. 117, 194–5.
3. Kosminsky, in *P&P*, no. 7, p. 28; R. H. Hilton, in *VCH Leics*, vol. II, pp. 186–7, and *The Decline of Serfdom*, pp. 32, 39–40.
4. See the summary of the debate over the security of copyhold in Tawney, *Agrarian Problem*, pp. 187ff. Also see A. Savine, 'Copyhold Cases in Early Chancery Proceedings', *English Historical Review*, vol. 17 (1902), and 'English Customary Tenure in the Tudor Period', *QJE*, vol. 19 (1905); I. S. Leadam, 'The Inquisition of 1517: Inclosures and Evictions', *Tr RHS*, new ser., vol. 6 (1892), and 'The Security of Copyholders in the Fifteenth and Sixteenth Centuries', *English Historical Review*, vol. 8 (1893); C. M. Gray, *Copyhold, Equity, and the Common Law* (Cambridge, Mass.: Harvard University Press, 1963), esp. intro. and ch. 1; E. Kerridge, *Agrarian Problems in the Sixteenth Century and After* (London: Allen and Unwin, 1969) ch. 3: 'Security of Tenure'.
5. See Savine, *QJE*, vol. 19, pp. 43ff. Other authors, such as Vinogradoff and Maitland, recognise the link between copyhold and villeinage.
6. Brenner, in *P&P*, no. 70, p. 52.
7. Hilton, in *P&P*, no. 31, pp. 64–9; C. Dyer, 'A Redistribution of Incomes in Fifteenth-Century England?', ibid., no. 39 (1968).
8. B. J. Harris, 'Landlords and Tenants in England in the later Middle Ages: the Buckingham Estates', ibid., no. 43 (1969).
9. Hilton, in *VCH Leics*, vol. II, pp. 191–5. R. Lennard documents medieval peasant resistance to enclosure in 'Agrarian History: Some Vistas and Pitfalls', *Ag HR*, vol. 12 (1964) pp. 85–8.
10. Hilton, *The Decline of Serfdom*, p. 49.
11. Ibid., p. 48; W. G. Hoskins, *The Midland Peasant: The Economic and Social History of a Leicestershire Village* (London: Macmillan, 1965) pp. 104–10.
12. Kerridge, *Agrarian Problems*, ch. 2.
13. Tawney, *Agrarian Problem*, pp. 297ff. Brenner makes this aspect central in his analysis of English development.
14. M. W. Beresford, *The Lost Villages of England* (London: Lutterworth, 1954) p. 148.
15. M. W. Beresford and J. G. Hurst (eds), *Deserted Medieval Villages* (London: Lutterworth, 1971) table II, p. 12. Warwickshire, 73 desertions; Northamptonshire, 60; and Leicestershire, 60. For the type of community vulnerable to desertion, see ibid., pp. 20–9; Beresford, *Lost Villages*, pp. 198–261, 427 (n. 35).

16. R. H. Hilton, 'A Study in the Pre-history of English Enclosure in the Fifteenth Century', *The English Peasantry.*
17. Beresford and Hurst (eds), *Deserted Medieval Villages*, p. 20. Beresford's discussion of Warwickshire villages is in *Lost Villages;* table 7, p. 251.
18. Hilton, 'A Study in the Pre-history of English Enclosure', *The English Peasantry;* C. Dyer, 'Population and Agriculture on a Warwickshire Manor in the Later Middle Ages', *University of Birmingham Historical Journal*, vol. 11 (1968).
19. Hilton, *The English Peasantry*, p. 168.
20. Ibid., p. 60n.; Dyer, in *P&P*, no. 39, pp. 14–17.
21. N. W. Alcock, 'Enclosure and Depopulation in Burton Dassett: a Sixteenth Century View', *Warwickshire History*, vol. 3, no. 5 (1977).
22. For Wormleighton, see H. Thorpe, 'The Lord and the Landscape', in D. R. Mills (ed.), *English Rural Communities: The Impact of a Specialised Economy* (London: Macmillan, 1973). For the other desertions, see M. W. Beresford, 'The Deserted Villages of Warwickshire', *BAS Tr*, vol. 66 (1945–6).
23. Hilton, *Decline of Serfdom*, p. 45.

NOTES TO CHAPTER 8: ENGLISH DEVELOPMENT, 1485–1640

1. Tawney, *Agrarian Problem*, esp. pt ı, ch. 1.
2. These figures for different forms of tenure are confirmed by Kerridge's work more recently (*Agrarian Problems*, pp. 36–8). However, Kerridge does not share Tawney's conclusions on the consequences of the tenurial situation. Kerridge asserts that the copyholder, protected by the courts, was secure in possession of land. As I argued in Chapter 7, no amount of protection in the courts could remedy an insecurity which was fixed by the law itself as a consequence of the working out of custom. Kerridge's argument in fact only applies to copies of inheritance with fixed entry fines.
3. P. J. Bowden concludes that a minimum of 30 acres was required for *profitable* operation of an arable holding in this period – P. J. Bowden, 'Agricultural Prices, Farm Profits, and Rents', in J. Thirsk (ed.), *The Agrarian History of England and Wales*, vol. ıv: *1500–1640* (Cambridge University Press, 1967).
4. R. H. Tawney, 'The Rise of the Gentry, 1558–1640', *Ec HR*, vol. 11, no. 1 (1941); H. R. Trevor-Roper, 'The Gentry, 1540–1640', ibid., Supplement 1 (1953); J. P. Cooper, 'The Counting of Manors', ibid., 2nd ser., vol. 8, no. 3 (1958) (for criticism of Tawney's method of enumeration of manors held by the landed class); L. Stone, *The Crisis of the Aristocracy, 1558–1641* (London: Oxford University Press, 1967).
5. C. Hill, 'Recent Interpretations of the Civil War', in *Puritanism and Revolution* (London: Secker and Warburg, 1958), and 'More about the Gentry, 1540–1640', *New Statesman*, 21 May 1965. This view is also expressed by Wallerstein (*The Modern World-system*, pp. 235–46) and Bowden (in Thirsk (ed.), *Agrarian History*, vol. ıv, pp. 694–5).

6. C. Hill, in *Puritanism and Revolution*, pp. 9–10, and *Reformation to Industrial Revolution* (Harmondsworth: Pelican, 1969) pp. 65–6.
7. L. Stone, 'Social Mobility in England, 1500–1700', *P&P*, no. 33 (1966). For the prominence of the yeomanry, see M. Campbell, *The English Yeoman Under Elizabeth and the Early Stuarts*, 2nd edn (London: Merlin, 1967). Indirect evidence for the widespread upward movement of lesser land-owners is provided by the 'Great Rebuilding' of their houses at this time – W. G. Hoskins, 'The Rebuilding of Rural England, 1570–1640', *P&P*, no. 4 (1953).
8. E. Kerridge, 'The Movement of Rent, 1540–1640', *Ec HR*, 2nd ser., vol. 6, no. 1 (1953).
9. For these points, see the discussion by Tawney (*Agrarian Problem*, pt ii, ch. 1), and Bowden, in Thirsk (ed.), *Agrarian History*, vol. iv.
10. E. Kerridge, *The Agricultural Revolution* (London: Allen and Unwin, 1967).
11. Debate over agrarian change has been vexed by much confusion over the meaning of the term 'enclosure'. Many historians have taken it to mean all forms of assertion of individual (several) ownership of land by creation of a barrier around it. This obscures the damage wrought by a particular form of agrarian change associated with depopulation and conversion to pasture, because this type of change is blended into other, non-contentious forms of enclosure. The usage I shall adopt is that implemented by the Tudor and early Stuart state and endorsed by Tawney (*Agrarian Problem*, pp. 170, 216–17). Enclosure in this sense involves the destruction of common rights, engrossing, depopulation, and conversion to pasture. In 1548, John Hales, a leading anti-enclosure government official, in his instructions to the enclosure commissions, defined enclosure in the following way:

> But first, to declare unto you what is meant by this word 'inclosures'. It is not taken where a man doth enclose and hedge in his own proper ground where no man hath commons. For such inclosure is very beneficial to the commonwealth . . . but it is meant therby, when any man hath taken away and enclosed any other mens commons, or hath pulled down houses of husbandry [depopulation], and converted the lands from tillage to pasture. This is the meaning of this word, and so we pray you to remember it.   (R. H. Tawney and E. Power (eds), *Tudor Economic Documents*, vol. i (London: Longmans, 1924) p. 41)

12. H. L. Gray, *English Field Systems* (Cambridge, Mass.: Harvard University Press, 1915); C. S. Orwin and C. Orwin, *The Open Fields* (Oxford: Clarendon Press, 1938).
13. For this section, see J. Thirsk, 'Enclosing and Engrossing', and Bowden, 'Agricultural Prices', in Thirsk (ed.), *Agrarian History*, vol. iv, pp. 247ff., 613, 637ff.; J. Thirsk, *Tudor Enclosures* (London: Routledge and Kegan Paul, 1959); Tawney, *Agrarian Problem*, pp. 24–5.
14. Beresford, *Lost Villages*; Tawney, *Agrarian Problem*; E. F. Gay, 'Inclosures in England in the Sixteenth Century', *QJE*, vol. 17 (1903), and 'The Midland Revolt and the Inquisitions of Depopulation of 1607', *Tr RHS*, new ser.,

vol. 18 (1904); E. M. Leonard, 'The Inclosure of Common Fields in the Seventeenth Century', ibid., new ser., vol. 19 (1905); L. A. Parker, 'Enclosure in Leicestershire, 1485–1607' (University of London, PhD thesis, 1948); E. C. K. Gonner, *Common Land and Inclosure*, 2nd edn (London: Cass, 1966).

15. A. H. Johnson, *The Disappearance of the Small Landowner* (Oxford: Clarendon Press, 1909) p. 90, gives a figure of 6.5 million acres enclosed by parliamentary means. In addition to this area, eighteenth-century enclosure by agreement is estimated at 4–7 million acres – R. E. Prothero, *English Farming, Past and Present*, 4th edn (London: Longmans, Green, 1927) p. 163. Thus, post-seventeenth-century enclosure involved some 10–15 million acres, only 35–50 per cent of the cultivated area. This broad figure is reflected in the proportion of land enclosed by parliamentary means in individual Midland counties. Figures range from 25 per cent in Warwickshire to 54 per cent in Northamptonshire – Gonner, *Common Land and Inclosure*, appendix B, pp. 268–9.

16. Gay, in *Tr RHS*, new ser., vol. 18, p. 234. Even a Marxist historian such as Christopher Hill fails to question Gay's figures – C. Hill, 'Land in the English Revolution', *Science and Society*, vol. 13 (1948) p. 29.

17. Tawney, *Agrarian Problem*, pp. 261–5.

18. The assumptions upon which Table 8.2 is based are detailed in Martin, 'Peasant and Landlord', pp. 651–2.

19. Gay, in *Tr RHS*, new ser., vol. 18, table ɪ, p. 233. For the section below, see Gay, in *QJE*, vol. 17, pp. 584–92. Concerning prosecutions in Exchequer in the period 1558–1603, 51 per cent of all places recorded and 73 per cent of the total acreage enclosed were in the Midlands. The three named counties alone accounted for 52 per cent of the acreage. Enclosure was particularly heavy in Northamptonshire.

20. L. A. Parker, 'The Depopulation Returns for Leicestershire in 1607', *Leicestershire Archaeological Society, Transactions*, vol. 23 (1947), and 'Enclosure in Leicestershire'.

21. Gay, in *Tr RHS*, new ser., vol. 18, p. 233. His figures for Warwickshire are an underestimate. I have derived the cited figures from documents in the PRO: C 205/5/4; STAC 8/15/21; SP 16/257/129.

22. V. F. Semeonov, *Enclosures and Peasant Revolts in England in the Sixteenth Century* (Moscow and Leningrad, 1949) in Russian.

23. M. W. Beresford, 'Habitation Versus Improvement: the Debate On Enclosure by Agreement', in F. J. Fisher (ed.), *Essays in the Economic and Social History of Tudor and Stuart England* (Cambridge University Press, 1961). I have criticised this view in some detail in J. E. Martin, 'Habitation for the Peasantry Versus Improvement by Enclosure for the Landlord – Reopening the Debate on Enclosure in the 17th Century' (unpublished paper). Therein (and in Martin, 'Peasant and Landlord') evidence drawn largely from Chancery decrees (PRO, C 78), is used to dispute this interpretation.

24. Such decrees were noted from the index to the Chancery decrees in the PRO, compiled under the aegis of Maurice Beresford. We should note that the index provides only partial coverage of the rolls. For this source, see M. W. Beresford, 'The Decree Rolls of Chancery as a Source for Economic History', *Ec HR*, 2nd ser., vol. 32, no. 1 (1979). He suggests that a total of 30 enclosures by decree were found for Leicestershire, 26 for North-

amptonshire, and 19 for Warwickshire, in a broader period than that under consideration here. The other two counties with many enclosures by decree (Lincolnshire with twenty-four and Yorkshire with twenty-three) are so large that they cannot be directly compared with this group of Midland counties in which decrees were a feature.

25. The place of early-seventeenth-century enclosure and state activity against enclosure at that time is considered in J. E. Martin, 'A Re-assessment of the Agrarian Policy of the Tudor and Early Stuart State' (in preparation), and 'Habitation for the Peasantry'. Also see Martin, 'Peasant and Landlord', chs 9 and 10. The major primary sources used were as follows: Calendar of State Papers, Domestic; PRO, SP 14 (James I), SP 16 (Charles I) – containing enclosure certificates, instructions of the Privy Council and petitions to the Privy Council; Acts of the Privy Council (APC); and HMC, Calendars and Indexes of Manuscript Collections.

26. Leonard, in *Tr RHS*, new ser., vol. 19, p. 130.

27. PRO, C 212/20 (Depopulation Fines). Gonner tabulates the aggregate sums paid by county in *Common Land and Inclosure*, table, p. 167.

28. For these aspects of the aspirations of the Tudor state in the 1530s, see the following: J. Hurstfield, 'Was There a Tudor Despotism After All?', *Tr RHS*, 5th ser., vol. 17 (1967); L. Stone, 'The Political Programme of Thomas Cromwell', *Bulletin of the Institute of Historical Research*, vol. 24 (1951); J. A. Youings, 'The Council of the West', *Tr RHS*, 5th ser., vol. 10 (1960).

29. See F. C. Dietz, *English Government Finance, 1485–1558, and 1558–1641*, 2 vols (London: Cass, 1964).

30. This relationship between the monarchy, Parliament and classes is trenchantly argued for by Hill in *Reformation to Industrial Revolution*, and in *The Century of Revolution, 1603–1714* (London: Cardinal, 1974). Also see Anderson, *Lineages of the Absolutist State*.

31. Hill, *The Century of Revolution*, pp. 36, 96, and *Reformation to Industrial Revolution*, p. 95; L. Stone, 'State Control in 16th Century England', *Ec HR*, vol. 17, no. 2 (1947); Tawney, *Agrarian Problem*, pp. 379–84.

32. G. R. Elton, *The Tudor Revolution in Government: Administrative Changes in the Reign of Henry VIII* (Cambridge University Press, 1953).

33. See C. G. Cruickshank, *Elizabeth's Army*, 2nd edn (Oxford: Clarendon Press, 1966); and L. Boynton, *The Elizabethan Militia, 1558–1638* (London: Routledge and Kegan Paul, 1967).

34. Many authors have observed that the state protected the peasantry for the reasons of political stability, and fiscal and military strength. See Tawney, *Agrarian Problem*, pt III, ch, 1, esp. pp. 343–7; P. Ramsey, *Tudor Economic Problems* (London: Gollancz, 1963) p. 37; W. H. R. Curtler, *The Enclosure and Redistribution of Our Land* (Oxford: Clarendon Press, 1920) p. 99.

35. Tawney, *Agrarian Problem*, pp. 314–17; Stone, in *Ec HR*, vol. 17, no. 2, pp. 111, 116; Hill, in Hilton (ed.), *Transition from Feudalism to Capitalism*, p. 121, and *Reformation to Industrial Revolution*, pp. 94–5.

36. More generally, the advance of capitalism in other spheres threatened to cause disorder and led to state regulation of the economy. The institution of poor relief, the Statute of Artificers of 1563, regulation of wages through the Statutes of Labourers, and in the seventeenth century the issue of

comprehensive instructions to JPs (the Book of Orders), all represented attempts by the state to control instability.

37. See Postan, *Medieval Economy and Society*, pp. 173–9; Hilton, *Bond Men Made Free*, p. 148; Kosminsky, *Studies in the Agrarian History of England*, p. 337. Villeins were protected by the legal doctrine of 'waynage': see Vinogradoff, *Villeinage in England*, p. 74. For the sixteenth century, see Tawney, *Agrarian Problem*, pp. 345–7; Hill, *Reformation to Industrial Revolution*, p. 106.
38. For this section, see Martin, 'Peasant and Landlord', ch. 10, and 'Reassessment of the Agrarian Policy'. Major primary sources used were as cited in n. 25 above. Comprehensive discussions of agrarian policy are to be found in Tawney, *Agrarian Problem*, pt III, ch. 1; Thirsk, 'Enclosing and Engrossing', in Thirsk (ed.), *Agrarian History*, vol. IV.
39. See, Tawney, *Agrarian Problem*, pt III, ch. 1; Beresford, *Lost Villages*, pt I, ch. 4.
40. Beresford, in Fisher (ed.), *Essays in the Economic and Social History of Tudor and Stuart England*; Thirsk, 'Enclosing and Engrossing', in Thirsk (ed.), *Agrarian History*, vol. IV.
41. Gay, in *QJE*, vol. 17; Beresford, *Lost Villages*, pt I, ch. 4, and appendix I.
42. See J. E. Martin, 'Enclosure and the Inquisitions of 1607: an Examination of Kerridge's Article "The Returns of the Inquisitions of Depopulation"', *Ag HR*, vol. 30 (1982). This constitutes a criticism of Kerridge's own article, which appeared in the *English Historical Review*, vol. 70 (1955). Major primary sources used: PRO, Star Chamber Proceedings (STAC 8), Chancery Warrants (C 82), Exchequer Decrees and Orders (E 124), State Papers, Domestic (SP 14 and SP 16), Depopulation Returns (C 205/5); HMC, Calendars and Indexes.
43. For this section, see Martin, 'Peasant and Landlord', ch. 10, and 'Reassessment of the Agrarian Policy'.
44. Thirsk, in Thirsk (ed.), *Agrarian History*, vol. IV, p. 213.
45. PRO, SP 16/187/95 (1631). This statement relates to the instigation of enclosure enquiries in the 1630s.
46. Gay, in *Tr RHS*, new ser., vol. 18, p. 219; Leonard, ibid., vol. 19, p. 133; Gonner, *Common Land and Inclosure*, pp. 154, 166, 175.
47. Hill, *The Century of Revolution*, p. 70. Also see Tawney, *Agrarian Problem*, p. 384.
48. Brenner, in *P&P*, no. 70, pp. 70–1.
49. Barrington Moore, Jr, *Social Origins of Dictatorship and Democracy* (Harmondsworth: Penguin, 1974) p. 28. More generally, see ibid., ch. 9. Skocpol, *States and Social Revolutions*, pp. 140–4, makes similar points. Her overall analysis, however, is intended to focus on peasant revolutions which *succeed*.
50. See A. Fletcher, *Tudor Rebellions*, 2nd edn (London: Longmans, 1973) ch. 3.
51. For the Pilgrimage of Grace, see Fletcher, *Tudor Rebellions*, ch. 4; M. H. and R. Dodds, *The Pilgrimage of Grace, 1536–37, and the Exeter Conspiracy, 1538*, 2 vols (London: Cass, 1971); R. B. Smith, *Land and Politics in the England of Henry VIII, the West Riding of Yorkshire, 1530–46* (Oxford: Clarendon Press, 1970); S. M. Harrison, 'The Pilgrimage of Grace in the Lake Counties' (University of Lancaster, MPhil thesis, 1975), which focuses

on agrarian aspects; M. R. James, 'Obedience and Dissent in Henrician England: the Lincolnshire Rebellion, 1536', *P&P*, no. 48 (1970).

52. W. R. D. Jones, *The Mid-Tudor Crisis, 1539–1563* (London: Macmillan, 1973).
53. These aspects of Somerset's protectorate are stressed by M. L. Bush in *The Government Policy of Protector Somerset* (London: Edward Arnold, 1975).
54. Jones, *Mid Tudor-Crisis*, p. 45.
55. This summary is based on the following sources: Gay, in *Tr RHS*, new ser., vol. 18, pp. 199–200; W. K. Jordan, *Edward VI: The Young King, the Protectorship of the Duke of Somerset* (London: Allen and Unwin, 1968) pp. 439–53; Semeonov, *Enclosures and Peasant Revolts*, map; S. K. Land, *Ket's Rebellion: The Norfolk Rising of 1549* (Ipswich: Boydell Press, 1977) pp. 27–9; J. R. Ravensdale, 'Landbeach in 1549: Ket's Rebellion in Miniature', in L. M. Munby, (ed.), *East Anglian Studies* (Cambridge: Heffer, 1968); L. Stone, 'Patriarchy and Paternalism in Tudor England: the Earl of Arundel and the Peasants Revolt of 1549', *Journal of British Studies*, vol. 13, no. 2 (1974); A. Vere Woodman, 'The Buckinghamshire and Oxfordshire Rising of 1549', *Oxoniensia*, vol. 22 (1957).
56. Stone, in *Journal of British Studies*, vol. 13, no. 2, p. 21. Land, *Ket's Rebellion*, pp. 29, 37–40, makes this a feature of his analysis.
57. See the recent recapitulation of this view of the revolt in the South West by J. Cornwall, *Revolt of the Peasantry, 1549* (London: Routledge and Kegan Paul, 1977).
58. Sources used for Ket's Rebellion: Land, *Ket's Rebellion*; Cornwall, *Revolt of the Peasantry*; Fletcher, *Tudor Rebellions*, ch. 6; S. T. Bindoff, *Ket's Rebellion, 1549* (London: Historical Association, 1968); R. J. Hammond, 'The Social and Economic Causes of Ket's Rebellion' (University of London, MA thesis, 1933); B. L. Beer, '"The Commoyson in Norfolk, 1549": a Narrative of Popular Rebellion in Sixteenth Century England', *Journal of Medieval and Renaissance Studies*, vol. 6, no. 1 (1976).
59. K. J. Allison, 'The Sheep–Corn Husbandry of Norfolk in the Sixteenth and Seventeenth Centuries', *Ag HR*, vol. 5 (1957).
60. Gay, in *Tr RHS*, new ser., vol. 18, p. 233.
61. Land, *Ket's Rebellion*, pp. 68–72; Tawney, *Agrarian Problem*, pp. 335–7.
62. For accounts of this rising, see D. G. C. Allan, 'Agrarian Discontent under the Early Stuarts and during the Last Decade of Elizabeth' (University of London, MSc (Econ) thesis, 1950) pp. 20–30; Gay, in *Tr RHS*, new ser., vol. 18. Details are given within the State Papers, Domestic, in the PRO: SP 12/261/10–13, 21–4, 27–8 and 32, and 262/4; SP 14/28/64. This abortive rising caused the government to instigate local enquiries concerning enclosure in the Midlands in 1597. Sources: APC, vol. 26 (1596–7) pp. 437–57, 483, and vol. 27 (1597) pp. 37–43; PRO, STAC 5: A 13/36 and 49/7.

NOTES TO CHAPTER 9: THE MIDLANDS REVOLT OF 1607

1. Other authors, in describing the Midlands Revolt, have largely relied upon Gay, 'Midland Revolt', *Tr RHS*, new ser., vol. 18. See Allan, 'Agrarian

Discontent', ch. 3; Thirsk (ed.), *Agrarian History*, vol. IV, pp. 232–6; J. Wake (ed.), *The Montagu Musters Book, 1602–1623* (Northampton: Northamptonshire Records Society, 1935) pp. xlv–xlix. Useful contemporary commentaries on the revolt are to be found in 'The Journal of Sir Roger Wilbraham', *Camden Society*, 3rd ser., vol. 4 (Camden Miscellany, vol. 10) (1902); G. B. Harrison, *A Second Jacobean Journal, 1607–1610* (London: Routledge and Kegan Paul, 1958) pp. 27–54. Readers should note that repetitive source references are not given for every detailed point made. I shall make an initial reference and then note further the same source only when required by the text. Detailed references can be found in Martin, 'Peasant and Landlord', pt III.

2. W. G. Hoskins, 'Harvest Fluctuations and English Economic History, 1480–1619', *Ag HR*, vol. 12 (1964). For the discussion of Midland grain-supply problems, see A. L. Beier, 'Studies in Poverty and Poor Relief in Warwickshire, 1540–1680' (Princeton University, PhD thesis, 1969) pp. 131–6; Bowden, in Thirsk (ed.), *Agrarian History*, vol. IV, p. 620.

3. In January 1607, there were massive floods in South Wales, and in Gloucestershire, Somerset, Devon, Bedfordshire and other (unspecified) parts of England – *Harleian Miscellany*, 12 vols (London: Robert Dutton, 1808–11) vol. III, pp. 64–71. In April 1607, there was a huge inundation in Warwickshire – Beier, 'Poverty and Poor Relief', p. 134n. As early as January 1607, there were fears of a dearth of grain in the South West – HMC, no. 8, 9th Report, vol. 1, pp. 268–9. By May in the same year these fears were realised – Beier, 'Poverty and Poor Relief'. By the end of 1607, the dearth was widespread – HMC, Salisbury MSS, vol. 20 (1608) pp. 127, 153–4, 160, 175.

4. Bowden, in Thirsk (ed.), *Agrarian History*, vol. IV.

5. BM, Harleian MSS, 787 (art. 11) fo. 9b. This petition is transcribed in J. O. Halliwell (ed.), *The Marriage of Wit and Wisdom* (London: Shakespeare Society, 1846) pp. 140–1.

6. BM, Lansdowne MSS, vol. 90, fo. 23.

7. R. Wilkinson, *A Sermon Preached at Northampton* (London: for John Flasket, 1607).

8. A. S. Standish, *The Commons Complaint* (London: W. Stansby, 1612).

9. E. C. Pettet, 'Coriolanus and the Midlands Insurrection of 1607', *Shakespeare Survey*, vol. 3 (1950).

10. Gay, in *TR RHS*, new ser., vol. 18, table II, p. 236.

11. PRO, STAC 8: 78/13, 87/7, 137/14, 163/6, 231/25, 244/14 and 295/11. The proceedings of cases in the Court of Star Chamber constitute the major source of information on the revolt. This court dealt with matters of riot, rebellious assembly and destruction of property. Many instances of enclosure riot, which together made up the Midlands Revolt as a whole, were recorded individually in Star Chamber as aggrieved enclosers attempted to prosecute those who destroyed their enclosures. I have largely relied upon the 'bills of complaint' brought by such plaintiffs against rioters, and occasionally on the interrogatories administered to defendants (where they have survived). Defendants' answers were invariably recorded in an illegible hand on sheets of paper attached to the major sheet of parchment (the bill) and were often missing. As a result, most information obtained was

that presented to the court by the plaintiff and should be assessed with this fact in mind. We should also note that very few verdicts of the court have survived.

12. HMC, no. 24, 12th Report, appendix IV, Rutland MSS, vol. 1, p. 405 (henceforth 'HMC, Rutland MSS'); BM, Lansdowne MSS, vol. 90, fo. 23.

13. BM, Additional MSS, 11,402, Abstracts of the Privy Council Register, 1550–1610, fo. 127. Unfortunately, the Privy Council registers themselves for the period concerned were destroyed by fire early in the seventeenth century. PRO, STAC 8/198/21, concerning riots at Shutlanger in Stoke Bruerne and at Ashton on 21 May and 6 and 9 June.

14. Ladbroke: PRO, STAC 8: 10/18, 61/35, 63/8, 68/3 and 159/6; C 82/1753, Feb 1608 (pardon granted to rebels gathered at Ladbroke). Dunchurch: PRO, STAC 8/16/4 (these riots must have been linked with the more serious disturbances at adjacent Hillmorton). Withybrook: PRO, STAC 8/221/1. We should also note that there was trouble in Lincolnshire at North Owersby at this time – PRO, STAC 8/18/19, concerning enclosure riots 1 June 1607 and 4 Apr 1608. For further details of Lincolnshire's involvement in the revolt, see Martin, 'Peasant and Landlord', appendix IV. For action taken in Derbyshire, see College of Arms, Talbot MSS, vol. L, fos 86–7, 89; *VCH Derbys*, vol. II (1907) p. 123. For action taken in Lincolnshire, see HMC, Salisbury MSS, vol. 19 (1607) pp. 196, 198, 208, and Rutland MSS, vol. 1, p. 406.

15. HMC, no. 45, Buccleuch MSS, vol. 5, the Montagu Papers, 2nd ser., p. 116.

16. J. Larkin and P. Hughes (eds), *Stuart Royal Proclamations*, vol. I: *1603–1625* (James I) (Oxford: Clarendon Press, 1973) no. 71, pp. 152–4.

17. Haselbech: PRO, C 205/5/5, cited by Gay, in *Tr RHS*, new ser., vol. 18, p. 216n. Newton: J. Bridges, *The History and Antiquities of the County of Northampton*, 2 vols (Oxford: T. Payne, 1762–91) vol. II, p. 322. Pytchley and Rushton: ibid., vol. I, p. 206; *Northamptonshire Notes and Queries*, vol. 1 (1886) p. 74. Coventry: PRO, STAC 8/144/24; HMC, Salisbury MSS, vol. 19 (1607) p. 175. Chilvers Coton: PRO, STAC 8/221/1. Welham: H. Stocks (ed.), *Records of the Borough of Leicester*, vol. IV: 1603–1688 (Cambridge: 1923) pp. 63, 71. Stowe's Chronicle cites large gatherings at Hillmorton and Cotesbach – Gay, in *Tr RHS*, new ser., vol. 18, p. 215.

18. J. Nichols, *The History and Antiquities of the County of Leicester*, 4 vols in 8 pts (London: Nichols, Son and Bentley, 1795–1811) vol. IV, pt 1, p. 83. Description of the battle at Newton.

19. PRO, STAC 8: 71/6, 245/15, 297/11, 256/20 and 76/16. See Martin, 'Peasant and Landlord', appendix IV.

20. BM, Additional MSS, 11,402, fo. 128. The formal order for commissions was issued later, on 27 August – PRO, C 82/1747.

21. Larkin and Hughes (eds), *Stuart Royal Proclamations*, vol. I, no. 74, pp. 161–2.

22. PRO, STAC 8: 105/1, 134/9, 148/7, 295/22, 61/33, 197/26, 159/18, 106/2, 249/15 and 279/9, 10 and 11. These cases are additional to those already noted.

23. Martin, 'Peasant and Landlord', appendix IV. Reference to the revolt is made in later Star Chamber cases such as PRO, STAC 8: 18/19, 148/7, 295/22, 61/33, 122/17, 260/17 and 25/6.

24. See note 14 above for references pertaining to Ladbroke. These quotations are taken from PRO, STAC 8/63/8.

25. This account is based upon the following sources: LRO, Hall Papers, vol. 4, nos 99–112, 115, 129–30, 132, 146 and 152; Stocks (ed.), *Records of the Borough of Leicester*, vol. iv, pp. 58–73; Huntingdon Library, San Marino, California, Huntingdon MSS, HA 4167–71, 4174, 5419–20, 5422–3, 5426–7 (some of these documents are calendared in HMC, no. 78, Hastings MSS, vol. 4, pp. 192–7).

26. This view of riot has recently been articulated by J. Walter in 'Grain Riots and Popular Attitudes to the Law: Maldon and the Crisis of 1629', in J. Brewer and J. Styles (eds), *An Ungovernable People: The English and their Law in the Seventeenth and Eighteenth Centuries* (New Brunswick, NJ: Rutgers University Press, 1980).

27. Martin, 'Peasant and Landlord', p. 686 (n. 44). For JPs, see J. H. Gleason, *The Justices of the Peace in England, 1558–1640* (Oxford: Clarendon Press, 1969).

28. As we have seen, John Meacocke, Constable of Harbury, was central in organising the riots at Ladbroke. In agitation at Hillmorton leading up to the revolt, Michael Carter, Chief Constable of Knightlow hundred in Warwickshire was a central figure. For these disputes, see PRO, STAC 5: A 18/18, 21/24, 42/3 and 3/3; STAC 8: 40/22 and 6/4; C 2 (Jas I): B 34/51, A 8/12, P 30/40. Hillmorton's links with other communities, as delineated in Map 1, have been drawn from these sources, rather than from sources which derive directly from the revolt itself. For the antagonistic attitude of constables to enclosure, see PRO, SP 14/35/52. For involvement by constables in enclosure riots after the revolt, see PRO, STAC 8: 71/6, 231/35, 295/22, 15/13, 121/20 and 260/17.

29. I have noted eight persons listed for the militia who were also in a list of rebels taken by Northamptonshire authorities – Wake (ed.), *Montagu Musters Book*; NRO, Buccleuch Letters, vol. 4, fo. 18a, b, and c. See Chapter 10 for involvement of the rich peasantry in the revolt. Of the 71 rioters recorded from Leicester town, 13 were listed for the town's force of 40 men.

30. The county stores of arms, etc., were held at Apethorpe in the easterly part of Rockingham Forest, about 10 miles from Newton itself.

31. PRO, STAC 8/221/1.

32. BM, Lansdowne MSS, vol. 90, fo. 23.

33. PRO, STAC 8/221/1.

34. Wilkinson, *Sermon Preached at Northampton*.

35. Gay, in *Tr RHS*, new ser., vol. 18, p. 215; D. H. Willson (ed.), *The Parliamentary Diary of Robert Bowyer, 1606–1607* (New York: Octagon, 1971) p. 366.

36. Gay, in *Tr RHS*, new ser., vol. 18, p. 217n.

37. See Walter's discussion of the involvement of women in riots, in Brewer and Styles (eds), *An Ungovernable People*, pp. 62–3.

38. Willson (ed.), *Parliamentary Diary of Robert Bowyer*, pp. 363–6.

39. Wilkinson, *Sermon Preached at Northampton*.

NOTES TO CHAPTER 10: TOWN, FOREST AND FELDEN IN THE REVOLT

1. J. Thirsk, 'The Farming Regions of England', in Thirsk (ed.), *Agrarian History*, vol. IV.
2. BM, Additional MSS, 25,084 (1547); NRO, Book of Fines and Estreats, Eliz. I and Jac. I (1564, 1595); PRO, C 205/5/5, (1607). For the enquiry of 1597, see above, ch. 8, n. 62. I am at present writing an article on sheep-farming and its relationship with enclosure in Northamptonshire in the second half of the sixteenth century. For further discussion of this point, see Martin, 'Peasant and Landlord', pp. 383–5, 693–5.
3. M. E. Finch, *The Wealth of Five Northamptonshire Families, 1540–1640* (London: Oxford University Press, 1956) pp. 17, 31n. This source is invaluable for study of the Northamptonshire enclosing and grazier families. Also see Bowden, in Thirsk (ed.), *Agrarian History*, vol. IV, pp. 639–40.
4. For this section, see H. J. Habbakuk, 'English Landownership, 1680–1750', *Ec HR* vol. 10, no. 1 (1940); A. Everitt, 'Social Mobility in Early Modern England', *P&P*, no. 33, (1966); Tawney, in *Ec HR*, vol. 11, no. 1; Finch, *Wealth of Five Northamptonshire Families*.
5. Ibid., ch. 4; Allan, 'Agrarian Discontent', pp. 42–4; BM, Additional MSS, 39,836, fo. 316, and 39,829, fos. 61–3; PRO, E 163/16/19.
6. PRO, STAC 8/18/12. See C 2 (Jas I): B 18/20 for immediate court proceedings brought by Great Houghton's freeholders against Baude.
7. See the section below, on forest villages. Tresham also held pastures in Brigstock, Oundle, Benefield and Pilton, his cousin's manor – all in the region of Rockingham Forest. See Finch, *Wealth of Five Northamptonshire Families*, pp. 69–70, 74.
8. NRO, Isham MSS, I (L), 3947. For Haselbech, see the following: PRO, STAC 8/18/12; BM, Additional MSS, 39,828, fo. 289, and 39,829, fo. 61; Finch, *Wealth of Five Northamptonshire Families*, pp. 70–92; Kerridge, *Agrarian Problems*, pp. 174–84.
9. For Rushton, see the following PRO papers: STAC 2/23/39; STAC 8/18/12; C 205/5/5; C 3/260/12; C 2 (Jas I): B 27/23. Also see BM, Additional MSS, 39,829, fo. 41; Finch, *Wealth of Five Northamptonshire Families*; Allan, 'Agrarian Discontent', appendix I.
10. For Newton, see the following PRO papers: STAC 5/A13/36; E 163/17/8; C 2 (Jas I): S 24/55. Also see Bridges, *History and Antiquities of the County of Northampton*, vol. II, p. 206.
11. For Pytchley, see the following PRO papers: STAC 8/18/12; C 78/279/3; C 2 (Jas I): C 8/16 and 24/52. Also see NRO, Isham Family Letters, Calendar I, 1563–1669, no. 97.
12. L. A. Parker, 'The Agrarian Revolution at Cotesbach, 1501–1612', in Hoskins (ed.), *Studies in Leicestershire Agrarian History*, pp. 71–3.
13. Many cases in Star Chamber arose as a result of rioting against enclosure in Leicestershire – for example, PRO, STAC 8: 219/23, Garendon, 1604; 87/7, Ullesthorpe, 1606; 249/15, Halstead, 1608–9; 296/22, Knossington, 1610; 204/7, Grimpston, 1611; and 260/17, Hallaton, 1617.

14. For Cotesbach, see Parker's detailed study in Hoskins (ed.), *Studies in Leicestershire Agrarian History*, and his 'Enclosure in Leicestershire'.
15. For Welham, see the following: Stocks (ed.), *Records of the Borough of Leicester*, vol. iv, pp. 63, 71; *VCH Leics*, vol. ii, p. 123, and vol. v, pp. 33–4; Parker, in *Leicestershire Archaeological Society, Transactions*, vol. 23, p. 284, and 'Enclosure in Leicestershire', pp. 127–8; M. W. Beresford, 'Glebe-terriers and Open-field Leicestershire', in Hoskins (ed.), *Studies in Leicestershire Agrarian History*, p. 114.
16. For Belton, see the following: PRO, STAC 8/71/6; Parker, in *Leicestershire Archaeological Society, Transactions*, vol. 23, p. 262n. S. M. Thorpe, 'The Monastic Lands in Leicestershire on and after the Dissolution' (Oxford University, BLitt thesis, 1961) pp. 47–8, 269–70.
17. For Hillmorton, see the following PRO papers: STAC 5: A 18/18, 21/24, 42/3, 3/3, 58/9 and 35/31; STAC 8: 15/12, 40/22 and 6/4; C 2 (Jas I): A 8/12, B 34/51 and P 30/40; E 178/4671. Also see WRO, D 31/22, 24 and 25, and CR 409.
18. For Chilvers Coton, see the following PRO papers: STAC 8: 221/1, 15/21, 152/20 and 157/18; SP 16/257/129. Also see *VCH Warwicks*, vol. ii (1908) pp. 217–22; E. G. Grant, 'The Spatial Development of the Warwickshire Coalfield' (University of Birmingham, PhD thesis, 1977) pp. 68–96, 113–35. Beier, 'Poverty and Poor Relief', pp. 126, 155.
19. PRO, STAC 8/144/24; HMC, Salisbury MSS, vol. 19 (1607) p. 175.
20. For Ladbroke, see the following PRO papers: STAC 8: 15/12, 10/18, 61/35, 63/8, 68/3 and 159/6; C 82/1753 and 78/396/13. Also see S. H. A. Hervey, *Ladbroke and Its Owners* (Bury St Edmunds: Paul and Mathew, 1914) – an essential source; WRO, Z 358 (map of Ladbroke, 1639); Thorpe, in Mills (ed.), *English Rural Communities*, map of Spencer pastures; Finch, *Wealth of Five Northamptonshire Families*, pp. 38–49; W. E. Tate, 'Enclosure Acts and Awards Relating to Warwickshire', *BAS Tr*, vol. 65 (1949) pp. 58–63.
21. J. B. Post, 'Courts, Councils, and Arbitrators in the Ladbroke Manor Dispute, 1382–1400', in Hunnisett and Post (eds), *Medieval Legal Records*; Hilton, *The English Peasantry*, p. 163; Harley, 'Population and Land Utilisation', vol. i, pp. 201–4.
22. These figures are derived in the following way: to the numbers assessed in the Subsidies of 1525 and *circa* 1550 I have added a further one-third in order to estimate the total number of households. For use of the subsidy see J. Cornwall, 'English Population in the early Sixteenth Century', *Ec HR*, 2nd ser., vol. 23, no. 1 (1970). For the figures circa 1550: WRO, microfilm MI 231/2, Subsidy Roll, c. 1550 from the Denbigh MSS. 1563: Beier, 'Poverty and Poor Relief', table 6, p. 247. 1603: taken from the number of tenants and cottagers recorded in the enclosure agreement of that year. Thus

1525	31 households assessed (plus one third = 41 households)
c. 1550	25 households assessed (plus one third = 33 households)
1563	34 households
1603	19 households

Note that the extent of depopulation recorded by the 1607 commission (18 households) is consistent with the above figures.

240 *Notes*

The changes in landholding discussed below are indicated by the
following changes in land held (in yardlands):

1596   Landlords – Catesby, 8; Spencer, 6¼, Grange, 7
          Tenants-at-will – 38

1599   Landlord – Dudley, 36¼
          Freeholders – Burton, 5½; others, 17½

1603   Landlord – Dudley, 40¼
          Leaseholder – Burton, 5½
          Freeholders – in total, 13

23. Huntingdon MSS, HA 4169, Privy Council to the Earl of Huntingdon, 12 June 1607. A modern author expresses puzzlement over the involvement of Leicester in the revolt – J. Simmons, *Leicester, Past and Present*, vol. I: *Ancient Borough* (London: Eyre Methuen, 1974) p. 74.
24. See P. Clark and P. Slack, *English Towns in Transition, 1500–1700* (London: Oxford University Press, 1976) pp. 101–9.
25. Ibid., p. 108.
26. J. Thirsk, 'Stamford in the Sixteenth and Seventeenth Centuries', in A. Rogers (ed.), *The Making of Stamford* (Hertford: Leicester University Press, 1965) pp. 63–4; L. Clarkson, 'The Leathercrafts in Tudor and Stuart England', *Ag HR*, vol. 14 (1966); W. G. Hoskins, 'English Provincial Towns in the Early-sixteenth Century', 5th ser., *Tr RHS*, vol. 6 (1956). Unfortunately, such occupational specialisation was related to agrarian changes which were in contradiction with the pressing needs of Midland towns for grain.
27. Hoskins, in *Tr RHS*, 5th ser., vol. 6, p. 18. Also see Clark and Slack, *English Towns in Transition*, pp. 92–108.
28. See E. Kerridge, 'The Social and Economic History of Leicester, 1509–1660', in *VCH Leics*, vol. IV (1958); W. G. Hoskins, 'An Elizabethan Provincial Town: Leicester', *Provincial England: Essays in Social and Economic History* (London: Macmillan, 1963).
29. Hoskins, in *Tr RHS*, 5th ser., vol. 6, table, p. 13; *VCH Northants*, vol. III, p. 23.
30. I have been able to gather together documented instances of riot by the inhabitants of Lincoln, Southampton, Huntingdon, Malmesbury, Nottingham, York, Newcastle, Norwich, London, Cambridge, Bristol, Witney, Leicester and Coventry – Martin, 'Peasant and Landlord', pp. 714–6. C. Phythian-Adams concludes that enclosure riots were endemic in towns in the early sixteenth century – 'Urban Decay in Late Medieval England', in P. Abrams and E. A. Wrigley (eds), *Towns in Societies: Essays in Economic History and Historical Sociology* (Cambridge University Press, 1978) p. 182. The evidence that we have suggests that this is true also until the mid seventeenth century at least.
31. M. D. Harris (ed.), 'The Coventry Leet Book', *Early English Texts Society*, nos 134–5, 138, 146 (1907–8); C. Gill, *Studies in Midland History* (Oxford: Clarendon Press, 1930) ch. 4; *VCH Warwicks*, vol. VIII, pp. 202–4.
32. Kerridge, in *VCH Leics*, vol. IV, pp. 108–9; Stocks (ed.), *Records of the*

Borough of Leicester, vol. iv, pp. xxxviii–xxxix, 140, 239–43; M. James, *Social Problems and Policy during the Puritan Revolution, 1640–1660* (London: Routledge and Kegan Paul, 1930) pp. 123–4.

33. For conditions in Leicester, Coventry and Northampton in this period, see Clark and Slack, *English Towns in Transition*, p. 95; J. Goring and J. Wake (eds), *Northamptonshire Lieutenancy Papers and Other Documents, 1580–1614* (Northampton: Northamptonshire Record Society, 1975) pp. xvi–xvii, 24–32; M. Bateson (ed.), *Records of the Borough of Leicester*, vol. iii: *1509–1603* (Cambridge, 1923) pp. 346–7, 372, 387, 396–7; Stocks (ed.), ibid., vol. iv, pp. 74, 140, 196.

34. Kerridge, in *VCH Leics*, vol. iv, pp. 107–8.

35. LRO, Hall Papers, vol. 4, nos 99–112, 115, 129–30, 132, 146, 152. Kerridge's excellent discussion of occupations and wealth in Leicester (drawn from analysis of inventories) clearly establishes that the occupations of rioters were at the poorer end of the scale – *VCH Leics*, vol. iv, pp. 83–99. Unfortunately (in contrast with forest and felden rioters), few positive correlations of wills and/or inventories with recorded rioters can be made, because of a lack of signatures or marks for identification. The positive identifications made are as follows.

John Smyth (Smith), carpenter, died in 1609; in his will, he left all his working tools to his grandson William Steeples, apart from an old whip-saw, which went to his apprentice. He also left 12*s*. 6*d*. to the poor and the church of St Martin's. John Smyth, carpenter, and William Steeples, his apprentice, are entered in the list of rioters. John Panke, tanner, died in 1620, and in his will left £20 to his eldest son, John, and a further £20 to his other son. Since there were relatively few tanners in the town, identification of either father or son is reasonably certain. (LRO, Wills, ser. 14, 1580–1649: John Smith, 1609, no. 1; John Panke, 1620, no. 70.) In terms of wealth these three rioters came from the upper end of the occupational groups represented in the revolt. John Smith would have been a master craftsman, perhaps worth at least £10–15. John Panke may have left an estate of over £60 but probably not much more, since the tanning business required little capital. The two legacies totalling £40 may well have constituted the bulk of his estate. Other less certain identifications are discussed in Martin, 'Peasant and Landlord', appendix vii (a).

36. PRO, STAC 8/144/23.

37. The predominant form of disorder engaged in by forest communities related to their wider location in the economic region. In the more advanced South and East of England, where strong and stable felden peasant communities had been replaced by consolidated and enclosed farms producing grain surpluses, the predicament of forest villages was expressed in grain rioting, rather than riots against enclosure. Protest was channelled into struggles to disrupt the market mechanism of grain distribution and prices to their advantage. See P. Clark, 'Popular Protest and Disturbances in Kent, 1558–1640', *Ec HR*, 2nd ser., vol. 29, no. 3 (1976); J. Walter and K. Wrightson, 'Dearth and the Social Order in Early-modern England', *P&P*, no. 71 (1976); Walter, in Brewer and Styles (eds), *An Ungovernable People*. The distinction between Southern and Midland forms of forest protest is clearly evident in maps drawn up by A. Charlesworth. In the South, food rioting on

the edge of forest regions predominated, while, in the Midlands, land (enclosure) riots remained prevalent in the period 1586–1640. See A. Charlesworth (ed.) *An Atlas of Rural Protest in Britain, 1549–1900* (London: Croom-Helm, 1982).

38. Thirsk, 'The Farming Regions of England', in Thirsk (ed.), *Agrarian History*, vol. iv.
39. A. Everitt, 'Farm Labourers', ibid., pp. 433–4.
40. Tawney, *Agrarian Problem*, p. 22n.
41. Harley, 'Population and Land Utilisation', vol. i, p. 203, and in *Ec HR*, 2nd ser., vol. 11, no. 1, pp. 13–16.
42. For this section, see the following. J. M. Martin: 'Marriage and Population Change in Tudor and Stuart Warwickshire' (unpublished, held in the WRO); 'Warwickshire and the Parliamentary Enclosure Movement', 2 vols (University of Birmingham, PhD thesis, 1965); and 'The Parliamentary Enclosure Movement and Rural Society in Warwickshire', *Ag HR*, vol. 15 (1967). Also see V. Skipp, *Crisis and Development: An Ecological Case-study of the Forest of Arden, 1570–1674* (Cambridge University Press, 1978).
43. M. J. Kingman, 'Markets and Marketing in Tudor Warwickshire: the Evidence of John Fisher of Warwick and the Crisis of 1586–7', *Warwickshire History*, vol. 4, no. 1 (1978); *VCH Warwicks*, vol. ii (1908) p. 137n.
44. For this section, see P. A. J. Pettit, *The Royal Forests of Northamptonshire: A Study in their Economy, 1558–1714* (Gateshead: Northamptonshire Record Society, 1968), esp. ch. 7 and appendix iv.
45. Ibid., p. 133. Quote from John Norden.
46. C. Hill, 'The Many-headed Monster in Late-Tudor and Early-Stuart Political Thinking', *Change and Continuity in Seventeenth Century England* (London: Weidenfeld and Nicolson, 1974).
47. NRO, Buccleuch Letters, vol. 4, fo. 18 a, b, and c.
48. Pettit, *Royal Forests of Northamptonshire*. In the period 1524–1670, Weldon experienced a 100 per cent increase to 300 households; Corby, 92 per cent to 480 households; Benefield, 65 per cent to 660 households; and Cottingham and Middleton an increase of 43 per cent to 570 households.
49. Ibid., pp. 171–4; L. Stone, 'The Fruits of Office: the Case of Robert Cecil, First Earl of Salisbury, 1596–1612', in Fisher (ed.), *Essays in the Economic and Social History of Tudor and Stuart England*.
50. We should note that the data contained in Table 10.4 represent a very rough estimation of wealth, as drawn from the wills left by rioters. Inaccuracies, if they occur, involve a consistent *underestimation* of wealth. Unfortunately, virtually no inventories have been preserved for this period. They would have given us a much better impression of wealth. Identification of rioter and testator is made largely on the basis of common signature/mark or occupation. For further discussion, see Martin, 'Peasant and Landlord', appendix vii (b). The full range of wealth of rioters is illustrated by the following two cases: John Hitchcocke, mason of Little Weldon, died in 1635 with debts greater than his goods; John Checkley, husbandman of Little Weldon, died in 1627 and was able to leave £60 to relatives other than his wife and son, who received the bulk of his estate. His sister, who received a cow, was married to Gyles Phillips, another rioter. Probably, Checkley

would be more accurately described as a yeoman in terms of his wealth.

The following testators were positively identified as rioters and data for Table 10.4 were taken from these sources: NRO, Wills of the Consistory Court of Peterborough: John Brown, Book G, fo. 19; Christopher Burrow, Book 13, fo. 124; John Baker, Book H, fo. 202; George Bull, Book I, fo. 285; William Checkley, Book B, fo. 224; Thomas Coles, Book I, fo. 5; John Checkley, Book L, fo. 2; John Dervile, Book D, fo. 104; John Hitchcocke, Book F, fo. 151; Henry Laxton, Book M, fo. 40; William Morris, Book E, fo. 146; Thomas Peake, Book B, fo. 154; Thomas Phillips, Book E, fo. 14; Richard Rowlatt, Book F, fo. 188; Lyon Rowell, Book I, fo. 170; and Hugh Taylor, Book L, fo. 21.

51. See Everitt, in Thirsk (ed.), *Agrarian History*, vol. IV, pp. 406–9, for discussion of agricultural labourers' involvement in enclosure riots. His comments are especially pertinent to forest-dwelling labourers.

52. Essentially, the distinction between open and freehold communities is contained implicitly within the work of Martin: 'Warwickshire and the Parliamentary Enclosure Movement', and in *Ag HR*, vol. 15. He contrasts their different experiences of enclosure in the eighteenth century. I have extended this distinction back into the sixteenth century and examined why such communities largely avoided enclosure until later. By the eighteenth century, open communities had become closely integrated into the labour requirements of adjacent enclosed or 'close' parishes. See B. A. Holderness, '"Open" and "Close" Parishes in England in the Eighteenth and Nineteenth Centuries', *Ag HR*, vol. 20 (1972).

53. B. K. Roberts, 'Field Systems of the West Midlands', in A. R. H. Baker and R. A. Butlin (eds), *Studies of Field Systems in the British Isles* (Cambridge University Press, 1973) pp. 192–4, esp. map p. 193.

54. For deserted villages and early depopulations in Warwickshire, see the following: Beresford, in *BAS Tr*, vol. 66; Tate, ibid., vol. 65; C. J. Bond, 'Deserted Medieval Villages in Warwickshire: a Review of the Field Evidence', *Birmingham and Warwickshire Archaeological Society, Transactions*, vol. 86 (1974).

55. Harley, '*Population and Land Utilisation*', vol. I, p. 205.

56. For this section, see the appropriate volume of *VCH Warwicks*; and Finch, *Wealth of Five Northamptonshire Families*, pp. 49n., 62, 178. For enclosure in Prior's Hardwick, see PRO, C 2 (Jas I) B 17/26. Depopulation in Bishop's Itchington: Beresford, in *BAS Tr*, vol. 66, p. 93; PRO, SP 16/257/129, STAC 8/15/21 and C 78/400/9; WRO, Sessions Order Books, vol. 1, p. 235. Depopulation in Burton Dassett; Alcock, in *Warwickshire History*, vol. 3, no. 5; E. F. Gay, 'The Rise of an English Country Family: Peter and John Temple to 1603', *Huntingdon Library Quarterly*, no. 4 (July 1938); Thorpe, in Mills (ed.), *English Rural Communities*, map.

57. WRO, DR 184/6, Southam 'enclosure agreement', 1625. This document lists at least 30 cottages, 10 of which were on parish wastes. Also see PRO, STAC 8/281/17.

58. PRO, E 178/4671, terrier of Hillmorton, 1608. Hillmorton was enclosed in 1754 and Southam in 1761. Also see Martin, 'Warwickshire and the Parliamentary Enclosure Movement'.

59. See the appropriate volume of *VCH Warwicks*, and the following sources:

Finch, *Wealth of Five Northamptonshire Families*, p. 49n; Thorpe, in Mills (ed.), *English Rural Communities*, map, pp. 53, 61–2.
60. Gay, in *Huntingdon Library Quarterly*, no. 4, pp. 389–90. Sessions Order Books in the WRO contain much evidence of such levies and the poverty of open parishes. See vol. 1, p. 88; vol. 2, pp. 8, 17, 19, 38, 82, 193–4, 206, 216; vol. 3, pp. 50, 71, 194, 304; and vol. 4, pp. 138–9. In 1563, Brailes contained 115 households; by the 1660s this had risen to 175 households, an increase of 52 per cent. See Beier, 'Poverty and Poor Relief', table 6.
61. P. Styles, 'A Census of a Warwickshire Village in 1698', *University of Birmingham Historical Journal*, vol. 3 (1951) (occupational analysis of Fenny Compton), and 'The Social Structure of Kineton Hundred in the Reign of Charles II', *BAS Tr*, vol. 78 (1962).
62. Martin, 'Warwickshire and the Parliamentary Enclosure Movement', vol. I, p. 14.
63. The burden of poor rates resulting specifically from enclosure was cited as a grievance by the rebels of 1607, together with the problems caused for those who had rights of common, by illegal settlement on the wastes – PRO, SP 16/307/2.
64. There has been little systematic work done on occupational structure in the felden. In these circumstances, the basis for comparison in Table 10.8 has been made with reference to the following sources: Hoskins, *The Midland Peasant*; A. J. Tawney and R. H. Tawney, 'An Occupational Census of the Seventeenth Century', *Ec HR*, vol. 5, no. 1 (1934); Pettit, *The Royal Forests of Northamptonshire* (sections on the felden); Styles, in *University of Birmingham Historical Journal*, vol. 3, and in *BAS Tr*, vol. 78; Everitt, in Thirsk (ed.), *Agrarian History*, vol. IV; Martin, 'Marriage and Population Change in Tudor and Stuart Warwickshire'; Tawney, *Agrarian Problem*, p. 22n. (data from Worcester Recognisances).
    Sources for Table 10.8: NRO, Buccleuch Letters, vol. 4, fo. 18a, b and c (pardon issued to Northamptonshire rebels); PRO, STAC 8/198/21 (riots at Stoke Bruerne, Northamptonshire). Occupations taken from wills and inventories of rioters at Ladbroke, Warwickshire (see below). Occupations gleaned from the Southam, Warwickshire, enclosure agreement (WRO, DR 184/6) and Southam Parish Register – Rev. W. L. Smith, *Historical Notices and Recollections Relating to the Parish of Southam, 1580–1629*, 2 pts (London: E. Stock, 1894).
    Sources for Table 10.9. Confirmed identifications of recorded rioter and testator of will and inventory, made by a process of elimination through consultation of relevant parish registers: Southam, Smith, *Historical Notices*; WRO, Parish Registers: Napton, N1/01, 1607–50; Harbury, DR 303/1, 1607–50; and Hillmorton, DR 256/1, 1595–1650. All wills and inventories are contained within the Lichfield Joint Records Office, referenced only in the form of name, parish, and date recorded. I was extremely fortunate in having inventories for virtually all wills located. This made an estimation of wealth much more accurate than by wills alone. I shall not list the more than fifty wills and inventories in detail. They are to be found in Martin, 'Peasant and Landlord', appendix VII (c). The three inventories mentioned in the text: William Chambers, Harbury, 27 Nov 1629; Ellis Burbury, Harbury, 10 July 1610; Nicholas Bodington,

Cubbington, 29 Nov 1636 – for a detailed study of the Bodington family, see W. F. Carter, *The Bodingtons of Cubbington in the County of Warwick*, (Birmingham: C. Cooper, 1896); and Henry Mister, Napton, 21 Oct 1634.

Index

absolute property, 102, 104, 109, 122, 129
absolutism, 50–1, 54, 98–9, 101, 150
  conditions of existence, 109–13 *passim*, 142–3
  in England, 140–2, 215
  as feudal state, 107–10
  institutional structure, 110–12
  relationship with peasantry, 113–14, 142–4
  theory of, 103–10
agrarian capitalism, 99–103 *passim*, 114–15, 130–2, 150, 156, 215
agrarian crisis (1315–22), 65, 70–1
agrarian policy, of the absolutist state in England, 113–15, 132, 141, 144–50
  impact of, 149–50
agricultural revolution, 132
Alavi, H., 100
Alcock, N. W., 125
alliance of classes, 99, 100
Althusser, L., xv, 52
Amin, S., 100
ancient demesne, 64–5
  status of, 72–3, 75, 86, 89, 121, 143–4
Anderson, P., xv–xxi *passim*
  and feudalism, 5–6, 46–51 *passim*, 56, 59
  and transition to capitalism, 98–9, 104–5
Arden (Warwicks), 79, 81, 82, 198–9, 201, 202
aristocracy, decline of, 130–1
army, *see* militia
articulation, of modes of production, 52–4, 98–101

Asad, T., 55–6
Ashby-de-la-Zouch (Leics), 171
Ashley, W. J., 119
Ashton (Northants), 166, 176, 202
Astley, Mary, of Hillmorton (Warwicks), 188, 206
auto-effectivity, 46, 48–9, 50, 53–7 *passim*

Balibar, E., xv, 4, 6, 51–5 *passim*, 98–9, 106
Banaji, J., xvii, 8–10, 21, 26, 59, 100
banalites: *see* monopolies; soke
Baude, Ferdinando, 183, 184
Beaumont, Sir Thomas, 187, 189
Bedfordshire, 82
  enclosure in, 135, 140
  enclosure riots in, 167
Bedworth (Warwicks), 177, 189, 202
Belcher, William, 173
Belton (Leics), 167, 186, 187
Benefield (Northants), 201
Bennett, H. S., 42
Beresford, M., xvi, 122–6 *passim*, 133, 138, 139, 147, 149
Berkshire
  enclosure in, 135
  riots in, 154, 168
Bettelheim, C., xv, 100
Bishop's Itchington (Warwicks)
  feudal development, 81, 84–92 *passim*
  and Midlands Revolt, 190, 205–8 *passim*, 212
Black Death (1348–9), 45, 47, 69–70, 71, 89, 91–2
Bloch, M., 38, 41

246

Index